Differentiation and the secondary curriculum

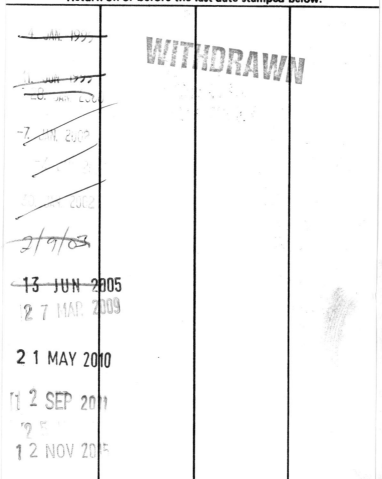

Differentiation and the secondary curriculum: debates and dilemmas

Edited by Susan Hart

with contributions by Sharon Camilletti, Kiran Chopra, Brigid Davidson, Judy Erwin, Janet Fawthrop, Michael Fielding, Nicola Hancock, Jean Mayala, Lynda McCall, Jan Moore, Neil Parr, Barbara Parry and Susanna Pickstock

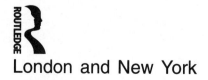

London and New York

First published 1996
by Routledge
11 New Fetter Lane, London EC4P 4EE

Simultaneously published in the USA and Canada
by Routledge
29 West 35th Street, New York, NY 10001

Routledge is an International Thomson Publishing company

Typeset in Palantino by Florencetype Ltd, Stoodleigh, Devon

Printed and bound in Great Britain by
TJ Press (Padstow) Ltd, Padstow, Cornwall

British Library Cataloguing in Publication Data
A catalogue record for this book is available from the British Library

Library of Congress Cataloging in Publication Data
A catalogue record for this book has been requested

ISBN 0–415–13201–0

Contents

Figures and tables

FIGURES

TABLES

Acknowledgements

We would like to thank the Institute of Education, Cambridge University, for funding teachers' release to be involved in this initiative, also to colleagues at the Institute who have supported our work in the drafting stage.

We extend our thanks to Karen Lewis, for her helpful feedback on early draft chapters, and also to Pauline Mason, for her support throughout the initiative and particularly in the preparation of the final manuscript.

We thank the following schools, organisations and support services for enabling the initiative to go ahead, and to staff and students for their contribution to the work described:

- Language and Curriculum Access Service, London Borough of Enfield
- Language and Curriculum Support Service, South West Herts
- Language Support Service, London Borough of Barking and Dagenham
- Learning Support Service, London Borough of Barnet
- Queen Elizabeth's Girls' School, Barnet
- Minority Ethnic Curriculum Support Service, Education Department, Hertfordshire
- Saffron Walden County High School, Essex
- Thurston Upper School, Suffolk
- Unesco International Teacher Education Project 'Special Needs in the Classroom'
- Uplands Middle School
- Walton Junior School
- Watford Girls' Grammar School
- Wheatcroft JMI School, Hertford.

Introduction

Since the late 1980s, the term 'differentiation' has increasingly entered the everyday usage of teachers and become a priority issue on many school development plans. Yet in the summer of 1994, when most of the co-authors of this book met together on an in-service education (INSET) course at the Institute of Education in Cambridge, a library research revealed only three books and a small collection of articles with 'differentiation' in their title. Of these, none provided any actual examples of practice and none asked the sorts of questions about differentiation that this group of teachers most wanted to raise.

This seemed a good enough reason for trying to write such a book ourselves. What was needed, we felt, was a book written *by* teachers *for* teachers that would reflect the living, breathing, frustrating, tiring, challenging, rewarding and occasionally inspiring reality of everyday work in schools. We have tried to write the kind of book that we wish had been available to us at the start of the course: one that reads easily but does not patronise, one that not only offers practical examples but also raises theoretical questions, one that recognises the pressures of practice and the need to get the task done, but does not shy away from acknowledging the complexity of the issues involved.

When we came together originally, as a group of professional people, all that united us was a shared interest in learning more about the issue of differentiation and its implications for practice in schools. As we have gradually built up a shared body of knowledge, experience and expertise, however, we have also gradually begun to elaborate some shared questions, concerns and principles relating to differentiation that give a distinctive flavour to the approach adopted in this book.

Perhaps the most important of these is a recognition that the new focus on differentiation in schools can lead not only to positive developments but also to developments that we would not necessarily wish to endorse. One of our main aims in this book, then, is to draw attention to some of these more controversial aspects of 'differentiation' and try to open these up to constructive discussion and debate. We do not pretend to have definitive answers to the questions we raise, or to offer clear solutions to the tensions and complexities that we acknowledge. What we can do is to provide honest accounts of how we have attempted to respond to them so far in the various contexts within which we work. All are part of a continuing enquiry: seeking to understand what 'differentiation' means and the part it might play in fostering children's learning.

In many cases, the accounts record the first tentative steps taken as we began to explore ways forward. Most are written by teachers who are describing their work for publication for the first time. We present them because we think that the questions they address are important and because examples of practice will provide food for thought to help readers reflect upon alternative possibilities and establish their own principled basis for choosing particular ways of working.

The overall structure of the book and the organisation of the case study chapters have been designed with this purpose in mind. It is possible to read or dip into the various parts of the book in any order, or use individual chapters as a basis for INSET, depending upon readers' particular needs, interests and purposes. All chapters begin with an editorial introduction which aims to highlight the key issues and questions addressed in each chapter at a general level. This could be used as a starting point for staff discussion, drawing first upon teachers' own experience and resources to reflect upon the questions and issues raised, and then developing the discussion further by engaging with the ideas in the chapter.

PART I: WHAT IS DIFFERENTIATION?

Many teachers on the course felt that a necessary first step for themselves and their colleagues was to demystify the notion of 'differentiation'. They talked to colleagues, observed in lessons, examined their own practices and took photographs round the school in order to clarify their own understandings of the term and the range of practices that might be included within it. They drew on their own existing understandings, plus the limited literature so far available, to begin to analyse and describe the many features of school and classroom practice which contribute to 'differentiation' and examine how these connected up with their own ideas of good practice.

In this first part of the book, we invite readers now to reconsider with us the question 'What is differentiation?' Our experience suggests that there is no simple answer to that question. Indeed, the term has a whole set of meanings and prior associations which are frequently unacknowledged in current debates. Three course participants, including the course tutor, make their own contributions to answering this question, linking it up to their own experience and practice.

Chapter 1 examines the origins of the new emphasis on 'differentia-tion' and some of the influences which have made 'differentiation' a major priority for development work in many schools. It highlights some of the controversial and problematic issues which the term 'differentia-tion' raises for the author, and proposes an interpretation of 'differenti-ation' which links it to equal opportunities issues.

Chapter 2 looks at how the different traditions, philosophies and forms of organisation of primary and secondary schools affect how 'differen-tiation' is interpreted and what kinds of 'differentiation' are possible. It considers the implications of these differences for children transferring to secondary school, and what can be done to ease the transition. The chapter takes the form of a dialogue between Brigid Davidson, a primary Year 6 teacher, and Jan Moore, a secondary teacher who is currently engaged in a major initiative to develop differentiation across the curriculum in her own school.

Chapter 3 argues for an interpretation of 'differentiation' that will help to ensure that the effort which teachers put into 'differentiation' will lead to a genuine improvement in children's learning. Drawing on her own experience, Sharon Camilletti analyses why the considerable effort that goes into differentiating work does not always achieve the goal of enabling children to learn more successfully and independently. She proposes an interpretation of 'differentiation' based upon an under-standing of learners' strengths, and offers a practical illustration of curriculum material which reflects these ideas.

PART II: DIFFERENTIATION THROUGH SMALL GROUP LEARNING

In this second part of the book, we invite readers to consider the impact upon children of different ways of organising teaching and learning in response to the diversity represented within any teaching group, and look in particular at the potential for using small group learning as a means of achieving differentiation.

In Chapter 4, Lynda McCall explains her own reasons for wanting to avoid approaches involving the separation of children into ability groups and sets, or the fragmentation of a mixed-ability class into groups working at different levels. She offers an example of a redesigned science lesson in which carefully planned and structured group work is used as a means of providing appropriate and challenging learning experi-ences for all children, while maintaining a worthwhile educational experience that the whole class can share.

Chapter 5 acknowledges the concerns that many teachers have about group work and considers what steps might need to be taken in order for group work to be effective. Janet Fawthrop describes how she involved the children in her class in setting up ground rules for group work, as a first step towards enabling them to reflect on and monitor their effectiveness in working together. She discovered that even children whom she had expected it would be difficult to include and involve could be successfully integrated with group work activities. A number of useful sources of ideas for supporting teachers in the development of group work are included in an appendix to this chapter.

PART III: DIFFERENTIATION THROUGH FLEXIBLE TEACHING

The third part of the book draws into the discussion and invites readers to evaluate the usefulness of research on different teaching and learning styles. Much of the emphasis, in current discussions of differentiation, is upon how best to provide for differences in attainment or ability within a group of learners. However, existing differences of attainment are themselves symptomatic of the extent to which other differences (including preferred learning style) have been taken into account in the educational experiences previously provided. In Chapter 6, Michael Fielding examines some of the available research on teaching and learning styles and relates this to his overall understanding of the conditions needed to support learning in any classroom.

In Chapter 7, Kiran Chopra describes how she used this work to support and inform two development initiatives in her school. She shows how a study skills programme was enhanced by incorporating into it an understanding of different learning styles. She elaborates particularly on mind-mapping techniques, showing how these are capable of accommodating a range of learning styles. She also describes how knowledge of different learning styles was incorporated into differentiation strategies used in the planning and implementation of a language awareness project.

In Chapter 8, Nicola Hancock shows how she used this research as a basis for INSET amongst staff. The chapter raises the more general question of how INSET needs to be organised in order to ensure that the time invested is felt by staff to be well spent. The author describes how she contributed to the planning and organisation of the INSET, using the outcomes of her own classroom research on teaching and learning styles, and presents detailed examples of both the activities which teachers undertook and the practical ideas which emerged.

PART IV: DIFFERENTIATION THROUGH SUPPORT

Current discussion on 'differentiation' often seems to take for granted that it is a relatively straightforward matter to establish what a child 'needs' educationally. Yet our experience suggests that the task is in fact a highly complex one, even when a support teacher is available for some of the time to provide one-to-one help. Though we may be prepared in principle to adjust our teaching in any way necessary to accommodate children's needs, it may be difficult to know how best we can help a child.

In Part IV, we acknowledge these complexities, and look at some of the tensions and dilemmas surrounding support teachers' work. Chapter 9 describes the efforts of one support teacher to understand and get to know a little better the 'needs' of a 14-year-old girl identified as having 'emotional and behavioural difficulties'. Barbara Parry describes how her perception of the ways support might best be used changed as a result of detailed observations of Kelly's participation in lessons.

Chapters 10 and 11 look at issues of support for bilingual children, and examine the case for and against providing support through withdrawal. Since the late 1970s, it has been argued that the best context for learning English is the mainstream classroom. In this setting, children are constantly exposed to the language that they are in the process of acquiring, used in real situations for real communicative purposes. Yet teachers are often concerned, particularly at secondary level, about accepting early stage bilingual students because it does not seem possible to provide for their learning in the context of subject teaching. In Chapter 10, Jean Mayala examines the part that an 'induction' class can play in supporting the transition into mainstream education of newly arrived bilingual pupils. He looks at what can be done in this withdrawal context to prepare pupils to cope more successfully within the mainstream, and raise their own expectations of what they can achieve. He also explains briefly the wider context of his work supporting teachers and learners in mainstream contexts.

In Chapter 11, Neil Parr explores what form support for bilingual learners can take if it is not something added on to existing provision, but developed as an integral part of schools' response to the cultural and linguistic diversity of their students. He explores what makes a learning environment more or less enabling for bilingual learners and puts forward some concrete suggestions to help mainstream teachers develop teaching approaches that are both supportive and inclusive.

PART V: DIFFERENTIATION AT A WHOLE-SCHOOL LEVEL

The final part of the book looks at issues relating to the development of differentiation at the level of overall school policy. Should there be a policy on differentiation? If so, what exactly is its function and what should it contain? How do we organise its development in such a way that it becomes more than just a paper exercise? How does or should it overlap with other policies, say on special needs, behaviour, equal opportunities or language across the curriculum? Chapter 12 describes one school's experience of developing a whole-school policy on differentiation. Susanna Pickstock outlines the processes of consultation that surrounded the development of a draft document, the content of the document eventually produced and the INSET activities used to raise awareness and stimulate further discussion amongst staff.

Chapter 13 looks at where a policy on differentiation fits within schools' wider commitment to providing equal opportunities for all children. Drawing attention to the National Curriculum Council's recommendation that a commitment to equal opportunities should permeate every aspect of the curriculum, Judy Erwin explores different perceptions of the importance of equality issues in schools. She draws on her own experience as an advisory teacher for equal opportunities to explain her own developing understanding of these issues, and identifies some approaches and activities to stimulate discussion and help schools develop policy and practice.

The book concludes with an appendix prepared collectively by the teachers participating on the course, reviewing materials for INSET currently available and identifying additional reading material which course members found useful in supporting the development of their own thinking and practice.

Part 1

What is differentiation?

Chapter 1

Differentiation and equal opportunities

Susan Hart

Without 'equality' there can be no 'quality' of education
(Runnymede Trust 1993)

INTRODUCTION

Since the introduction of the National Curriculum in the late 1980s, the notion of 'differentiation' has entered our professional vocabulary and become widely accepted amongst many teachers and other educators as an essential feature of 'good practice'. Any scheme of work or collective learning experience must be 'differentiated', it is claimed, if it is to provide appropriate and challenging learning opportunities for all children.

But what exactly is meant by 'differentiation' and what does it entail in practice? Is it just a new word for what teachers have always done to take account of the diversity of learners in their classes? If so, why do we need a new term for it? Why does it need to be made such a priority issue for discussion and development in schools? If not, how is it different from what we have always done? What else does it imply that we need to do or think about? Where does this imperative come from and why is it important?

These are some of the questions that we set out to examine at the start of the in-service course which led to the idea of this book. Course participants were attempting to clarify their understandings of the term by relating it to their previous experience and to their existing thinking and practice. As course tutor, my aim was to encourage debate, rather than impose my own interpretations. Nevertheless, I felt that it was relevant to share with participants my own difficulties in coming to terms with the new focus on 'differentiation', if only to demonstrate that it was legitimate, within the course, for contrary view points to be voiced and debated in an open, exploratory and constructive way.

This is again the spirit in which this chapter is written. In it, I outline my own understanding of the meaning and origins of the term 'differentiation' and engage in debate with these meanings based on my own previous understandings and experience. I explain why it has been problematic for me to assimilate it into my own ways of thinking, and make explicit the particular meanings which I need to invest in it in order for it to fit with, and constructively serve, my own aspirations for children's learning. Again, the intention is to encourage discussion and examination of alternative perspectives, rather than to try to impose a particular view or way of interpreting 'differentiation' in practice. I am not speaking on behalf of other contributors to the book. They will elaborate their own perspectives and ideas, and the particular questions which they felt it important to pursue, in their own chapters.

Briefly, I had problems in coming to terms with the emergence of 'differentiation' as a new discourse of 'good practice' because all my thinking about teaching and learning, throughout my professional life, had been developed within a framework which identified 'differentiation' not as a solution to but as a major cause of inequality and under-achievement. My ways of conceptualising and responding to 'differences', and my perceptions of the scope available to teachers for enhancing learning and achievement, were informed by, and developed explicitly to counteract, the adverse effects that my training and profes-sional experience had led me to associate with 'differentiation' practices in schools. This concept of 'differentiation' was clearly born of a different era, a different political agenda, a different set of debates. Yet it raised questions and concerns about entitlement and opportunity which seemed to me still to have power and relevance today, and particularly since many of the old tensions between selective and comprehensive principles have emerged afresh in the debates surrounding current legislative reforms.

In this chapter, then, I explain how I have tried to work through these problems and reach a new understanding of 'differentiation': one which not only acknowledges and addresses my original concerns but also extends and enriches my earlier thinking. I hope that exploring these links and tensions between the idea of 'differentiation' and my own previous thinking and practice will provide a stimulus for readers to review their own understandings and join with me in grappling with the more problematic aspects.

ORIGINS OF THE TERM

My research suggests that the new focus on 'differentiation' – as a discourse of 'good practice' – has its origins in a series of reports by Her Majesty's Inspectorate (HMI) following surveys carried out in secondary schools in the late 1970s and early 1980s (Department of

Education and Science (DES, 1977, 1978a, 1978b, 1979, 1984). These reports expressed concern that much of the teaching observed was insufficiently challenging for pupils of all abilities. Teachers' expectations were often too low; teaching approaches were too narrow, exam-focused and overly directive; teaching tended to aim at the middle (however pupils were grouped) rather than seek to accommodate successfully a broad range of attainment and prior experience. The term 'differentiation' was used by HMI to try to pinpoint what it was that was felt to be lacking: namely that the 'more able' and 'less able' pupils in the group were inadequately catered for; in some cases, even the 'middle' group remained under-challenged because expectations of the notional average underestimated what pupils were really capable of achieving.

Although mixed-ability classes were not the sole target of criticism, the problem was noted to be particularly acute in 'mixed ability' situations because the range of 'ability' was so wide.

> It was surprising to find that in a large number of cases mixed ability classes were taught as though they were homogeneous groups. The work was usually pitched at a level thought appropriate for the majority of the class, and inevitably this was unsuitable for pupils at each end of the spectrum. Sometimes, the level aimed at was below what the average pupil could attain, and the result was a slow pace, undemanding work and general underachievement.
>
> (DES 1978a p. 49)

However, 'teaching to the middle' was observed to be a common practice, whatever the mode of grouping. Grouping by ability, *per se*, was not a sufficient basis for ensuring that pupils' abilities were appropriately provided for. A 'gifted' child was not catered for, simply by being placed in a top stream or set (DES 1977), nor were the 'least able' children necessarily appropriately helped by being taught together in a selected group:

> They frequently had the advantage of being taught in smaller classes, with the possibility of receiving greater individual attention, but the programmes offered to them were seldom successfully pitched at a level which both retained interest and demanded worthwhile achievement.
>
> (DES 1979 p. 40)

Where explicit steps had been taken to adapt teaching to accommodate differences within a teaching group, these had in many cases succeeded only in catering for a different pace of working. HMI noted, too, that the use of worksheets and individual assignments often had the effect of reducing opportunities for genuine intellectual challenge, for using personal initiative and for engaging in independent thinking:

Even when they were genuinely matched to the abilities of pupils –
and this was rare – the assignment sheets had certain disadvantages.
They had to be explicit to enable work to proceed without reference
to the teacher, and as a result were often over-directive and reduced
opportunities for pupils to think for themselves and to use resources.
For the same reason, they tended to over-emphasise transfer of
information and to encourage intellectual conformity rather than
intellectual curiosity and independence of thought. By asking for a
written response to a written stimulus they reduced opportunities for
discussion, with the result not only of limiting progress in oral skills
but also of restricting opportunities for the development and understanding of concepts that can arise through talking round a subject.

(DES 1978a p. 54)

In setting their expectations of pupils, teachers needed to bear in mind
that 'more able' pupils often disguised their capabilities from teachers,
levelling their performance down to the average of the group. The
limitations of the teachers' own experience could also lead them to
underestimate pupils' potential:

A not inconsiderable number of teachers had no experience of the
level and quality of work that can be achieved by able pupils in setted
or streamed groups, and found it difficult to appreciate their potential
and meet their needs when they encountered them as individuals or
as a small minority in a mixed group.

(DES 1978a p. 51)

Equally, it was important to ensure that children perceived as 'less able'
were not underestimated and given an impoverished curriculum, either
because of their weaknesses in the 'basics' or because it was felt that
they could not cope with challenging tasks:

It is not merely a matter of seeing that a range of subjects appears
on their timetable but that they, as much as any other children,
maintain contact with stimulating experiences. . . . Academically less
able pupils need to have plenty of opportunity to exercise their
imagination and reasoning power through a variety of subjects.

(DES 1984 pp. 44–6)

Thus, HMI's concern about 'lack of differentiation' in teaching was in
effect a concern about entitlement and opportunity at all points of the
notional ability range. What was being proposed did amount to quite
a significant departure from teachers' existing practice. It involved a
concerted effort to develop practice at two levels. At the level of method,
the task was to introduce greater variety and flexibility into teaching
approaches in order to cater for differences (here defined in terms of

notional 'ability'), and in a way that would genuinely enhance the quality of learning opportunities provided for all children. At the level of expectation, the question was how to ensure that demands made on pupils were sufficiently challenging: neither underestimating their capabilities nor making unrealistic demands that would prevent them from participating fully and gaining a sense of achievement in their work.

In the wake of these surveys, 'differentiation' became a recurring theme in HMI documents during the course of the 1980s. It was seen as a necessary corollary of the simultaneous move towards greater coherence, commonality and continuity in the curriculum provided for all children throughout the years of compulsory schooling:

> Enabling all pupils to achieve a comparable quality of education and a comparable quality of adult life is a more subtle and skilled task than taking them all through identical syllabuses or teaching them all by the same methods. It requires careful assessment of children's capabilities and continuing progress, and selection of those experiences and activities that will best enable them to acquire the skills and knowledge they need in common and to develop to the full their potential.
>
> (DES 1980 p. 2)

These concerns and recommendations for enhancing 'differentiation' were clearly influential in the debates about educational standards which preceded and precipitated the governmental drive toward reform. The document *Better schools* (DES and Welsh office 1985a), which presented government's view of what needed to be done to raise standards of achievement generally, includes 'differentiation', alongside 'breadth', 'balance' and 'relevance', as one of four key principles to be reflected in the curriculum offered to every pupil:

> there should be careful differentiation: what is taught and how it is taught need to be matched to pupils' abilities and aptitudes. It is of the greatest importance to stimulate and challenge all pupils, including the most and least able: within teaching groups as well as schools the range of ability is often wide.
>
> (ibid., p. 15)

'Choice' and 'diversity', two key themes of 'differentiation' , were to be the means of achieving equality of opportunity for all:

> I want to ensure that we actively recognise pupils' differing abilities and aptitudes and create the means for this diversity to flourish. That is the way to genuine equality of opportunity
>
> (John Major, speech, 1992)

ANOTHER POINT OF VIEW?

However, HMI's critique of existing practice and recommendations for improving teaching were not themselves without their critics. The report on mixed-ability teaching, for example, was taken to task by Simon (1979) for its treatment of children 'as segments of "the whole ability range" [who] must be given an education "appropriate" to their place in this range' (p. 54).

A leading critic of theories of IQ and intelligence testing, Simon argued that schools (or their teachers) who had made a conscious and deliberate move to non-streaming would be unlikely to think of their pupils in these terms:

> Such a move is based on the concept that the child develops in the process of his [sic] education, and that it is highly undesirable from an educational point of view to predetermine that development by forming teaching groups based on a judgement (however made) as to the child's present level at a given moment in time. Groups so formed determine the child's scope for development by ensuring differentiated environmental stimuli. This is why Douglas, Vernon (and others) found over 20 years ago now that stream placement affected intellectual development, the differences between streams becoming exacerbated over time.
>
> (Simon 1979 p. 54)

The idea that in order to provide appropriate and challenging teaching for all requires that teachers categorise their pupils by 'ability' in their minds 'misses the whole point of unstreaming', Simon argues, and indeed is 'in contradiction to its very purpose':

> Certainly there should be scope for the pursuit of individual (or group) interests, and each child encouraged to make his own unique contribution. But that contribution cannot be pre-determined on a rigid classificatory model – the unexpected may occur and should be allowed for; particular children may develop particular interests and enthusiasms. In short, the situation must allow for growth, for developments which cannot be predicted. . . . This concept differs fundamentally from the structuring of 'programmes' for differing levels of ability as the pre-condition for success in the non-streamed situation.
>
> (Simon 1979 p. 54)

The case for differentiation argued in the reports was not, of course, concerned solely with provision for diversity in unstreamed or mixed-ability groups. Nevertheless, Simon's principle that our ways of formulating and responding to diversity must 'allow for (unpredictable) growth' helps clarify and confirm my own sense that we were working with a different conception of 'differences' and their significance for teaching and learning, which did not involve comparing and fixing children's abilities in our minds or ranging them along an imagined continuum, as a strategy for organising and planning 'appropriate' teaching.

Working with this conception of 'differences' did not mean ignoring differences of attainment, but rather taking them into account in a way that would leave every opportunity open and, hopefully, spur the child on to transcend existing limits. It meant keeping a resolutely open mind about every child's capabilities and therefore looking for approaches to teaching which would avoid prejudging outcomes in ways which might be limiting. Hargreaves (1972) summed up the principle as follows:

> All teachers are committed to the improvement of their children. It seems that improvements can occur, even dramatically and *contrary to the evidence*, if the teacher can go on believing that the potentiality for improvement is always there within the child waiting to be released. And an important part of promoting the release of these potentialities consists in the teacher's communication of his faith in the pupil to the pupil.
>
> (Hargreaves 1972 p. 68, my emphasis)

Indeed, more than just communicating faith, it was about taking active steps to try to engage children's learning powers more fully. One of the challenges of this way of approaching the task, however, was how to ensure that children did in fact take up and pursue all the opportunities which the topic presented rather than being satisfied with a minimum contribution. It could be that what HMI saw and condemned as 'teaching to the middle' was in fact teachers' not-yet-entirely-successful attempts to develop approaches to teaching which deliberately sought to avoid prejudging capability based on existing attainment. The opportunities for more challenge may have been present in the teacher's mind and planning, but not realised in practice because the material did not succeed in engaging learners' interest in sufficient depth for the more challenging aspects of the topic to be opened up. The success of the approach depended upon winning pupils' interest and willingness to take up and pursue as fully as possible the learning opportunities provided.

Thus, if it had been part of HMI's brief to probe teachers' own analyses and agendas for development at the time, it might have been noticed that there were other ways of conceptualising the problem of under-achievement and the scope available to teachers for addressing it, based on less problematic assumptions. Certainly, it was not difficult to believe that most children (even those deemed academically successful) were capable of far more than they currently achieved in the context of formal schooling. An enduring experience for me of working with secondary age children was that most engaged only a fraction of their available resources most of the time in the tasks of school learning. In many cases, the energy and emotional investment in school work was minimal. To borrow Mead's (1934) analogy:

> It is as if a generator with enough electricity to power an elevator were used to run an electric light bulb.
>
> (Mead 1934)

Many put their best efforts, as Pye (1988) observes, into simply coping with the 'predicament of being in school', finding ways of defending themselves against learning which were directly at odds with teachers' intentions and aspirations. There was clearly enormous scope for enhancing learning and achievement, irrespective of differences between individuals' capabilities, if we could find ways to enlist more of pupils' emotional and intellectual resources in the tasks of school learning.

In my own modern languages field, dreary and inappropriate text-books, which were all that were available in the early 1970s, were gradually replaced by lively, multimedia materials with an authentic flavour that were able to engage children's interests and facilitate active involvement in a variety of ways. Teachers adapted and developed these materials themselves, continually searching for better ways of engaging learners' interest, imagination and commitment to learning. Similar developments were taking place in subject teaching throughout the school. Maths teachers were experimenting with the development of individualised learning materials suitable for mixed-ability groups, and trying to come to terms with both the management and pedagogical problems which these raised. Humanities and English teachers combined resources to produce an integrated 'world studies' curriculum designed to support and stimulate independent learning, giving pupils more time to become absorbed in tasks and pursue their own personal lines of investigation.

None of us would have claimed that our efforts were entirely successful or that we had even come close to 'cracking' the problem of how to win more of children's emotional and intellectual commitment to the tasks of school learning. Nevertheless, much was learnt during this period of relevance to today's discussions on 'differentiation'. For instance, we discovered the risk of 'death by a thousand worksheets' and the danger of reducing the teacher's role to a mere manager and marker when individualised approaches are used. We discovered the many problems associated with the development of simplified printed materials intended for poor readers within the group: the loss of redundant text which paradoxically makes the text more difficult to read; the isolation of those children from the stimulus of working with peers;

the stigma attached to simplified material if made available to just some children; alternatively the problem of preventing those who did not need them choosing the easy option if we made them freely available to all.

We began to think differently about ways of responding to diversity: viewing a class of learners not as thirty independent units but as a learning group capable of benefiting individually and collectively from the enormous variety of personal resources contained within the group as a whole. The question now became how to organise learning in such a way as to bring each child's resources into interaction with those of others, and with the curriculum, so as to support and enhance their own and one another's learning (Hart 1989).

This analysis of the scope and focus for development was endorsed in an important review of secondary education carried out in London schools in the early 1980s (Inner London Education Authority (ILEA) 1984) with a view to developing a strategy for combating under-achievement. Interestingly, this made no use of the term 'differentiation' either in presenting its analysis of the problem (following extensive consultation with pupils and teachers) or its 104 recommendations for improving secondary schools:

> Much of the boredom cited by ILEA pupils relates to [the] view that too little effort is made to engage them in active learning, that they are required to spend too much time listening or copying, or completing worksheets. ... Boredom leads to resentment and that resentment is expressed either by passive withdrawal of attention or by disruptive behaviour. In the case of the latter a 'double-bind' situation is all too often created: rebellious pupils are seen as too irre- sponsible to be given opportunities for discussion, working in pairs, or in small groups and are meted out with yet more of the very kind of silent solitary activity that has stimulated their original rebellion. ... Our evidence suggests that pupils wish to be given much more responsibility for their own learning and to have the opportunity to negotiate much more of both its content and its process.
>
> (ILEA 1984 p. 69)

The implication of the overall report was that in order to raise standards of 'achievement', schools needed to open up some fundamental ques- tions about curricula, teaching and learning: about how 'achievement' itself is recognised, defined and valued, about how we conceptualise learners and about the part that learners have to play in their own education. At the heart of the problem, the report suggested, was a passive view of learning and the learner which leads to low-level engage- ment on the part of most students and disaffection on the part of a significant number, particularly those who do not see themselves as likely to achieve 'success' in conventional terms. To focus on catering

more effectively for 'differences', without raising these more fundamental questions, would still leave the most important features of the
situation unchanged.

To summarise, then, my training and teaching experience had led to
a different way of thinking about 'differences' and a different analysis
of the scope available to teachers for enhancing learning and achievement from that presented by HMI. Their recommendations for enhancing
'differentiation' were born of their analysis and ways of thinking about
differences, and did not correspond to my own agenda for change and
development. Indeed, 'differentiation' suggested to me a separating
out process, whereas my experience had brought me to a point where,
in my mind, what I was trying to achieve was better thought of as a
process of bringing learners together, into purposeful and fruitful interaction with one another, so that the diversity of knowledge, experience,
prior skills and interests within a class could provide a resource and
stimulus for the whole group. Obviously, this way of formulating the
task does also include a need to take account of such differences, since
it would not be possible to achieve the goal of enhancing pupils' active
involvement in learning unless they had the means to undertake the
tasks, and perceived tasks themselves to be interesting and worthwhile.

ADVERSE EFFECTS OF DIFFERENTIATION?

The ways of thinking about 'differences' and about the scope for
enhancing learning that informed my teaching were influenced by a
powerful and accumulating body of evidence, generated by research and
reinforced through experience, highlighting the inhibiting effects of the
ways in which schools have traditionally defined, identified and
provided for 'differences' in learners' perceived abilities and needs.
Research claimed that these practices had a seriously limiting effect upon
many children's long-term development and life-chances both by irrev-
ocably closing off options (either formally through grouping or informally through expectations formed in teachers' minds) and by setting
up a complex set of social and psychological reactions which led to
lowered expectations, loss of dignity, confidence and motivation, and
the progressive alienation of a significant proportion of the school's
population. These effects were found to be associated, moreover, not just
with situations where children were formally separated into groups on
the basis of similar attainment or perceived ability, but also in mixed-
ability or unstreamed situations, through well-intentioned steps taken
to accommodate 'differences'.

It seemed to me that it was vital to work through these concerns and
their implications for differentiation practices today, if developments
undertaken in the name of equality and entitlement were genuinely to

contribute to that aim. Indeed, a recent study has produced up-to-date evidence to reconfirm and develop some of its main theses (Abraham 1995). Yet it is rare in my experience for this prior history even to be acknowledged let alone given serious theoretical consideration in current debates. Meanwhile, many schools in both primary and secondary sectors, who (under the influence of this research) had previously abandoned differentiated grouping systems, are now in the process of recreating them, in the belief that this will allow the more effective and efficient teaching of the National Curriculum. What grounds are there to reassure ourselves that these groupings will not produce similar effects, undermining the very aims of entitlement and achievement which they are intended to promote?

Of course, the idea that children should receive an education based on ability and aptitude, and *not* on the basis of privilege and social background, was originally intended as a means of promoting equality of opportunity. Justice meant ensuring that children's abilities and needs were accurately identified, so that they could be guided towards the appropriate provision. The practice of sorting children, formally or informally, on the basis of perceived ability therefore began almost immediately upon entry into school. Gradually, however, research began to expose the errors and injustices inherent in these processes.

Jackson (1964) argued that we create 'types' of children by believing that there are 'types' and hence treating them differently. The characteristics of a 'c' stream child come into being through the existence of 'c' streams, not because of common inherent characteristics of children allocated to those categories. Since movement between streams was rare, the process of sorting children by ability meant that decisions that would have irrevocable consequences for children's long-term development and life-chances were being made within a year or two of starting school. The expectations created by the labels, once applied, seemed to become self-fulfilling. Procedures that were intended to promote a fairer distribution of educational opportunities were actually reproducing existing patterns of inequality (Coard 1971; Rist 1971).

Hargreaves (1967) drew attention to the effects of selective grouping upon pupils in a secondary modern school. He showed how the stream to which a pupil was allocated affected their attitudes and expectations and those of teachers towards them. Gradually a polarising effect occurred, with pupils allocated to the lower streams becoming increasingly oppositional and resistant, while those allocated to the top streams remained closely identified with the aims and values of the school. Lacey (1970) found similar processes operating in a grammar school. He used the term 'polarisation' to describe the social processes set in motion by, and bound up with, institutional processes of 'differentiation'. Like Hargreaves, he traced how groups formed a social identity (or subculture), with its own norms and values, that reflected their position in the status hierarchy, leading to the progressive alienation from the school's aims and values of groups assigned to low status positions.

I believe that most teachers will have had at least some experience to call on which corroborates the findings of this research: the damage which can be unintentionally done to learners' confidence, self-image, attitudes and commitment to learning through the impact of labels and more subtle messages conveyed to them through differential treatment. In my own case, on teaching practice in a grammar school, I remember being greeted by pupils in the second 'ability' set out of four with the information that they were 'useless' and I would be better advised to request to teach the top set. I remember, in my own grammar school education, how polarisation began to occur, in attitudes and behaviour, as classes went up the school, with those selected to continue with Latin becoming the elite, and those taking cookery instead becoming disillusioned and occasionally even rebellious as a result of their perceived second-class status. I remember, too, during my teaching career, salutary encounters with 'sink' groups of disaffected youngsters (groups created with the best of intentions to cater for those perceived to be in need of 'extra English') who had long given up any hope of gaining any personal sense of achievement and satisfaction from school learning.

This is not to deny that opting for 'mixed-ability' or undifferentiated approaches to grouping can create its own problems. Research pointed to similar processes operating within comprehensive schools, and even where classes had been organised on an unstreamed or mixed-ability basis. The problem, it began to emerge, was more to do with particular ways of thinking about learners, and responding to perceived 'differences', rather than specifically with how pupils were grouped. Ball (1981, 1986) studied the shift from a system of banding to mixed-ability grouping in one comprehensive school, and found that the processes and effects were even more marked in mixed-ability settings. He concluded that this was, paradoxically, because of teachers' heightened awareness of differences in this situation, and more concerted effort to make provision to accommodate them. This was, as we have seen, precisely what HMI were recommending as 'good practice' in responding to diversity within a teaching group.

FROM CATEGORIES OF 'ABILITY' TO 'INDIVIDUAL NEEDS'

Nevertheless, a significant change has certainly taken place in the terms in which 'differentiation' is now formulated in National Curriculum documents. Since the original series of HMI reports, the use of broad categories of 'ability' to formulate diversity within a teaching

group has given way to a more individualised and diversified interpretation of 'differences', couched in the more descriptive language of
'attainment' and focused upon assessing and meeting 'individual
learning needs'.

This shift was already noticeable in an HMI discussion document
(DES 1985b) published in the same year as the government document
Better schools, which introduced the section on 'differentiation' as
follows:

> A necessary first step in making appropriate provision is the identifi-
> cation of the learning needs of individual pupils by sensitive obser-
> vation on the part of the teacher.
>
> (DES 1985b p. 47)

The meaning of 'learning needs' was clarified in the following paragraph,
emphasising that 'differences' other than those of attainment or ability
in a particular area also need to be acknowledged and provided for:

> Individual work and assignments can be set to allow for different
> interests, capabilities and work rates so long as this does not isolate
> pupils or deprive them of necessary contact with other pupils or the
> teacher. Finally there should be differentiation in the teaching
> approaches; some pupils need to proceed slowly, some need a
> predominantly practical approach and many concrete examples if they
> are to understand abstractions; some move more quickly and require
> more demanding work which provides greater intellectual challenge,
> many have a variety of needs which cannot be neatly categorised.
>
> (ibid p. 47)

This shift towards a more diffuse, individually focused understanding
of differentiation, guided by observation and assessment of individual
'needs', was maintained and consolidated in the first pronouncements
on differentiation made by the National Curriculum Council (NCC
1990c). A set of documents intended to introduce school staffs and
governing bodies to the principles underpinning the National
Curriculum linked 'differentiation' to processes of assessment, planning
and evaluation, as follows:

The National Curriculum will help teachers to:

(a) assess what each pupil knows, understands and can do
(b) use their assessment and the programmes of study to identify the
    learning needs of individual pupils
(c) plan programmes of work which take account of their pupils'
    attainments and allow them to work at different levels
(d) ensure that all children achieve their maximum potential.

(NCC 1990c)

LIMITATIONS OF THE NEW FORMULATION

However, the fragility of this formulation, as a solution to HMI's concerns about underachievement, is highlighted when it is set against the background of the research reviewed earlier. More carefully differentiated assessment and provision to build on existing attainments will reinforce a cycle of low attainment and demoralisation if it is not undertaken as part of a wider endeavour to understand the dynamics of demoralisation and limited achievement and to discover what can be done, within the context of the school, to break into that cycle and influence those dynamics in a positive way.

One major contribution of this research is to illustrate that existing ceilings of achievement are the outcome of complex dynamics in which school experience plays a key determining role. The research on the impact of differentiation processes provides one powerful example of how these dynamics can operate in a way that limits and constrains learning. This happens not only through formal institutional structures, but also through invisible psychological processes: the multi-layered intermeshing of expectations and interactions between teachers and learners, and between learners themselves as they negotiate and respond to the requirements of the formal school curriculum.

In the intervening period, moreover, much other research and development work has been carried out which has opened up awareness of previously unnoticed constraints upon children's full participation and learning in many other areas of school experience. These are not a result of conscious or intentional action on the part of teachers and schools, but arise from ways of thinking and practices that are so familiar and taken for granted that it has not previously occurred to us to consider what their effect might be upon learning.

We have become increasingly aware, for instance, of the impact of classroom language upon children's learning. This can present a barrier which affects all children to some extent (Barnes 1976; Hull 1985; Wells 1987). However, it affects some children more than others, since for some there is a much greater distance between teacher and learners in terms of the shared knowledge and assumptions upon which communication depends (Edwards and Mercer 1987; Heath 1983; Tizard and Hughes 1985).

We have become aware, too, of the unintended messages that can be conveyed to pupils through the selection of particular curriculum content and by the images presented in reading materials and textbooks. These may reinforce perceptions of who is (and who is not) recognised and valued in the school's scheme of things. We have begun to acknowledge and challenge practices in schools which reinforce gender stereotypes, thus limiting aspirations and motivation towards achievement in school to particular spheres of interest and work associated with masculinity and femininity.

We have become aware of the way that the social world of the school impacts upon children's learning for better or worse, with peer group relationships operating to include or exclude children, generating a dominant pro-school or anti-school ethos which it is difficult for individuals to stand out against. Issues of bullying, racism and sexism and their effects upon children's well-being, upon their attendance at school and their feelings and attitudes towards learning have been the subject of much research, debate and development work in schools.

We have become aware of the ways in which the content and methods of assessment affect children's performance, and ability to reveal the full extent of their existing attainments. We know that the way questions are phrased can significantly affect test outcomes, and that different styles of assessment and examination favour boys and girls differentially. For bilingual learners, the opportunity to use their first language both in learning and for assessment purposes has been raised as an important equal opportunities issue.

It is only by keeping constantly on the alert to such unseen constraints, and working to overcome them as we become aware of them, that we can genuinely claim to be taking steps to be promote 'equality of opportunity' and 'ensuring' that children 'reach their potential'. For to claim to know a child's 'potential' may be to attribute limitations to the child that are in fact limitations of our own understanding of possible factors that might be constraining learning. This, according to Gould (1981), constitutes one of the greatest injustices of all:

> We pass through this world but once. Few tragedies can be more extensive than the stunting of life, few injustices deeper than the denial of an opportunity to strive or even to hope, by a limit imposed from without, but falsely identified as lying within.
>
> (Gould 1981 p. 29)

DIFFERENTIATION AND 'EQUAL OPPORTUNITIES'

If by 'equality of opportunity', we mean a professional concern, commitment and responsibility to ensure that, within the context of formal education, all children have an equal chance to develop their personal resources as fully as possible, then we cannot achieve this goal unless our endeavour to achieve it is informed by all that we know and have learnt over the years (through experience and research) about how the dynamics of schooling can operate in ways that are constraining as well as enabling of children's learning. Despite its limitations, HMI's view of 'differentiation' was indeed presented as a means of overcoming constraints upon children's learning that arose, according to their analysis, from approaches to teaching which paid insufficient attention to differences. While disagreeing with the terms in which their vision of 'good practice' was formulated, I would certainly agree with the spirit in which their concerns were expressed. I now realise that 'differentiation' can be used in the service of a more powerful vision if, informed by all that we know about potential 'limits from without', it is used as a tool for probing the limits of existing provision: helping us to appreciate what in a particular situation might be preventing children from revealing, using and developing their personal resources more fully, and discover what might be done to enable them to use these more fully and effectively in support of their learning.

The pressure which the new focus on differentiation has placed upon my thinking has helped me to appreciate that we need a differentiated as well as a more general analysis of the scope for enhancing learning and achievement. The dynamics which shape children's responses and help to determine the extent and limits of their achievements work themselves through in a way that is unique to each child. What presents a constraint for one may be enabling for another. Teaching needs to acknowledge and take account of such differences, continually adjusting and developing in the light of feedback provided by children's responses in an endeavour to provide for all children an equal opportunity to learn in ways which are most enabling for them.

Understood in this way 'differentiation' would always imply a development beyond existing practice, because its whole function would be bound up with seeking out ways to enhance learning for children individually, within the collective provision made for all. Any steps taken to make learning conditions more enabling do, of course, need continuous and careful monitoring. For what we think may be enabling may turn out to be quite the opposite once it has been filtered through children's experience and been interpreted in their terms. Moreover, what we imagine will be helpful based on the best of our current understandings may, in the light of further experience, be perceived as misconceived. In the 1970s, for example, reading was used less and less for learning (Moy and Raleigh 1985) in order to ensure that poor readers were not denied access to learning across the curriculum. With hindsight, this strategy was revised and alternative approaches to the use of texts in learning began to be developed in order to try to ensure that those children who most need to use and develop their literacy skills have the opportunity to do so as a regular part of learning activities.

The conclusion that I have reached, then, in my attempts so far to come to terms with 'differentiation' is that, if such development work is genuinely to serve children's interests, our definition needs to be inspired by a refusal to set limits in our minds to the potential for future development of any child. Existing levels of attainment tell us only what a child has been able to achieve given the particular set of learning opportunities to which he or she has already been exposed. They cannot tell us what a child *might* have been able to achieve, if previous learning opportunities had been significantly different, or what a child might *now* be able to achieve if learning opportunities were to be extended or enhanced in ways that would be particularly enabling of the child's learning. Existing limits are determined by complex dynamics that are at least partly within our control. There is always potential, then, for opening up and moving beyond existing limits, if we can reach a better understanding of how those dynamics are operating and features of them that are constraining and enabling of children's learning. Differentiation is *one* of the means by which we can continually probe the dynamics that determine these existing limits and enable children to transcend them. As Jackson (1964) says:

> Excellence may have genetic limits, but we may alter circumstance a great deal before the genes finally stop our growth. Meanwhile, our colossal technical resources can serve an imaginative approach to education and rediscover what every great civilisation of the past stumbled on. In favourable circumstances, excellence is not static or severely limited. It multiplies.
>
> (Jackson 1964 p. 143)

Chapter 2

Across the primary–secondary divide

Brigid Davidson and Jan Moore

EDITOR'S INTRODUCTION

Each new article or set of guidelines that becomes available on the topic of 'differentiation' seems to offer its own definition of the term. However, so far little attention has been paid to the effect that differences in philosophy, organisation and approach at primary and secondary level might have upon how differentiation is interpreted in practice in the two situations. The exchange of ideas between primary and secondary teachers on our course highlighted significant differences. Teachers in both phases felt that there was scope for learning from one another by sharing interpretations and examining the different opportunities and constraints.

Pursuing this idea, one of the co-authors of this chapter – a Year 6 primary teacher – arranged to spend a day shadowing a class in a secondary school. She found that this experience not only helped to update her knowledge of teaching and learning in a secondary context, but also provided a useful vantage point from which to review and clarify her understanding of 'differentiation' and how it is achieved in her own primary context. The contrast helped her to see her own familiar practices with new eyes and also to raise new questions with respect to primary–secondary transfer that might not otherwise have occurred to her.

In order to explore further the similarities and differences, this chapter takes the form of a dialogue between Brigid Davidson, the primary teacher who made the visit described, and Jan Moore, a secondary teacher whom we invited to respond to Brigid's questions from her secondary perspective. Jan was not a participant on the course, but was known to be leading a major initiative on differentiation in her school, and we were keen to draw on her experience.

Brigid offers insight into her own current understanding of differentiation and how it is achieved in a primary setting. She explains the differences that were highlighted for her by her visit, and begins to consider their implications for children moving to secondary school. Then Jan takes up the questions Brigid raises and explains the kinds of developments that are taking place in her school to support the learning of Year 7 pupils. She shows how these are helping to create more flexibility within a secondary, subject-based form of organisation, while nevertheless interpreting the task of 'differentiation' in a way that is realistic and manageable in a secondary context.

◆ ◆ ◆

THE PRIMARY PHASE

Brigid Davidson

As a Year 6 teacher, I have responsibility for preparing children for transfer to secondary school, and so I was keen to have more up-to-date knowledge of the new situation that I am preparing children to enter. I spent a day shadowing a Year 7 class in a neighbouring secondary school in order to explore the kinds of new experiences, expectations and opportunities that await my class in September.

The experience brought home to me the differences that there must inevitably be between what primary and secondary teachers mean by 'differentiation' because of the different organisation and structure of the secondary school day. It made me realise, in a way that was not so obvious before, that what I understand by 'differentiation' depends upon flexibility built into the overall organisational structure of primary schools and classrooms which is not similarly built in at secondary level. In the first section of this chapter, I shall use the example of my own school and classroom to explain and illustrate these differences and begin to explore their implications for children transferring to secondary school. I shall then pass over to Jan to respond to the points raised from her secondary perspective.

My school has both an infant and junior department, and has 180 children on roll. At Key Stage 1, there are three classes grouped by year, working in a large open-plan area, each with a home bay. Key Stage 2 children work in two open-plan double units, one housing mixed Year 3 and 4 children, the other mixed Year 5 and 6. Each unit is team-taught by two colleagues. For the purposes of this case study, I draw on my specific experience as a Year 5 and 6 teacher in this school.

This basic organisation of the school creates a flexible framework within which individual needs can be recognised and catered for. This is what staff in my school mean by differentiation. Mixing children across two age groups allows for greater flexibility of grouping according to a common curricular, social or emotional need. For example, my colleague and I group children by attainment (or perceived ability) for maths activities, according to interest in thematic work, and by age for gymnastics and dance. The presence of two teachers in a classroom allows for further flexibility of organisation: for example, one of us can spend intensive, extended time with an individual or with a small group of children brought together for a specific purpose, while the other works with the majority of children on other activities.

In our classroom a variety of activities takes place throughout the day and at the same time. This makes it easier for the teacher to match the curriculum to the child through group work. Differentiation occurs, for example, through the nature of the task set, the pace at which a group works, the content chosen as the medium for practising or learning a new skill, according to interest, ability, prior experience, and so on. There is also scope for differentiation in the degree of autonomy accorded to individual children to make choices with respect to their own learning. Whereas one child might work to a fairly structured timetable which is teacher-directed, another might be allowed to work independently and choose to move from one activity to another more freely, resources permitting.

Differentiation also occurs through the allocation of teacher time and through flexible use of additional adult support in the classroom. Teacher support is available in our unit (traveller support, classroom assistants) and these staff are used widely in a variety of contexts dependent on a temporary or long-term need. One child with a physical disability, for example, has a full-time teaching assistant who is able to support not only that child but also those engaged in a similar activity. We also have support for traveller children which can be used on a one-to-one or group basis depending on the traveller child's social or academic need.

Classroom language is a further important means through which differentiation occurs. One-to-one dialogue between adults and children allows for individual children's thinking to be expressed, explored and extended, for adults to achieve a better understanding of each child's understandings, purposes and concerns. Flexible and varied forms of classroom organisation create many different opportunities for developing children's language, and using language for learning in different contexts. Children who rarely dare to express themselves at any length in a whole-class setting, may open up in a small, supportive group of friends or in one-to-one conversation with an adult. Ideas once rehearsed in a small group setting may be more readily shared with a wider group. Children who find it difficult to sustain concentration when working individually may be stimulated and supported by regular opportunities to discuss their ideas and get feedback on their work from others.

The organisation of resources in our room is also planned to accommodate differences. Resources are clearly labelled and freely accessible to the children, who select from them according to their need and preferred style of learning (for example, auditory, visual or kinaesthetic). A wide variety of reading material and textbooks (for instance, a few copies drawn from several maths schemes) is a further attempt to answer individual needs. The area in which children work is arranged to reflect and celebrate differences in the class, for example, through displays.

These are some of the ways in which we use the flexibility built into primary forms of organisation and teaching approaches to try to meet individual needs. Knowledge of individual children, advance planning and flexible forms of organisation are what makes 'differentiation' possible. However, the enormous range and number of differences between children in any one class makes the task challenging for teachers to say the least. Differentiation is never straightforward because children's learning is always unpredictable. We can never be sure in advance what tasks, groupings, materials, timings will be appropriate for a particular child on a particular day, and so have to be ready to make adjustments and vary our plans in the light of children's responses. We have to think on our feet and respond to children's comments, questions and reactions in a way that is individually supportive and enabling. That is perhaps the most demanding aspect of differentiation, and the part that it is hardest to describe because so much of the thinking involved is intuitive in nature.

This interpretation of 'differentiation' is one which I believe fits in with a child-centred philosophy and is consistent with traditions of primary education as they have evolved in Britain since the Plowden Report (DES 1967). It is a pedagogical principle which examines the needs of the child before attempting to provide learning experiences (consistent with statutory requirements) which will best meet those needs and enhance learning.

My visit to a secondary school made me realise how much less flexibility there is for secondary teachers to adjust experiences to take account of individuals' needs. At secondary level, the timetable imposes a pre-set pattern of learning that must stand, irrespective of individual children's interests, inclination and concentration. Secondary teachers have to teach set topics at set times. They have responsibility for five or six times the number of children, yet meet them only intermittently, and have little time or opportunity to discover what they have been doing and learning in between. What 'differentiation' means in a secondary context is necessarily shaped by this framework of subject teaching.

Children transferring to secondary school must learn to fit in with ways of working which do not allow the same freedom that they have perhaps been used to. Primary teachers can, if they judge it appropriate, redirect a child to a different activity if it does not seem that productive learning is going to occur on the task in hand, and make a note to return to the problematic task on another occasion or tackle it by an alternative means. They can allow children to choose the order in which tasks are accomplished, and negotiate longer-than-anticipated time being spent on a particular task if a particular interest has emerged and seems likely to be productively pursued. Since primary teachers work all the time with just one class of learners, there is plenty of time to get to know the children individually and come to appreciate the contexts and tasks which best suit each child. As we are responsible for the whole of a child's (school-based) educational experience, we can notice and build on a child's strengths to develop other areas of learning. We can teach mathematical concepts and develop literacy through topic areas that are of high interest to the child, if the child is making slow headway with regular reading and maths activities.

Recognising these differences, it strikes me that the transition from primary to secondary school may require even more adjustment than we have previously appreciated. How do children experience and adapt to these changes? What are the implications for helping children to make the adjustment successfully to the new demands and expectations of the secondary curriculum? To what extent is it possible for teachers to meet individual needs within a framework of subject teaching?

THE SECONDARY PHASE

Jan Moore

At our school, we have been working since 1993 on an initiative to develop differentiation within the curriculum, with a particular focus on the style and content of teaching in Year 7. The kinds of developments which we have introduced so far while working on this project illustrate that considerable scope can indeed be found for meeting individual needs more effectively within subject teaching.

The school is a rural 11–18 comprehensive with nearly 1,600 students. Its intake comes from primary schools in the immediate town and surrounding villages, which can mean liaising with over twenty primary schools in a typical year. The 'Differentiation Project', as the initiative is called, was set up in response to a concern that the mixed-ability teaching predominant in the school's organisation was possibly not as effective as it might be. Writing courses for the National Curriculum had meant that many teachers and curriculum areas had become so involved in the content and 'what' to teach, that the 'how' had really taken a back seat. Talking about teaching had become a thing of the past. It was time for teachers to consider their practice and rediscover many of the skills that were there within the subject departments.

The project's aim is to maximise the achievement of all students. We are trying to improve the way in which the curriculum areas meet the needs of individual students by providing relevant, stimulating, appropriate and challenging work for all abilities. This is our working definition of 'differentiation', and covers issues of resourcing, teaching materials, teaching styles and schemes of work. The project is planned to run over three years, gradually working its way through the curriculum areas. We have been fortunate in that considerable resources have been invested in creating timetable remission for the teachers directly involved in development work. I shall explain the management of the project in more detail at a later point, since my main purpose here is to explain and illustrate in a concrete way the kinds of developments in our teaching that the project has led to so far.

In the first year of the project, we decided to concentrate on English, mathematics and humanities teaching. Pairs of teachers from each of these curriculum areas met together and decided to begin by carrying out some observations of each other's classes. The focus of our observations was to explore the skills needed by pupils coming into Year 7 to cope with the curriculum in each of these areas. Teachers looked at the way pupils worked, the difficulties they encountered in the unfamiliar secondary environment and the gap between acquired and required skills. They used a check sheet to record information while observing three pupils of varying abilities (see Figure 2.1).

Carrying out these observations helped to open up productive dialogue about children's learning and how different features of classroom practice contribute to this. They also led us to a number of conclusions about how existing practice might be improved:

1 There were often too many verbal instructions given and pupils found it difficult to carry out and sequence basic instructions without continual reference to the teacher.
2 Having instructions available for reference was helpful but there was less confidence when worksheets were given to pupils with special needs.
3 Class discussions worked well if all pupils were involved but often there were silent pupils.
4 The composition of groups makes a significant difference to the commitment and involvement in the lesson.
5 Some pupils benefit from working with a regular partner, but some weak pupils hid behind the work of their friends.
6 There was an inability to transfer or use skills, even within a lesson where the skill has been actively taught.
7 Resources were often inappropriate for pupils with poor basic skills.
8 Pupils did not have the research skills and higher order reading skills that teachers thought they had already acquired.
9 There was confusion amongst pupils about teacher expectations and ways of working in a secondary classroom.

The group's observations confirmed that there was considerable scope for positive action to enhance learning in Year 7 classes. They also helped partners to pinpoint priority areas to work on in their own practice. Alongside a gradual review of Year 7 schemes of work, the English teachers decided to concentrate on improving the quality of pupils' participation and learning during cooperative group work. They developed and piloted a series of role and support cards, designed to enable pupils

FORM   TEACHER   OBSERVER   DATE

Pupil 1 —————— Pupil 2————— Pupil 3 ————— Pupil 4 —————

Mark if pupil is using skill: Yes ☑   No ☒   *Sometimes* ☐

Comment if the skill is specifically taught as part of the lesson

ENGLISH OBSERVATIONS

**Personal organisation/ P1 P2 P3 P4
listening**
Books
Correct equipment
Ready for work
listens to:
        class instructions
        group instructions
        other pupils
stays on task
self-motivated
independent working
collaborates
seeks help from
        staff
        pupils
Other
Comments

Reading
Silent reading
For information
        alone
        in group
From board/OHP
        worksheet
        textbook
Range of books
Other
Comments

Recording/writing
Drafting
Note taking
Report writing
Other

Written work:
clear handwriting
paragraphs
sound spelling
well planned
use of dictionary/thesaurus
relevant terminology
Comments

Speaking
articulates ideas/problems
uses relevant terminology
actively involved
Other
Comments

MATHEMATICS OBSERVATIONS

Practical skills   P1 P2 P3 P4
Uses ruler to
        draw
        measure
Mapwork – specify
Drawing chart/diagram/graph/
  pie chart
Using equipment – *specify*
Calculator
IT – *specify type*
Other
Comments

Style of lesson
Group work
Pair work
Silent, individual work
Presentation to class
Discussion: groups/class
Question and answer
Teacher led
Comments

Number work
Four rules – *specify*
Tables
Angles – drawing
Measuring
Area
Decimals
Money
Other
Comments

Brief outline of lesson content

Any additional skills needed by pupils

Skills that pupils had most difficulty with or
did not have

Skills specifically taught by teacher

Any other comments

Figure 2.1 Year 7 pupil skills check sheet

of all abilities to work together and have their place in the group valued. They tested them out in each other's classes and asked the department for volunteers to join in the trial. This worked so well that the 'trial classes' were able to replicate the group work in other subjects without the cards (see Chapter 5).

The maths department also eventually moved to a focus on cooperative work. They started by taking a critical look at their use of language in the classroom and its relationship to the pace of the lesson. They decided that they talked too much and were in danger of losing pupils' concentration. This was a real test of a critical partnership. They then moved on to spend a significant amount of time with their Year 7 classes improving group work. Pupils were randomly grouped to start with, which meant that no one felt selected and eventually all of the class had worked together. This allowed the teacher gradually to introduce more structured groupings without confrontation or concern. Pupils willingly accepted that seating plans and group choices were part of the lesson structure. Work was planned by the teachers together and strategies for meeting the range of abilities within the classes were written into the schemes of work.

The humanities area decided to write study guides for project work within the Year 7 history curriculum. Their goal was to provide a variety of resources to encourage and enable pupils of differing abilities to work independently. The teachers experimented with supportive groupings and some roles within groups to complete the work. Planning each lesson with a clear view of pupils' different skills and abilities was the focus for the remainder of the project.

Returning to Brigid's questions, several points of similarity can be noted between the methods which she uses for achieving differentiation in a primary classroom and developments undertaken within our Differentiation Project. By developing the students' (and their own) skills in, and commitment to, learning through cooperative group work, teachers in our school have dramatically increased the flexibility available to them for varying their teaching and accommodating individual needs within a variety of groupings. By developing the resources to support independent project work, they have begun to open up scope for choice and the open-ended pursuit of individual interests and purposes which are not available where pupils are dependent upon the teacher to define the next steps of their learning. In both situations, by increasing the students' ability to work independently of the teacher and support one another's learning, they have created quality time for themselves to give to individuals and groups, offering the kinds of support and challenge which only the teacher can provide.

The project is now into its second year, and has moved on into science and technology, while work in the other three areas continues. The aim in both science and technology is to establish the baseline of individual pupil skill and experience and look for ways to build on this. Pupil autonomy through differentiated tasks and approaches is enabling the development of teacher tutoring allowing for both support and extension.

In technology, three teachers from different parts of the area are working together. Each of the technology staff was given a questionnaire which considered skills taught, teaching methods and differentiation in their Year 7 modules of work. This enabled staff to look at the assumptions that are made about pupils' skills and to start to look in detail at how those skills are taught. The technology staff are observing each other's lessons, focusing on two pupils and how they tackle the tasks set. Support and practice materials to develop independent use of basic machinery and techniques are in process.

I am working with one technology teacher on a repeated unit of work using resistive materials. Two groups at a time cover a fifteen-hour project to make a pencil box. This repetition is enabling us to trial and refine teaching methods, supportive and extension materials, tasks and grouping strategies using our partnership of observer and teacher. The aim of this work is to encourage and enable independent working and to develop skills and strategies that can be generalised across this disparate area.

From observation of the initial group it became obvious that pupils were dependent upon the teacher and working with a great range of pace and skill. Some pupils need practice and confidence before sawing or chiselling, others could move ahead independently. The pack of materials was devised to enable both pupil and teacher to plan their work. There is not an expectation that every pupil will need every sheet, but they are available to aid independent learning.

Science also started with a questionnaire (see Figure 2.2) which was devised to assess how much pupils already knew about measurement, one of the early course modules. My science colleague and I were aware that science at Key Stage 2 has developed since the introductory course was written and we felt a need to review and rewrite. The questionnaire showed that most pupils had a working knowledge of methods of measurement but needed experience in problem solving. A measurement circus on three levels was devised, ranging from purely prescriptive work, through experiments with instructions, to open-ended work. Pupils can decide where they start; they must cover four elements and use the same equipment but for different purposes

Science teachers have also been experimenting with developing schemes of work which offer a range of tasks with a different degree of challenge and invite students to choose themselves what degree of difficulty they will attempt for any one task (see Figure 2.3). They have

MEASURING — WHAT DO YOU KNOW?

This sheet is to help us to plan work for you.
It is not a test. Ask your teacher if you are not clear
what to do.

We measure using an instrument — like a ruler.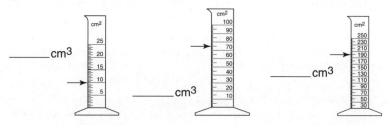

We use units to show what we are measuring in — like metres.

Complete as much of the sheet as you can

1. What would you use to weigh an apple?

_____

What units would it be weighed in? _____

2. Have you used an instrument like this before? _____

What is it used for?

_____

Can you read the scale on the drawings below? Write
your answer in the spaces.

_____ cm³   _____ cm³   _____ cm³

How would you find out how much water a glass holds?

Figure 2.2 Year 7 science questionnaire

YEAR 7   SOLAR SYSTEM WORK PLAN

This topic has been designed for you to work through on your own. As you can see, there are three levels of difficulty. You do not have to choose the same level for each task. Try to choose the most challenging level that you can manage for each row.

Stick this sheet in you book and use it to record the work you choose to do.
Choose one or more tasks from each row.
Shade the box when you have finished the task.
References (for information) are in italics.

Row	A OK	A Challenging	A More challenging
1	Make a poster or collage of what the solar system is (*Understanding Science 3* p. 57)	Make a model of the solar system (*Understanding Science 3* p. 57)	Make a scale model of the solar system or a mobile (*Science Companions 1* p. 9 Try it yourself)
2	The mysterious universe – sheet A2	Solar system disc – sheet B2 (*Understanding Science 3* pp. 56–9. Also *Earth in Space*)	Planets – sheet C2 (*Active Science 3* pp. 133–5)
3	Size of planets – sheet A3 1 bar chart to plot	Planets – sheet C3 using help sheet B3 2 bar charts to plot	Planets – sheet C3 using graph paper only 2 bar charts to plot
4	Night and day and the seasons – sheet A4 (*Understanding Science 3* p. 58)	Day and night – sheet B4 (*Understanding Science 3* p. 58)	Make your own notes about night and day and the seasons (*Earth and Space* pp. 4–5 and pp. 10–11)
5	Phases of the Moon – sheet A5 (*Science Companions 1* p. 3)	Phases of the Moon – sheet B5 (*Earth and Space 3* p. 8)	Read and keep. Why does the moon change shape? – sheet C5. Explain it to someone else
6	Draw a poster with as much information about the sun and/or starts as possible (*Active Science 3* pp. 136–7)	Give an illustrated talk on the sun as a star (*Science Companions 1* p. 58)	Sun sums Read *Understanding Science 3* p. 150 Do experiment (it needs to be sunny!) and answer question 2

Homework Project: Research space travel or satellites and write a leaflet or booklet on it. Include as much information as possible and make it attractive and fun to read

Figure 2.3 Year 7 solar system work plan

also been trying out different ways of grouping pupils and exploring if and how boys and girls approach practical work differently. This area has now started to develop graded assessments with all pupils answering a core test and then moving on to more advanced papers where appropriate. This will ensure that lower attainers will be able to score well on the core test and no longer face inevitable failure.

To summarise, then, I have described the kinds of developments which teachers in our school found ourselves undertaking as a result of examining the extent to which the curriculum areas were currently providing relevant, stimulating, appropriate and challenging work for all abilities. We built on current practice by observing and evaluating the responses of selected pupils to the learning experiences currently provided, and then used this information to help us decide what to work on in order to enhance learning and achievement. Working in partnerships and focusing on the review, evaluation and development of teachers' own classroom practice continue to be our central strategies.

The support which we received in the form of release from timetable in order to carry out this work has been a key factor in these developments. We also received outside support from Maggie Balshaw, a consultant working with the UNESCO 'Effective Schools For All' project. During the year, the team met regularly with Maggie, who gave encouragement when we felt that we were making little headway and helped us to plan the inclusion and involvement of the rest of our area colleagues. This was without doubt the most difficult part of the project. It is only too easy to think that you are developing your own classroom practice, making new discoveries and gain missionary zeal. It is important to remember that differentiation is not new but awareness needs raising amongst secondary teachers who are often more involved in the 'what' of teaching rather than the 'how'. Nevertheless, they are also skilled practitioners with heavy workloads feeling under pressure. Few things are more guaranteed to offend the teacher in the next classroom than the idea of yet another new initiative.

At the end of the first year of the project, a training day was set aside to consider differentiation. With Maggie Balshaw and Mel Ainscow from the Institute of Education, Cambridge University, the staff shared their classroom practice and the work of the project team. This was the first time for many years that the school had spent a training day discussing classroom practice in cross-curricular groups. Sharing the work of the project continues in the current year, through the network team (consisting of current project members, their partners and representatives of other curriculum areas) whose function is to keep all areas in touch with the work that is going on and to share experiences.

Whatever else it may or may not have achieved, the Differentiation Project has certainly succeeded in opening classroom doors and creating opportunities for dialogue about teaching. We believe that, more important than putting into place any particular structures, strategies or approaches, the key to enhancing children's learning is to put in place conditions which support and promote professional dialogue. It is professional dialogue which helps us to see new possibilities, which gives us the courage and impetus to try out new possibilities and which supports us in honestly evaluating and refining developments.

CONCLUSION

As a result of our work so far, we are now in a much stronger position to ease the transition of pupils from primary to secondary school because we have a more explicit awareness of the knowledge and skills that different areas of the curriculum demand. We have begun to develop the means to assess pupils' entry skills and enable them to develop the skills which they need in order to participate fully in the learning opportunities provided. Though the structure and organisation of secondary teaching make it impossible to recreate the flexibility and intimate knowledge of each child's learning that is possible at primary level, nevertheless our project has demonstrated that there is very considerable scope within secondary teaching for enhancing individual learning opportunities.

All the developments that we have undertaken have been concerned with introducing into our work with the whole-class specific developments (such as enhancing individual participation group work) that have the potential to open up enhanced learning opportunities for children individually as well as collectively. This seems to us to be the way to make the task manageable at secondary level, yet keep working systematically to enhance the learning and achievement of all students.

ACKNOWLEDGEMENT

Jan Moore would like to acknowledge the contribution made to the developments described in the second section of this chapter by Iain Walker, Sara Tulk, Andy Clark, Sally Harrison, Stewart Poole, Ruth Fothergill and Hilary Bradbury.

Chapter 3

Bringing out the sparkle

Sharon Camilletti

EDITOR'S INTRODUCTION

'Differentiation' is often described as a process of 'matching' learning tasks to pupils' differing abilities and needs. Difficulties occur, it is said, as a result of a 'mismatch' between learners' resources and the demands made by tasks. Better learning will result from achieving a better 'match'. But what exactly is it that we are trying to match, and how do we know when an adequate match has been achieved?

A reading book or learning text, for instance, might be 'appropriate' for a particular child in terms of the skills needed to read it independently, but mismatched in its content and presentation to the child's age, interests and/or social maturity. A task which makes seemingly 'appropriate' cognitive demands may be inaccessible because it makes assumptions about features of shared cultural experience which are not in fact shared by the child. One of the HMI reports referred to in Chapter 1 (DES 1984) mentions the case of a child who was observed doing a worksheet devised by a remedial teacher in an English class where the rest of the group were engaged in a stimulating activity in which the child could easily have taken part. In this case, considerable time and thought had clearly been invested in trying to recognise and meet the child's individual needs. Yet the effect was to isolate the child and reduce the range and quality of learning experiences to which he or she was exposed.

Sorting out what we understand by 'differentiation' and how we intend it to serve children's learning is clearly more than just an academic exercise. It can help ensure that the considerable time invested by teachers in planning for differentiation does make a significant contribution to children's learning. This is not necessarily always the case, as these examples show. When planning for differentiation, then, how can we be sure that our efforts will be genuinely enabling?

Sharon Camilletti examines this question from her perspective as an advisory and support teacher for children with special educational needs. In her work, she is expected to support mainstream colleagues in providing successfully for children experiencing difficulties in learning, and is increasingly asked for help on differentiation. She found that colleagues were becoming discouraged because the efforts that they were putting into differentiating their teaching often did not seem to lead to significant improvement in the quality of children's engagement with learning tasks.

Revisiting her experience, she tried to work out why this might be the case, in order to be able to offer more constructive support in future. In this chapter, she explains the conclusions she reached and proposes an interpretation of 'differentiation' intended to help ensure that teachers' efforts are rewarded by evidence of children's more sustained and productive engagement with learning activities provided. Though her focus is upon children with learning difficulties, we believe that the concerns she raises and ways of thinking about differentiation which she proposes in the study have relevance to teachers' work with all children.

♦ ◆ ♦

As an advisory and support teacher for children with special educational needs, my work continually brings me into contact with teachers and learners in mainstream schools. By virtue of my responsibilities, I have many opportunities not so readily available to other teachers to observe closely how children engage with the curriculum experiences provided, to examine the sense that they are making of tasks and to listen in to the ideas and questions which occur to them as they are working.

This opportunity for close observation generates many questions and ideas about what might be done to support and enhance children's learning – by no means exclusively those deemed to have learning difficulties. Sharing them with colleagues, however, is sensitive territory because suggestions can so easily seem to imply criticism of colleagues' work. I want to emphasise, therefore, that the concerns and ideas expressed here are presented in an attempt to give colleagues an insight into my thinking about ways forward in supporting both teachers and pupils, with success for both being the ultimate goal. I know that I do not have all the answers, nor would I be so rash as to say that I have!

I have called my chapter 'Bringing out the sparkle' because that is what I believe differentiation is trying to achieve. We know when we have been successful in differentiating learning experiences because children do light up with interest, understanding, confidence and a sense of success. Maybe it is unreasonable to think that we can achieve that on every occasion with every learner. But for some children, it seems so rarely, if ever, to happen that we cease to believe that it is actually a realistic possibility.

This conclusion seems all the more justified when teachers know that they have gone to considerable lengths to try to provide experiences adapted to children's individual needs, and yet still the children do not seem to understand what they are doing and demand constant support. It is hardly surprising that at this point teachers begin to feel that the problem must lie with the children themselves: that they are lazy, or did not pay attention, or are just not able to cope with or have success in school-based learning. Teachers can become more and more despondent when, despite hours spent differentiating work, their pupils still do not achieve independent learning and success. In the end, teachers begin to feel that they have 'done enough'. The children, too, become increasingly demoralised at their failure to do and learn what the school expects and eventually switch off altogether. Once that has happened, it is no simple matter to switch them back on to school learning, no matter how carefully the teacher has differentiated the work, because they are not prepared to take the risk of failing once more.

From my experience, observations and my own work with children, I have become convinced that there is much that we could do to free such children from dependence upon the teacher, to enable them to experience success and to gain confidence once again in their own ability to learn. For this to be possible, we need to know their strengths and use that knowledge to devise learning experiences which allow them to use and build on their strengths as their principal resource for learning and demonstrating learning. It is only if differentiation practices are directed towards the goal of making it possible for children to learn in the way that is most positive and meaningful for each individual that teachers will be rewarded by the progress and success that they so earnestly want for their pupils. The vehicle for this success is appropriately 'matched' or differentiated work. Interpreting the task of differentiation in this way ultimately benefits all children, since the time made available through appropriate differentiation can then be used by the teacher to work with other pupils.

In this case study, I try to explain and justify this view. I use some examples drawn from my experience to help illustrate why steps taken to differentiate learning experiences often prove not to be as enabling as teachers intend. I then suggest some strategies that in my experience can be helpful in 'bringing out the sparkle'.

THE LITERACY BARRIER

We know that the vast majority of children identified as having special educational needs are so identified on the basis of limited literacy skills. Yet in many if not most secondary school subjects, the opportunity to learn is dependent upon the ability to read and write, which it is generally assumed pupils ought by now to have acquired. Pupils with limited literacy are therefore continually at a disadvantage because they constantly have to rely for learning on their weakest resources.

Acknowledging this problem, many secondary subject departments are responding by attempting to introduce differentiated reading material and writing tasks graded to take account of limited writing skills. A great deal of time is being put into this work, and clearly it can open up learning opportunities for children who previously were unable to participate in lessons because they could not read the material provided or attempt more complex writing tasks. Unfortunately, though, easier-to-read texts and structured writing tasks do not fundamentally change the situation whereby children are obliged to learn and demonstrate learning via their weakest resources rather than their strengths. The work is 'matched' to their literacy levels but not to the pattern of their strengths and weaknesses that will best facilitate their learning.

Sometimes, when I am observing children or working with them on a one-to-one basis, I am struck by the quality of the thinking aloud that they do as they engage with a learning activity, the speculation that goes on, the questions they ask, the comments that they make in response to my answers and explanations. I know that they will never be able to write any of this down, and because they cannot, it frequently passes unnoticed. The quality of their thinking, learning and potential is generally judged through written outcomes and these in my experience are frequently a poor reflection of their actual knowledge and understandings.

There is a danger that we may significantly underestimate the abilities and potential of children with literacy difficulties because they are rarely in a situation where they can learn and demonstrate their learning via their strengths. We adapt our teaching to their attainments mediated through their limited literacy skills, rather than exploring how those attainments might be transformed if other modes of learning and demonstrating learning were more routinely allowed, indeed positively encouraged and valued.

There is also a danger that when we rely on written outcomes we may gain the impression that children have successfully learnt what we intended, when in fact the outcomes mask a significant lack of understanding. Most teachers are familiar with the problem of comprehension questions which can be answered simply by locating and copying the correct portion of text, and therefore tell you nothing about the child's actual understanding or engagement with the ideas the text contains. I observed a group of children carrying out a mathematics task which they interpreted in a way which was quite different from the teacher's intentions. The teacher's monitoring of the group during the lesson did not alert her to the fact that they were not doing the task as she had intended, and therefore not gaining what she had intended from its completion. Indeed, the finished product looked much as she expected. The group received justified praise for having cooperated well, and were themselves pleased with what they had produced, thinking it was exactly what the teacher wanted.

I believe that we could explore the more routine use of tasks that involve outcomes other than writing, for instance:

- purposeful observation
- drawing
- modelling

- model-making
- drama
- oral discussion and presentations of various kinds
- poster making.

We need to look again at the function of writing as a means of learning and demonstrating learning, so that we can use it discerningly and appropriately. In acknowledgement of different teaching and learning styles, we need to recognise when the same ends can be just as well achieved by alternative means. An example of learning material which addresses these issues and provides for differentiated learning across a whole-class group is provided in the concluding section of this chapter.

GROUPING BY ATTAINMENT OR PRESUMED ABILITY

The issue of literacy is linked to the issue of grouping, since the level of text difficulty is less significant if groups are not always or generally organised on the basis of attainment or presumed ability. It often seems to be taken for granted that grouping by ability is necessary if we are to ensure that children's individual learning needs are met. However, my observations suggest that groups made up of children who all have difficulties with literacy and lack confidence in their abilities as learners do not make productive learning groups and absorb a disproportionate amount of teachers' time. Many other forms of grouping – friendship, interest, mixed-ability, mixed-gender, mixed-language – can actually be far more successful as a learning unit and foster far more productive learning, as long as they contain individuals who are confident in taking the lead in reading, writing, drawing, etc., and each child is assigned a particular task in the team, that is, individual children are using their particular strength to contribute to the team as a whole.

When children learn in groups formed on some basis other than attainment or ability, the use of textual material and writing tasks is supported by members of the group, so pupils with literacy difficulties are able to tackle material together with others that they would not be able to tackle alone. One research project, for example, found that once the barrier of decoding was overcome – by reading texts collaboratively – children perceived as less able could contribute to the problem-solving task related to the text as effectively as their more confidently reading peers (Lunzer and Gardner 1979). It could be, then, that many of the learning difficulties attributed to children are actually a result of a largely literacy-based curriculum. Of course, it is also important that they should have opportunities to use and develop their reading and writing skills as part of normal curriculum activities. However, they are more likely to take up such opportunities once they have begun to feel confident and successful as a result of developing their learning through other modes.

INCIDENTAL DEMANDS THAT PRESENT BARRIERS

We need to look carefully at the demands of a particular task and our intentions for children's learning, and make sure that these present no barriers that will impede participation or unnecessarily divert children's efforts into activities that form no part of our intentions for their learning. I saw one group, for example, struggling to copy into their books the format for a game intended to provide insight into some mathematical principles. Copying the detail accurately became the central endeavour of the group and most of the lesson was taken up with doing it, with some frustration because they were quite keen to get on and play the game. Yet the copying was no part of the teacher's intentions for the children's learning. It would not have detracted from the task at all to have provided ready-made formats for playing the game, so that the group could have moved straight into the mathematical activity.

TASK PURPOSE AND STRUCTURE

Linked to the preceding point, we need to have a clear sense of what the purpose of a particular task is and ensure that the task is structured in such a way that it reflects this purpose. If we can achieve this, and succeed in communicating it to the children, then we put them in a position where they can exercise control over the task and take initiatives to develop it in ways that are helpful and productive to them. In my experience, children are frequently engaged in tasks where they do not understand or have any sense of control over what they are learning and why. They simply submit to whatever they are asked to do, without any attempt to engage actively their intellectual resources. One familiar example of this is children who have handed over control to the teacher and therefore do not notice themselves that what they are reading aloud makes no sense, or that an answer they have come up with to a sum is quite ridiculously impossible because they have made some simple slip.

PREFERRED TEACHING STYLES

We need to be aware of the impact of our own preferred teaching style upon the learning opportunities we make available for children, and how this affects children who might learn more successfully by other means. We need to recognise that children learn in different ways and that we may not yet have made available, or at least not sufficiently, the ways that would enable the least successful children in our classes to become independent and confident learners. This is a point which is taken up and developed more extensively in a later section of the book (pp. 81–137). So I shall do no more than acknowledge it here. It is important for all learners, and most especially for those seen to have special educational needs, that they should have available many different possible routes to learning, so that they can travel along those that they find most comfortable whilst exploring new experiences. We can then build on the sense of confidence and success thus created to work on the more problematic features of their learning.

SUMMARY

To summarise, I have argued that in order to give children confidence and ensure that they are able to have control of their learning, we need to give careful thought to how we build on their strengths and enable them to use all the resources they have available to support their learning to the full. In order to do this, we need first to identify their strengths and use them to influence the production of appropriately differentiated learning activities and materials. This includes thinking about:

- the balance between the different language modes used for learning
- the balance between teaching styles
- the range of outcomes that we expect
- the range of groupings that we routinely encourage
- the demands of the task and their relationship to our purposes
- our purposes, and how the structure of the task reflects these
- how we communicate our purposes to learners and enable them to take over control
- the different styles of learning that are possible and encouraged in our classrooms.

EXAMPLE: CLASSICAL STUDIES

A good example of a text-based resource which supports differentiated learning along the lines suggested in this chapter is the British Museum publication *The Romans* (Jackson *et al*. 1986). I have seen this used successfully for work in classical studies, with a Year 8 class which included children with learning difficulties. As the book is primarily visual, it instantly removes the tension which weaker readers experience on being presented with a textbook. Although the instructions have to be read, they are not particularly long or difficult, and paired or shared reading could overcome this, as would the teacher reading the instructions out loud.

Activities are provided which invite children to engage with the subject matter in a range of different ways, including opportunities to use and develop abilities in:

- visual discrimination
- sequencing numbers
- conceptual reasoning
- addition
- multiplication
- tracking
- using contextual clues
- spatial awareness
- eye-hand coordination.

By using this type of resource, the pupil who is weak in literacy skills but good orally, visually and/or aurally is able to contribute to the lesson, access information in the same way as the rest of the group/class and experience success in the same way as their peers, who have also benefited by the reinforcement of learning strategies through the subject material. Hence it is not necessary to differentiate other material, or produce separate worksheets. A more manageable approach is to consider alternative ways of presenting the topic, and the range of resources needed to encompass different teaching styles appropriate to the varied learning modes represented in the classroom. This way, everyone benefits.

CONCLUSION

I believe that a central aim of all education and teaching should be the development of self-confidence and independence. We have to try to create an environment where all children are given equal opportunity to use their ability and experience as a tool to becoming independent learners. Obviously, such a working environment cannot develop by itself or overnight and requires a good deal of teacher planning, not only of the work to be covered within the National Curriculum, but also of the organisation of the classroom's learning areas and resources. Discussion with the class as a whole is essential in order to agree the rules regarding the use of the classroom, by everyone, as a learning resource. In this chapter, I have drawn on my experience to explore some of the other essential ingredients which might go to create such a learning environment: one where all children can experience success and where teachers feel less pressured and so are more able to work with individual pupils when they require teacher intervention.

Part II

Differentiation through small group learning

Chapter 4

Differentiation without fragmentation
Lynda McCall

EDITOR'S INTRODUCTION

Once we have acknowledged the diversity of experience, interests, strengths and weaknesses that is represented in any teaching group, the teacher's task can suddenly seem an impossibly daunting one. If we take seriously the aspiration to acknowledge and build on this diversity, how can it realistically be achieved? Teaching the class as a class, with the same content, materials, tasks, homeworks, tests and assessment criteria for everyone, no longer seems to be a viable option. Logically, it seems that we have to find some means of breaking the whole-class group down and providing different tasks and materials for groups and individuals.

However, breaking the class down has disadvantages too. From the point of view of preparation, it seems to be requiring of teachers that they prepare what amounts to several different lessons for the same class. As was noted in the HMI reports referred to in Chapter 1, worksheets and other differentiated material may offer a poor substitute for a good teacher (DES 1977, 1978a, 1978b, 1979, 1984). It is very difficult to devise worksheet-based tasks that are sufficiently open-ended, stimulating and engaging to hold children's attention and challenge their thinking. Using worksheets extensively as a substitute for teacher–child interaction can lead to an impoverishment of learning experiences instead of the enhancement that is intended in breaking free from the constraints of whole-class teaching. Assignments intended to be carried out individually make considerable demands upon children to sustain concentration and persevere with tasks for extended periods. As Sharon Camilletti argued in Chapter 3, it can mean even more pressure upon children with limited literacy skills to rely on their weakest resources rather than their strengths.

Breaking the class down into groups or individuals working on different assignments also creates a considerable managerial problem for the teacher. The more complex the arrangement, the more time teachers may spend overseeing the management of the lesson rather than actually teaching. Research evidence at primary level (Bennett *et al.* 1984; Galton *et al.* 1980) has drawn attention to these dangers, showing that the majority of teacher–pupil interaction was of a low-level, procedural nature in classes where teaching was organised on an individual basis.

One of the well-rehearsed arguments against streaming and setting is that breaking the class down into groups on the basis of one criterion (usually attainment, ability or literacy skills) does not really take account of diversity, because it ignores all the ways in which pupils differ apart from the one common feature which provides the basis for a given grouping. Even supposedly individualised learning materials, such as mathematics schemes, are not really individualised since the nature and sequence of learning activities are predetermined and so cannot take account of individual interests, strengths, learning styles and patterns of development.

Many teachers also express concern that differentiated tasks targeted at different levels of attainment or ability may impose unnecessary constraints upon children's learning, and limit the possibilities for collaborative interaction between pupils working on different tasks. Research has highlighted the problem of 'matching' tasks to pupils' estimated capabilities, even at primary level where teachers have so much more opportunity to get to know the learning needs of each of their pupils as individuals (Bennett *et al*. 1984; Bennett 1991). Moreover, work which is successfully 'matched' academically may fail to promote learning if it reinforces a learner's low self-esteem and limited attainments in comparison with others in the group.

In addition, there is concern about the social effects of breaking classes down into groups who carry out differentiated work according to perceived levels of achievement. These groupings tend to form identities which then shape their work patterns, attitudes to learning and relationships within the group (Ball 1981; Pollard 1985), and can have a significant impact on children's long-term development.

For all these reasons, then, it is important to be cautious in the way that we set about developing differentiated learning. As HMI acknowledge, differentiation can be achieved through whole-class activity, with everyone ostensibly doing the same thing at the same time, provided that this activity has been conceived in such a way as to create appropriate, stimulating and challenging learning experiences for everyone:

> For example, a class pursuing integrated studies in the humanities were presented with a film strip which gave opportunities for noting differences between present and past and making deductions. The teacher helped with sensitive questioning, and pupils of all abilities were able to contribute to and benefit from the work.
>
> (DES 1978a p. 37)

Thus differentiation need not necessarily entail fragmentation. Indeed, if we see the diversity of knowledge, experience, backgrounds, interests and talents represented in a single class group as a positive resource, then we will be looking for teaching approaches and methods which recognise and build on this diversity for the benefit of the learning of the whole group.

In this chapter, Lynda McCall describes how she and a colleague in the science department worked together to try to develop mixed-ability approaches to learning science that would allow flexibility, yet maintaining a common experience that all could share. She explains why it was important for her to approach differentiation in this way and offers as an example a series of activities which they developed incorporating 'jigsaw' group work.

◆ ◆ ◆

I recently joined a Suffolk middle school which incorporates a double Area Support Centre (ASC) for twenty-four children. My post is funded by the county, but it is the wish of the head teacher that ASC staff and children (who are said to have moderate learning difficulties) are fully integrated into the school.

Being a support teacher means, above all, being adaptable. Described by Will Swann (1992) as 'pedagogic schizophrenia', the need for the support teacher to adopt different styles when working alongside different teachers is a well-known one. Nevertheless, support teaching also offers a privileged insight into the even greater complexities and adaptions necessary for pupils to cope as they move from subject to subject and teacher to teacher. Support teachers are uniquely able to identify with the child who experiences boredom and frustration in the classroom. If we are totally honest we have been there, looked out of the window, done that, read the book and seen the film – twice! I feel sure that part of the answer is to participate as much as possible in the curriculum planning of a subject.

In this chapter, I describe a scheme of work which a science colleague and I developed together, moving towards the two-way learning advocated by Bourne and McPake (1991):

> There are activities that make the whole of the curriculum accessible to everybody. Open learning is part of that . . . it becomes a two way process (between teacher and pupil) when you're negotiating things and you're both learning from each other.

Our aim was to enable all children to participate and learn successfully through greater use of oracy skills and through the development of worksheets that are suitable for all children when combined with carefully organised group work. Our thinking was influenced by ideas in *Access to Science* (Humberside County Council 1992) and the *Partnership teaching* project (Bourne and McPake 1991), which is a professional model for teachers working collaboratively to develop a curriculum appropriate to the needs and abilities of all pupils (see appendix).

I was particularly interested in being more closely involved with planning in science, partly because my own knowledge of science is limited and partly because many of the pupils I was supporting seemed to experience difficulties in that area. Being relatively new to the school, I did not feel confident enough to foist myself upon the science coordinator. However, I did discover that an equally new science teacher who was interested in mixed-ability group work was also concerned that the children who had difficulties were unable to cope with science in particular. Based on these joint concerns we felt that working collaboratively could be successful and that together we would feel more confident about providing lesson plans.

Consequently we have worked on some science lesson plans, based on the development of mixed-ability group work and suitable worksheets. We hope that making these plans available to colleagues might encourage more teachers to explore the value of alternative ways of working. All teachers are capable of adapting aspects of their work, the content, the delivery and the assessment, according to the strengths and weaknesses of their pupils. We can try to achieve a balance whereby pupils are helped to realise their capabilities as fully as possible without being segregated from their peers. I firmly believe that success can be achieved by the teacher who is flexible enough to be able to accept, and use to the group's advantage, the wide and varying experiences that children bring to the classroom.

We must remember that all children, whatever their strengths and limitations, are legally entitled to a broad and balanced curriculum, and that we as teachers must do our best to provide access to that curriculum. If some pupils are removed from the mixed-ability classroom in order to achieve this then they no longer have access to other equally important experiences such as further development of socialisation skills with their peers. If we are to differentiate successfully, we must avoid closing off opportunities from which children might significantly benefit. We need to safeguard equal opportunity for all.

In attempting to differentiate, we also deal with staff development. We need to find ways of breaking down barriers between subject staff and support staff, achieving equal status, and enabling staff to learn from each other and from pupils. Flexibility is the key.

BEYOND THE 'THREE-TIER WORKSHEET' APPROACH?

My colleague and I set out to expand on the lesson plan provided by the science coordinator and to provide group activities and worksheets which would be meaningful to all the children in the group. We particularly wanted to place increased emphasis on the use of talk in learning, and we were in agreement that we did not wish to produce what we called the 'three-tier worksheet.' We wanted to avoid the mechanical production of graded worksheets: either containing a main body of knowledge, with extension work for the more able and reinforcement work for the children who experience difficulties, or three separate worksheets for the three 'bands'. We agreed that such approaches can simply segregate the children within the classroom. The alternative was to provide either an open-ended worksheet or a cloze-style sheet which everyone could tackle. The idea of the two styles of worksheets is to offer flexibility to the teacher. For example, if time is short the cloze exercise may be completed very quickly.

We aimed to meet twice weekly to discuss the methods. My colleague would check on the content of the worksheets that I had prepared, as my concern was primarily with the needs of the children who experienced difficulties and my science knowledge, although expanding, still limited! Unfortunately, due to the usual constraints we rarely achieved this.

The activities we developed involve children working in pairs or groups, with much emphasis on oracy skills. The aims are as follows:

1 Children learn to work together in a variety of groups, gaining confidence, thus enabling them to become independent learners.
2 They accept each other's strengths and weaknesses.
3 They also help each other.
4 They learn to share resources, ideas and their results.
5 They gain confidence in talking to groups and to the whole class.
6 They work to deadlines.
7 They develop AT1 listening skills at all stages.

Access to Science (Humberside County Council 1992) was helpful in suggesting how we could differentiate yet still provide a broad and balanced curriculum. From this, we derived the following principles:

1 An appropriate starting point will affect the extent to which a child will learn and should be considered carefully.
2 Selection of a common experience such as a question at the beginning of an activity can be aimed at a specific concept or target.
3 Activity should be open-ended in order that it can be discussed and investigated and hypotheses can be formulated.
4 Child ownership of the investigation is important.
5 Building on pupils' existing knowledge and ideas and valuing what they bring to the classroom rather than leaving it all at the door are also important.
6 Verbal responses can be valued alongside written ones.

A range of techniques can be used to help pupils consider their ideas, for instance brainstorming, pair work, group work including 'jigsawing', and class discussion. It may be helpful at this stage to explain the uses of brainstorming and jigsawing as techniques.

Brainstorming is a useful method of introducing a new topic by letting pupils draw on their own existing knowledge and encouraging the sharing of ideas and beliefs. It helps to set the scene. It is vital that the teacher stipulates that all suggestions are of value and that no one is to pass judgement on other pupils' ideas. If this is a whole-class activity the teacher should aim to get a contribution from everyone; if it is a paired or grouped activity try to monitor this aspect if at all possible.

Jigsawing is a group activity which is broken down into individual or paired tasks. The class is divided into a number of groups, according to the number of areas to be covered. Group A, for example, have to work together to find out a body of information. Each child in this group must gather the information because everyone will later be regrouped amongst a new set of children who have been looking at different source material. Each child is now the 'expert' within the new group and will help by completing the part of the second task that concerns his or her expertise. All the other children in the new group have different information to contribute and will be the experts on the work that they studied initially, in their first group.

Our thinking was also influenced by the science indicators of good practice, as described in the Runnymede Trust document (1993), *Equality assurance in schools*. Nine indicators are listed in the document. We highlighted two indicators which relate to the topic we are working with:

> All pupils are given access to the specialist language of science. . . .
> Where necessary work is made intelligible by context and through practical tasks and activities so that learning is not wholly dependent on competence in English.

> Materials, tasks and activities reflect the pupils' own first hand experience of life, including cultural, linguistic and social experiences.

The main resource for this topic is the Bath Macmillan Science 5-16 textbook called *Investigating Life Key Stage 3* (Thompson and Hollins 1991).

The topic comprises five units set in the context of Sc. 2 'Life and Living Processes', strands (i) and (ii):

Unit 1 That's Life
Unit 2 Key the Difference
Unit 3 Classification
Unit 4 Pollen Power
Unit 5 Local Study.

One of the difficulties that arises in a middle school is that a subject may be taught by a non-specialist. We felt that we could provide further resources to supplement the lesson plan and the textbook. We also anticipate that this work will be helpful to new colleagues who may join us in the future. Here is an example from the work so far.

LEARNING TO CLASSIFY

The two lessons described in detail here are part of a sequence of lessons on classification. Pupils will previously have carried out a number of activities, beginning to examine and classify things based on perceived similarities and differences. They will have met the terms 'classify' and 'genes' and reached a suitable definition of 'characteristics'.

Lesson A: Shopping Spree!

This lesson was selected as our starting point because it had not been as successful as my colleague had hoped last time she had taught the topic and we hoped to improve it for the future. In previous sessions the pupils have worked from the textbook, but we felt that a wider variety of planned learning activities would be more meaningful to more pupils and 'hands-on' experience would add an element of fun.

In order to prepare the children for classifying animals it is important that they appreciate the need to sort things into groups in other situations. The aim of this introductory lesson is therefore to give them a sorting activity based on a common experience, using a scenario that is familiar to them. Because of the practical nature of this work and absence of written work, the children with learning difficulties should be able to integrate successfully. There is also ample opportunity to develop oracy skills. Based on the example given in the textbook we decided that a supermarket would be a suitable starting point.

Activity 1

On arrival each group is faced with a carrier bag full of miscellaneous shopping items. They are asked to group these items in any way that they like but to remember that they must all agree on how they have achieved this and should all be able to explain to others. The collection would include items reflecting different cultures aimed to encourage further discussion. It is a matter of choice (or convenience) as to whether each group has the same items to sort or different selections.

After five to ten minutes a spokesperson for each group explains the groups that they have made.

This activity encourages discussion and decision making within the group.

Activity 2: class discussion

The staff can remind pupils of the previous lesson when they talked about characteristics, genes and classification and emphasise the importance of knowing the correct scientific terms and the need for such classification.

Activity 3

In groups, repeat the grouping exercise but this time the children are scientists and have to sort a selection of shells and fill in a chart accordingly, inventing names for each type.

Activity 4

The homework is another sorting activity aimed at reinforcing the need for order and criteria for it. An example would be: 'Ways you might sort clothes'.

A simple sheet could be available that the teacher may prefer to use.

Lesson B: criteria for classification

This lesson provides an illustration of how we redesigned a lesson so that it would be accessible to all children, through the use of worksheets combined with carefully organised group work.

Before being able to sort animals into taxonomic groups, pupils need to be able to understand some of the criteria used to classify animals in this way. The session is aiming to encourage pupils to read actively, for a purpose, so that they become the expert on one specific group of animals. The experts then work together to produce a simple chart of typical characteristics. The groups could be given an appropriate name such as 'Robert's reptiles'.

The jigsawing technique is used for this exercise. We suggest that the groups are mixed-ability so that the more competent readers can help the pupils who experience some difficulty. It may also be helpful to note that the texts are of varying lengths: birds and insects being shorter than the others. In these initial groups the pupils work on the appropriate information worksheets (Figures 4.1 and 4.2) and answer the accompanying questions. There is a choice of a cloze-style exercise (Figure 4.3) or a more open-ended one (Figure 4.4). These worksheets have been written as simply and clearly as possible, guided by principles for making texts more readable. (We worked from an unpublished pack of material, *Better worksheets*, produced by a local education authority (LEA) colleague, Mike Oldfield, but see also, for example, Essex County Council 1993.)

Regrouping

When the expert groups have completed their task, children regroup so that members of each group representing mammals, fish, birds and insects come together to complete the chart (see Figure 4.5). All the children have the opportunity to pass on their expertise orally to the rest of the new group. It is not essential that each child writes down his or her own information: there are often other willing scribes.

The earth is crawling with insects, in fact they make up the largest group of animals. There are at least one million different species, including beetles, butterflies, ants and bees. Insects have been on earth for 500 million years.

HABITAT – WHERE THEY LIVE

Insects are found all over the world in every kind of habitat, from cold mountains to hot tropical rain forests. Many insects can fly and others live in water as well as many being on land.

APPEARANCE – WHAT THEY LOOK LIKE

All insects have six legs (so do you think that a spider is an insect?) and a body covered in a hard exo-skeleton. That means that the skeleton is on the outside not the inside like a human, who is a mammal.
A typical insect has a body divided into three parts. At the front is the head, in the middle is the thorax and at the back is the abdomen.

VARIETY – THE DIFFERENCES

They vary a lot in size and shape. The Goliath beetle weighs more than 100 grams (3.5 ounces) or a small bar of chocolate, the tiny fairy fly is almost invisible to the human eye.

FEEDING – WHAT THEY EAT

Insects feed on almost anything – wood, blood, nectar, paper, shoe polish, seaweed, dung and other insects.
The mouth parts of most insects, however, are specially adapted for a particular kind of food. Some are designed to suck, to stab, to pierce, to scrape and to probe.

BABIES

Insects lay eggs. How much the parent insects care for these eggs varies. Ants and bees live in colonies or large groups and the eggs are carefully looked after but most insects lay their eggs and then fly away.

Figure 4.1 Insects information worksheet

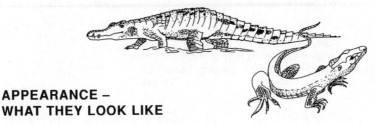

APPEARANCE –
WHAT THEY LOOK LIKE

Animals with scaly skins are called reptiles. Examples of reptiles are:

alligators   crocodiles
snakes   lizards
turtles

A reptile's scales give good protection against enemies and also stop the animal drying out.

HABITAT – WHERE THEY LIVE

Some live in water and some on land and most of them live in the warmer parts of the world such as India, South America, Africa and Australia.
  Reptiles are one of the most ancient of animals; dinosaurs were reptiles!

VARIETY – THE DIFFERENCES

Today, there are more than 6,500 kinds, or species, of reptiles, from a long python that measures 10 metres (33 feet) to the tiny dwarf gecko which is only 33 mm (1.3 inches long).
All these animals are reptiles:
Snakes – pythons, grass snakes, boa constrictors.
Lizards – the Komodo dragon, the skink, the gecko.
Crocodiles – alligators, caimans, gavials.
Turtles – the leatherback turtle, the common mud turtle.
Tortoises – giant tortoise, terrapin.

WARM OR COLD BLOODED?

Reptiles are cold blooded; they need the warmth of the sun to give them energy to move. They sunbathe to absorb (soak up) heat and hide in the shade when they get too hot.

BABIES

Most reptiles lay eggs, although a few do give birth to live babies, because they keep the eggs inside their bodies until the young are ready to be born. Snakes and lizards have leathery, flexible shells, which means that they don't break easily. Crocodiles, alligators, turtles and tortoises have eggs more like birds' eggs but they do not have nests; they often bury them in sand.

Figure 4.2 Reptiles information worksheet

GROUP . . . .

THINGS FOR YOU TO FIND OUT ABOUT REPTILES.

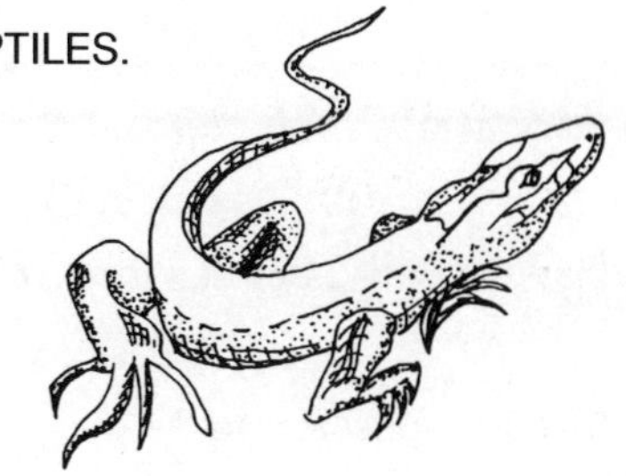

1. A reptile is
                 warm blooded.
                 cold blooded.

2. Reptiles are covered in
                        feathers.
                        skin.
                        scales.

3. Scales help stop the reptile from
                                slipping.
                                drying out.

4. Reptiles produce
                    live babies.
                    eggs.
                    live babies or eggs.

5. Snakes' and lizards' eggs are
                          live birds' eggs.
                          like leather.

6. Most lizards live in
                  colder
                        parts of the world, such as India and Africa.
                  hotter

7. There are more than
                    65
                    650   species of reptiles. The dinosaurs were reptiles.
                    6,500

8. These animals are reptiles
     lizard   snail   crocodile.
     lobster,   snake   and   camel.
     lion,   seal   cockatoo.

9. Turtles, tortoises and terrapins all have shells and they are
                                                          rodents.
                                                          reptiles.

10. Turtles are likely to bury their eggs in the
                                       water.
                                       sand.
                                       garden.

Figure 4.3 Reptiles cloze exercise

WHAT DO YOU KNOW ABOUT REPTILES?

1. Describe the body heat of the reptile.

    . . . .
    . . . .
    . . . .

2. What is the body of a reptile covered in?

    . . . .

3. What are scales for?

    . . . .
    . . . .

4. How does a reptile produce its young?

    . . . .
    . . . .

5. Give some examples of reptiles.

    . . . .
    . . . .
    . . . .

6. Where do they live in the world?

    . . . .
    . . . .

7. How many species are there?

    . . . .

8. Can you describe the eggs of reptiles?

    . . . .
    . . . .

9. Do turtles care for their eggs? How?

    . . . .
    . . . .

10. Explain how long reptiles have been on earth.

    . . . .
    . . . .

Figure 4.4 Reptiles open-ended exercise

ACTIVITY 2   GROUP.............

What to do.
Each "expert" must fill in their animal classification group in box 1, 2, 3, 4 or 5
Next fill in the details of your group using your worksheets to help. Look at the boxes
carefully

Animal Classification Group.	Warm blooded or cold blooded?	Describe the body covering.	Lays eggs, live babies or both?	Write down one more fact about your animal group	Name one animal that belongs to your group	Draw another animal which belongs to your group.
①						
②						
③						
④						
⑤						

Figure 4.5 Animal classification group chart

Follow-up

This lesson should lead on to using and making simple keys. The first part of this lesson could be a sorting activity, placing pictures of animals into the correct classification. It is envisaged that this will be a group and then whole-class activity to make a wall display.

Towards the end of the lesson the teacher could introduce the idea that pupils are explorers and they have just discovered ET or Gremlins. How would they classify them and how could this be shown clearly and precisely as a diagram?

SUMMARY

I believe that differentiation has been achieved in these lessons by using a familiar starting point and building on existing knowledge. Equal opportunity for every child to participate in each science lesson is created through a combination of

- mixed-ability group work
- open-ended worksheets which use language suitable for everyone
- non-written activities
- emphasis on oral work.

The teacher's role has been that of facilitator and adviser and children have been encouraged to feel a sense of ownership and responsibility for their learning.

Evaluation is a vital part of any new work and it is important to invite feedback from pupils and non-specialist staff. We planned to develop an evaluation sheet and carry out some on-the-spot tape recording.

CONCLUSION

Personally, I have benefited a great deal from much closer liaison with colleagues and feel more confident and clearer about my role in the classroom. Our relationships have strengthened and we can be far more direct and honest than previously. As I have become involved in the science department I have become familiar with a considerable amount of the syllabus, far more than I have dealt with here. This highlights the immense amount of work necessary in trying to differentiate, so that our philosophy is now 'bit by bit, little by little we will get there!' Ultimately, we would like to team-teach with all members of the science department. A more group-based approach would allow the special needs staff more time with members of the class and the science teacher greater familiarity with the children from the Area Support Centre.

As a result of this work I am even more positive that flexibility and tolerance are the key to successful differentiation and thereby successful teaching, but most importantly we cannot all be differentiating every-thing all of the time and expect to survive. So class-teach the same thing, in the same way, to everybody now and again and do not feel guilty: there is another day tomorrow. Do not forget that differentiation happens almost despite ourselves; teachers cannot help adapting as they go along. Simply to tell a child to omit a section of a worksheet, or tape rather than write a story, is differentiating. Knowing your pupils well, their strengths and weaknesses, means you can accept and acknowledge a variety of outcomes in their work – and this too is differentiation.

Chapter 5

Developing group work skills

Janet Fawthrop

EDITOR'S INTRODUCTION

In Chapter 4, we looked at the part that group work can play in organising teaching and learning to acknowledge and build on the diversity of experience, interests and needs within any teaching group. The approach described assumes that children have much to learn from one another as well as from the teacher, and that they benefit from the opportunity to work out ideas together through talk in a small group.

However, teachers are often wary of group work because children do not necessarily have ready-made the skills needed to work very constructively together. Where individual written work has been the most common form of classroom activity, children may not automatically appreciate the value of group work. They may not regard opportunities for talk as 'proper' work and so do not take group activities seriously. Group work can quickly break down into individual activity and/or become chaotic if the children lack the commitment and skills to work together effectively.

Teachers also express concern that some children will opt out of group activities and allow the others to do all the work, or that those who are slower to grasp ideas may be denied the opportunity to work through ideas sufficiently thoroughly to reach an adequate understanding of new material for themselves. Equally, there is concern that the more confident, knowledgeable and experienced learners will either dominate groups or be held back because of continually having to explain ideas to others. Whilst recognising that the act of explaining usually benefits the explainer as much as the recipient of the explanation, there is also concern that the more confident learners should not be exploited as substitute teachers to support the learning of those who are less confident or less committed to learning than themselves.

In addition, it is important to consider the social demands which group work makes upon those who find making relationships difficult, who are isolated within the group or at least not spontaneously included by others. There is some evidence that one of the effects of cooperative learning is to enhance children's liking for one another and positive acceptance of individuals within a class group. However, in the early stages of introducing collaborative activities, there are often individuals who actively disrupt the work of groups or whom other children do not spontaneously choose to work with.

For all these reasons, then, it is important to plan carefully for group learning and monitor closely its impact upon individual children's learning experience. Deliberate steps may need to be taken to develop the skills and understandings needed for successful collaborative learning. This chapter invites you to consider what teachers can positively do to help children to work successfully as part of a group and so be able to realise in practice the potential benefits of collaborative working. Before reading the case study material, you may wish to take some time to reflect on your own experience of group work and the kinds of steps which you take to enable cooperative work to be successful.

This chapter describes the steps which one teacher took to help children in her class to take responsibility for thinking about and managing group functioning. Janet Fawthrop decided that pupils' sense of responsibility for their own learning was the most important issue to tackle. She describes how she used some ideas from the book *Small group learning in the classroom* (Reid *et al.* 1989) as a stimulus for raising discussion about learning through group work in her class, and helping pupils to develop the tools and language that would enable them to monitor and evaluate group learning for themselves. Though the work described took place with 9 and 10 year olds, the activities described could be adapted to class groups consisting of learners of any age.

I learn best by talking to other people.

Natalie

I learn the best by talking and working in a group.

Kayleigh

I learn the best in a group when nobody bosses you around, because you work hard in a group.

Leslie

These are some of the comments from my new Year 5 class after we had talked about how we learn. I wanted to give my mixed-ability class of thirty-one girls and boys a tool to help with their learning experiences, but first I wanted to try to raise the children's awareness of how we learn and particularly how we can use small groups to help in this process. Ultimately I wanted children to begin to take the responsibility for their own learning and realise that to work in a group is a method of helping them do this.

By using small group learning as a means of classroom organisation, I hoped to develop cooperation amongst my pupils and a caring atmosphere. As well as exploring the potential for differentiating the curriculum through group work, I wanted to see if special educational needs could be met in an integrated way, rather than providing specially designed activities that might isolate children from the rest of the group.

Spillman (1991), in an article 'Decoding differentiation', warns about the difficulties of attempting the sort of differentiation associated with individual learning programmes. She suggests that it would become too complicated for the class teacher to manage, as all children 'would be working on different materials and different levels'. Small groups encourage children of all abilities to work together. By working in small groups I wanted to avoid the children with special needs becoming isolated in their learning.

Small groups encourage children to feel more confident, to speak and discuss work. Where children do not feel confident in the class, in a small group they can often feel more secure and valued. Children are more likely to listen and attention is less likely to wander if they feel their contribution is worthwhile. My aim was to establish that all children have something to offer and each group should work collaboratively. Children are learning to help each other, organise themselves and take responsibility as individuals and as group members.

Small group learning allows children to develop at their own pace, and by allowing children to become actively involved in information gathering I hope they will begin to develop a greater understanding of their work and develop independence. All children will bring their own strengths to the group and feel that they are valued.

Throughout the school year, groups would differ in composition depending upon the outcome of previous work and what was the focus of the group. It was not intended that groups should be permanent, as I wanted to be able to introduce a variety of groupings and give the children the experience of working with different people. The period of time that the children remain together varied, because group work was only one of the ways in which I was trying to achieve differentiation.

Group work can be used throughout the curriculum and because some children will do well in certain subjects and not in others, it gives children the chance to do well in front of their group and develop in confidence. In certain areas of the curriculum, group work lends itself more readily than in others, such as humanities or topic work. Investigative work in maths, science and technology is also best carried out cooperatively in order to facilitate the exploration of ideas.

LEARNING TO WORK IN GROUPS

The children had had previous experience of working in groups, but had not discussed how groups worked. I thought that they would benefit from a discussion about the value of working in groups and about how they work together. I used the suggestions in the book *Small group learning in the classroom* (Reid et al. 1989) to do this, modifying it to meet my needs.

As a first step, I decided I would ask the children how they thought they learnt the best. I intended to do this in groups, but it was obvious by their hesitant manner when I talked to them that they were unsure what I meant, so I decided to use a brainstorming session. I asked the whole class to say how they thought they learn and quickly wrote down their ideas. Once a few suggestions had been made, such as reading books, listening, watching TV, more were added. This was quite successful and as a result they were able to discuss in small groups and write down their ideas. At the end of the session I held up each group's work and we looked for similarities. Overall, the groups thought that they learn best by asking questions, talking and discussing their work with others in a small group.

I told the children we would probably be working in groups quite often over the year, and so I thought it might be a good idea to formulate some rules for group discussions. Individually they all made up their list of about five rules, and after sharing it with their group came up with a common list. When this was done I asked the children to number their rules in order of importance. We then talked about the rules as a class and decided upon a class list. The following list evolved.

1 Cooperate.
2 Involve everyone! Listen.
3 Think before you talk.
4 Don't interrupt.
5 Always have a say so that you can't grumble afterwards.
6 Don't think you'll get your own way all the time.
7 Ask if you don't understand.

'Cooperate' was felt to be the most important as it seemed to lead to the other rules. Everyone has something to offer, so we must all try to work together.

Whilst the children were discussing the rules for group work, several groups began to talk about what went wrong with groups. I felt that this was very important to talk about, as we would have to deal with these problems if group work was to be effective. It seemed that some children do not want to accept what others suggest; they always want their own way, hence the inclusion of number 6, 'Don't think you'll get your own way all the time.' There seemed to be the general opinion than some children 'mess about'. The children found this difficult to define and in the end decided it meant not listening, wandering about and teasing other members of the group both verbally and physically. I wanted the groups to try to decide why this happened and the outcome was that those children did not feel involved, hence the inclusion of numbers 2 and 3:

Involve everyone! Listen.
Think before you talk.

Some children had felt excluded from the group and had felt that their input was not important. Number 5 – 'Always have a say so that you can't grumble afterwards' – was included because some children said it would prevent members of the group complaining afterwards that their work was not included or they did not agree.

Number 7 – 'Ask if you don't understand' – included asking not only me the teacher, but also other members of the group. By doing this everyone understands and feels involved. The work is owned by everyone, not just by one individual.

We went through the rules again talking about what they meant. They were then copied down for class display and everyone signed the poster.

DIFFICULT-TO-INCLUDE PUPILS

Within my class, as in most classes, there are a few children who have very considerable difficulties with learning. One child, whom I shall call Danny, has a statement of special educational needs. He has limited oral and reading skills and finds it difficult to concentrate for any length of time. He is used to the individual attention of a learning support assistant (LSA) who is assigned to work with him for 50 per cent of the school time. His former teacher had been aware of his over-reliance upon the LSA in that he demanded all her attention and had begun to expect any newcomer, visitor or helper coming into the class to help him solely. To deal with this problem she had decided to use the LSA to include other children, so that Danny would get used to working alongside others. I have carried on with this approach, but very often he has found it difficult to cooperate and work with others. A lot of patience is needed by adults and his peers as he is slow to develop responses, and ideas have to be explained several times. When he does not have the support of the LSA he finds it difficult to keep on task. When working on a project, after one or two periods, his attention wanders and he loses interest.

Although I thought that it would be enormously beneficial for him to work in a group that was expected to operate independently of the teacher, I was not confident at first that I would be able to involve him successfully. Nevertheless, I found that other children were more than willing to accept him into their group and identify positive contributions that he could make to the overall work of the group.

The topic which the year group were working on was Space and Light. During Book Week where the theme was 'Using Reference Books' my colleague and I decided to use friendship groups of three or four children who would take one of the planets and produce a poster about this planet. The final product was to be presented to the year group first and then a vote by the children would decide which posters would be presented to the school during a whole-school assembly. The work was discussed. We were doing the poster to enable us to use the new school library as it would help to develop reference skills – the purpose of the Book Week. The children had a pre-arranged time in which to work

In fact, Danny was accepted into a group without any direct intervention from me. Although he made no attempt to join a group himself, some children took the initiative and asked him to join them. I went to this group first, as I felt that they might need my help. The group recognised Danny's talent for drawing, and he was chosen to draw the planet. I kept returning to this group to encourage Danny to remain on task, as he is inclined to wander. On this occasion, though, his sense of commitment and participation seemed to be much higher than usual and he found it easier to sustain concentration. There was a real sense that he had become part of the group when he played a full part in the presentation. It would be important, of course, to ensure that Danny (as other children) took turns in fulfilling other roles, opening up other opportunities for learning and cooperating. However, this first successful involvement in independent group work brought out a side of Danny that was not often in evidence and provided a positive basis upon which to build.

As the children were allowed to work with whom they wanted, one group was made up of children who all were identified as having special educational needs (one at Stage 3 and two at Stage 1). This group required a lot of teacher input: help assessing information, reading and presenting their work. However, I felt that they were very proud of their completed work and were quite willing to present it to their year group. As a result these children have shown their peer group that they are capable of completing their work and presenting it.

The rest of the children worked mainly in single-sex groups, with the exception of one when two boys and two girls worked together. The children in this group are confident in their abilities and worked extremely well together, cooperating, suggesting ideas, helping each other and dividing up the workload fairly. They presented a completed piece of work for class and year group display. They later explained and talked about their work in a school assembly.

If children are being encouraged to take responsibility for their own learning, this means also learning to evaluate their own work and the work of others. By doing this, children have the opportunity to see how they have progressed and also how and what they need to improve. By looking at the work of others they can share ideas and look more closely at how they have worked in a group. It also helps me, the teacher, to assess the children in what they have done.

After completing their poster I decided to ask the children to review their work and how well they had worked in groups. The children were not used to doing this so we talked about it first. I also felt it was necessary to assure the children that they could answer honestly. They also commented on how they felt about working in a group. Most of them said they enjoyed working together because they had worked with their friends. One boy felt that his group did not talk as much as other people did. Generally, the children did not give many negative points; one girl did not enjoy working with someone because that person did not listen, whereas others in the group did. This process was new to the class and one which would be developed throughout the year.

THE INDIVIDUAL

Although group work is only one of the strategies which teachers can use to meet individual learning needs within a large class, I believe that it does have some significant advantages to offer, if we can create conditions where children are able to work effectively together. If children learn how to take responsibility, not only for themselves but also as a group member, this will relieve the teacher from a certain amount of classroom organisation and allow more time to help with individuals who may need skills breaking down into more manageable parts. It will also allow for the more able children to work at their own pace, thus differentiating by outcome.

In allowing all pupils to take part in small group work, then, we are encouraging all to use investigational skills – asking questions, predicting outcomes. If work was to be done on an individual basis then children become isolated and discouraged, which may lead to boredom. With the help and support of the peer group this can be overcome.

By working in small groups children need to use language to communicate. This will help to make learning more personal and because children are talking through the work then the individual can be helped with any difficult reading material.

Andrew Pollard (1987) in an article about social differentiation in primary schools reminds us that, in school, children have to cope with the social world of the playground and peers, as well as the more formal requirements of teachers. We need to be aware of the pressures on children to conform to what is expected of them in school, but also to maintain their dignity and self-esteem with their peers. By working in small groups and building on what children feel capable of then their self-esteem and worth can be developed. Children can explore and make mistakes which are more acceptable in a small group than in front of a class, thus allowing them to maintain their dignity.

When working in groups some children find it difficult to do so and tend either to dominate or become very quiet. In the case of the dominant child I found it necessary to talk with the child individually and explain the necessity to work cooperatively. I would also avoid putting the child with groups containing very shy and quiet children. I find that very quiet children work better with friendship groups where they feel more confident.

CONCLUSION

Once the initial rules for group work have been established and agreed, these can become the focus for continued discussion, feedback and comment by teachers and children. More sophisticated understandings of the roles that individuals play in groups and of the kinds of questions and contributions that help to sustain and promote learning in groups can begin to be opened up. The book which I used to support my work with my class (Reid *et al.* 1989) contains examples of activities which can be used with pupils of any age to discuss and evaluate group learning.

In one secondary school (see Chapter 2), teachers have been experimenting with role cards covering group roles such as 'note-taker', 'reporter', 'encourager' or 'observer'. On each card is written a description of a role (Figure 5.1) which individuals can play within the group, and the assumption is that individuals will take turns in fulfilling the different roles within the group. The descriptions help to extend pupils' language and insights into the functioning of groups, how they can organise themselves to achieve a successful outcome, and criteria with which to evaluate processes as well as outcomes. These are positive ways of increasing pupils' ability to take responsibility for their own learning.

Similarly, work can be done to highlight pupils' awareness of the interactional skills by drawing attention to skills of questioning, brainstorming, summarising and so on which can be used at different stages of group work. Some of the published material available to support teachers' own thinking in this area is presented in an appendix to this chapter.

APPENDIX TO SECTION 2: SUPPORTING COLLABORATIVE LEARNING

There are now many published materials available which teachers can use to extend and develop their own thinking about how to organise for successful collaborative work as part of their usual repertoire of teaching approaches. This appendix presents a selection of those that we have found directly useful in supporting our own teaching.

Small group learning in the classroom (Reid *et al.* 1989)

This book offers a clearly worked-out rationale for group learning and for making groups the basic unit for planning and organisation of classroom tasks. Learning is seen as an essentially social and language-based activity. Therefore the collaborative group provides the most appropriate basic structure, although this structure is flexible. The class is divided into 'home groups' which subdivide into pairs and individuals as appropriate

CHAIRPERSON

Your job is to chair the meeting. You have to encourage everyone to speak, and summarise the feelings of the group for the note-taker. You have to start and end the discussion, and make sure the group stays on the subject!!

IDEAS PERSON

You have to inject ideas into the meeting, and come up with as many good ideas or answers as possible. This is a very important job.

REPORTER

When your group is asked a question by the teacher it will be your job to report the group's answer to the class. Speak loudly and clearly. You also have to take part in the discussion.

NOTE-TAKER

Your job is to take careful notes based on what the group has to say. The notes must be written clearly, so that the reporter can read them.

OBSERVER

You can take part in the discussion, but you will be asked to tell the class how well the group worked. You need to mention the positive and negative aspects of the work.

ROLES/SKILLS IN GROUPS

1. GIVE INFORMATION ABOUT THEM

2. PRE-TEST SELF-RATING

4. TEACH SKILL – pairs
   fours
   circle

5. PRACTICE – role cards
   observer
   feedback

6. RE-ASSESS

Figure 5.1 Group role cards

for different purposes, and sometimes reform into different groups, made up of representatives of different 'home groups' to share ideas across groups, or report on the outcomes of activities in other groups. This flexibility means that there is still plenty of opportunity for individual work and whole-class work within an overall group structure.

Decisions about how to group, and how to sequence different kinds of groupings, are determined partly by the content and aims of a particular activity. They are also chosen, in the context of a particular task, on the basis of those forms of grouping that seem most likely to sustain and promote activity through the five stages identified by the authors as necessary in order for significant learning to take place. These five stages are as follows:

1 Engagement: Time during which students acquire information and engage in an experience that provides the basis for, or content of, their ensuing learning.
2 Exploration: Time for students to explore new ideas for themselves, before being closely directed to explore them in a specific way by the teacher.
3 Transformation: A structured task requiring the students to use or to work with information in order to move towards a closer understanding of it.
4 Presentation: Sharing findings with an interested and critical audience in groups other than those in which the task was originally carried out. The requirement to do this puts pressure on 'home groups' to ensure that all members of the group are sufficiently clear about what has been achieved to be able to explain this to another group. The process reinforces students' understanding and provides an opportunity to discover how well they really understand what they are presenting. The feedback they receive from peers enables them to determine how successful their work has been.
5 Reflection: The opportunity to look back at what has been learned and the process of learning itself. Taking time to do this reflection allows students to gain a deeper understanding of both the content and the learning process itself.

Learning together through talk: Key stages 3 and 4 (Kemeny 1993)
Teaching, talking and learning in key stage three (National Oracy Project 1991)
Thinking voices: The work of the National Oracy Project (Norman 1992)

These National Oracy Project materials and reader provide a wealth of ideas for developing, evaluating and assessing group work and other collaborative activities. They are designed to be used for INSET purposes, or by teachers working on their own initiative, either alone or with other colleagues.

The part that talk plays in personalising learning for each child is underlined in a chapter in *Thinking voices* (Norman 1992). Jenny DesFountain and Alan Howe sum up the kinds of possibilities that are opened up for children when we put more emphasis on learning through talk:

A readiness to learn can be created because:

- pupils can, through talk, recall and review what they already know and can define what more they want to know about a topic;
- pupils have contributed their own ideas and therefore have a greater stake in the learning;
- the input from teacher, text, or other resources can be matched more accurately to the pupils' current understandings;
- pupils who are struggling with literacy can use talk to work on their understanding and to gain access to new areas of knowledge.

Pupils can work on ideas together because:

- talk 'loosens the cement' of previously established ways of thinking;
- ideas can be tried out to see how they 'sound', how far they'll stretch ('How do I know what I mean until I hear what I say?');
- 'provisional' meanings are likely to be made as a group feels its way towards some shared understanding;
- tentativeness can be valued and supported, and judgement can be deferred;
- (in this context they) are more likely to say 'I don't understand'.

Opportunity can be created for pupils:

- to make sense of new information
- to renegotiate ways of handling a topic, allowing their own voices and other voices (text, teacher, parent, friend, etc.) to be tried on for size;
- to share their own set of cultural references, into which ideas can be accommodated;
- to learn in the variety of English or the community language which best suits their needs and purposes.

Pupils working together provide social support for the learning process because:

- they can provide each other with an authentic audience;
- there is the possibility of an immediate and engaged response;

- there can be a sympathetic, but not sentimental valuing of each other's contributions;
- there can be a tolerance of the need to take time out (involving social talk, or silence) which can actually enhance their ability to return to the task after some 'thinking time';

Tentatively expressed thoughts can become clearer in well-structured group activities because:

- pupils are more likely to interrogate peers than their teacher;
- one person's ideas can be interpreted and expanded by others;
- group talk can place pupils where they represent and make explicit their thinking to others;
- encouraging pupils to cross-question each other about their work may result in a clearer definition of meanings;
- pupils will take longer 'turns' in expert role, providing opportunities to clarify and consolidate their own understandings.

(Norman 1992 pp. 144–6)
(Reproduced with permission of Hodder Headline PLC)

Learning together – Working together (Cowie and Ruddock 1988)

- Volume 1 *Co-operative group work: An overview*
- Volume 2 *Co-operative group work: School and classroom case studies*
- Volume 3 *Co-operative learning: Traditions and transitions*
- Volume 4 *Co-operative group work in the multi-ethnic classroom*
- *The co-operative group work training guide*

This work arises from a research project based at Sheffield University and funded by BP. The project has produced a useful collection of material, including theoretical discussion, practical advice and detailed accounts of practice. It is particularly useful in offering insight into the views that teachers and learners hold about group work, the kinds of reservations that both may have about the value of cooperative learning and how these may be constructively addressed. Volume 1, in particular, provides a detailed study of the kinds of problems that may arise in the management of group work and summarises strategies that can help to overcome them.

Learning together and alone (Johnson and Johnson 1987)

A substantial body of research on cooperative learning has been carried out in the USA. This is one of many publications which draw on that research, amongst other purposes, to explore and explain in a detailed and concrete way steps that teachers can take to ensure that group work is successful and productive.

The book looks at the advantages and disadvantages of competitive, individualised and cooperative approaches and puts forward a view relating to the positive role which each can play in learning. The main emphasis of the book is on the conditions that need to be created in order to realise the potential benefits of cooperative work in practice. Central to these is the idea of 'positive interdependence', meaning that learners are linked in such a way that the contribution of each benefits the others, and the success of each individual depends upon the success of all. The authors explain what teachers can do to create this 'positive interdependence' through the way in which they structure, organise and evaluate group learning.

Changing behaviour: Teaching children with emotional and behavioural difficulties in primary and secondary classrooms **(McNamara and Moreton 1995)**

As the title suggests, the main focus of this book is concerned with the development of positive responses to the challenges presented by children with emotional and behavioural difficulties. Part of the approach proposed involves the encouragement of discussion in random pairs, and specific help for pupils to develop the skills needed to work successfully in groups. The emphasis is upon developments that can be introduced into the overall learning environment to make it more supportive of and responsive to the emotional as well as cognitive needs of students. It is a highly readable book, full of practical ideas, suggestions and photocopiable material to support teachers' own thinking and practice.

Developing effective classroom groups: A practical guide for teachers **(Stanford and Stoate 1990)**

This book offers a different view of how teachers might approach the task of enhancing children's ability to work productively together. Drawing on theory relating to group dynamics, the book suggests activities which teachers can use at each stage of group development to help to address the needs of group members individually and collectively. The idea is that if the needs of the group are taken into consideration and successfully met, through appropriately planned activities, then the power of the group to support and promote learning will be significantly enhanced. The book provides a readable account of the theory underpinning the approach, plus many practical suggestions for activities which can be incorporated into ongoing curriculum work.

The Collaborative Learning Project, 17 Barford Street, London N1 0QB (Tel: 0171 226 8885; Director: Stuart Scott)

Since 1983, the Collaborative Learning Project has been building up a resource bank of materials, developed by teachers, for collaborative work across the curriculum. The project is run by Stuart Scott, who is also available on a consultancy basis to work with groups of teachers on the development of collaborative approaches. A catalogue of materials for sale at the cost of photocopying, and continually updated, is available from the above address. The purposes and principles underlying the materials are described as follows:

1 The materials place high value on what children can offer to each other on a particular topic.
2 Teacher instructions are kept to the minimum. Children work out what to do by sharing/reading written instructions.
3 The materials give children the opportunity to participate in their own words (or language) in their own time, without pressure.
4 They encourage children to respect each other's views and formulate shared opinions.
5 They aim to be anti-racist, avoid gender stereotyping and promote equal opportunities.
6 They develop study skills in context and must be used with a range of appropriate information books.
7 They are suitable for a wide age group, because children can bring their own knowledge to an activity and refer to books at an appropriate level.
8 All the activities have been produced by teachers working collaboratively, and are disseminated to encourage other teachers to do likewise.

ActionAid resources for development education: catalogue available from Kate Turner, ActionAid, The Old Church House, Church Steps, Frome, Somerset BA11 1PL

High quality learning materials, including photo and video packs, are available for purchase from ActionAid. Developed and trialled by teachers, they include background information booklets for teachers and suggestions for how the materials might be used, linked to National Curriculum programmes of study. All materials make extensive use of group activities.

The English and Media Centre: catalogue of materials available through the National Association for the Teaching of English, 50 Broadfield Road, Sheffield S8 0XJ (Tel: 0114 255 5419)

These materials offer a wide range of publications containing stimulating and imaginative ideas for teaching English which take for granted the use of talk and collaboration between pupils. The approaches used to foster exchange of ideas and yield a range of outcomes other than writing could be adapted to group learning in other areas of the curriculum.

Differentiation through flexible teaching

Chapter 6

Why and how learning styles matter
Valuing difference in teachers and learners

Michael Fielding

EDITOR'S INTRODUCTION

In this third part of the book, we open up to examination what is meant by 'difference', and the range of 'differences' that need to be acknowledged, valued and taken into account in our teaching. The differentiated framework of the National Curriculum tends to encourage an emphasis upon different levels of existing attainment as the foundation upon which new learning must build. However, there are other important differences which have implications for teaching and learning and which need to be recognised, valued and built upon, if individuals are to have the opportunity to use and develop their powers of learning as fully as possible. What are these other important differences, and what are their implications for the organisation of learning and teaching?

Discussion in the next three chapters focuses specifically upon differences of learning style and what research may have to contribute to the development of practice in this area. The author of Chapter 6, Michael Fielding, came to lead a session on learning styles in the early weeks of the course. As a result of this session, many participants decided to pursue the implications of the theories discussed in their own teaching. Two of the studies that resulted are described in Chapters 7 and 8. In this chapter, Michael summarises some of the background ideas upon which he based his session, and explains what he considers to be the most important issues and questions raised by this work. He proposes a broad framework for valuing difference, which includes acknowledgement of differing learning styles and has at its centre negotiation and dialogue between teachers and students as the most crucial features of an environment designed to empower and facilitate learning.

◆ ◆ ◆

When differentiation is understood as a process of understanding, valuing and responding to differences in how people learn, it can be a largely positive experience. Differences are woven into the fabric of classroom practices which are richly textured, imaginative and supportive of all those involved. However, the lived reality of differentiation can also be a diminishing and demeaning experience, involving segregation and disillusionment. Setting, work schemes and stepped resource material can (unwittingly) become substitutes for human encounter and the making of meaning in the learning process. As one teacher has remarked, 'One of the most powerful weapons is teacher–pupil discussion, and the administration of mixed-ability differentiated learning schemes leaves little time for this' (Simpson 1995 p. 10).

In this chapter, I consider how theory and research on different learning styles can be used as a resource to raise expectations and aspirations, and to help widen horizons in teaching and learning. My argument will be that a learning-styles-based approach to differentiation has considerable potential to enrich the teaching and learning process, providing it is set within the wider context of humanistic psychology – and has dialogue between teachers and students as persons at its centre.[1]

WHY LEARNING STYLES?

There are two kinds of reasons why I would want to argue that a learning-styles approach to differentiation might legitimately claim our professional attention. The first has to do with the imperative of research evidence which shapes our obligations as reflective professionals. The second has to do with a philosophical commitment to ways of working which place the principle of equal value at the heart of all we do.

The first of these reasons is addressed by Entwistle (1991) in his admirably clear overview of the development of work on cognitive styles in the UK. He argues that there are some compelling messages which come through from the literature on learning styles. These are that teachers should:

- take account of the range of learning styles their students will inevitably exhibit
- recognise that their own learning style is likely to be reflected in their teaching
- acknowledge the dangers of allowing one particular approach to teaching to exclude the voice of others.

He is uncompromising in his underscoring of this last point arguing that:

> The decision to adopt an extreme teaching method, or to espouse a particular philosophy of education to the exclusion of any other, could be seen as an unjustifiable self-indulgence. That style of teaching might well be personally satisfying to the teacher and to like-minded students, but would impose on other students an alien way of learning.
>
> (Entwistle 1991 pp. 144–5)

He ends by suggesting it might be interesting and worthwhile for teachers to:

- help their students to identify their own learning styles with a view to them being able to develop their strengths still further, but also extend the range of their learning repertoire by attending to those aspects of their style which hold them back or cause frustration.

Theory and research on learning styles provide additional insight into the relationship between teaching and learning, and a new perspective from which to review and evaluate pedagogical decisions in order to help ensure that they do provide equality of opportunity for all students. It provides a means of addressing constructively occasions where some sort of difficulty in learning is occurring, by suggesting a range of alternative routes that might lead to greater success, rather than assuming the difficulty arises from ineptitudes of learners or teachers.

This body of work is also important because, at its centre, lies the fundamental belief that different styles of learning are of equal value and of equal worth. One particular style of learning is no better or worse in a comparative sense than another; it is simply different. Furthermore, and equally importantly, these differences are seen as not only legitimate, but also potentially enriching. Here, then, we can see the possibility for developing an approach to differentiation which is centrally concerned with understanding and utilising the different processes of learning, which values them equally, and which seeks to develop future learning in ways which extend and expand existing preferences and capacities.

I shall examine two approaches to understanding learning styles which teachers often find helpful: first, David Kolb's (1984) learning style typology (diverger, assimilator, converger, accommodator) which has steadily gained in popularity since the mid-1980s;[2] secondly, the learning modality strengths approach (auditory, visual and kinaesthetic) associated with the work of either Walter Barbe and Raymond Swassing (1979) or Rita and Kenneth Dunn (1975).

THE WORK OF DAVID KOLB

In developing his work on learning styles, Kolb draws on the writings of Jung, Dewey, Lewin and Piaget. He argues for a four-fold model which incorporates differences in the ways that individuals perceive or grasp the nature of experience and then process or transform it.

Four learning styles

The way we perceive or grasp experience (see Figure 6.1) ranges from immersing ourselves in that experience in intuitive ways which engage our *senses* and *feelings* and attend to the uniqueness of the experience itself – the Concrete Experience orientation – to a preference for Abstract Conceptualisation which favours use of *logical* and *analytical* powers.

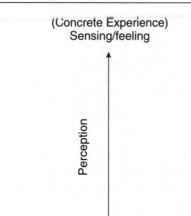

Figure 6.1 Kolb's model of Experiential Learning: the grasping dimension

Having engaged in perception and the attempt to grasp the nature of the new experience we then endeavour to understand it by processing or transforming it (see Figure 6.2).

Figure 6.2 Kolb's model of Experiential Learning: the transforming dimension

At the processing stage, responses range between a predilection for *doing*, an Active Experimentation orientation which urges us to act on information immediately and see how things work out in practice, and a preference for *watching*. This preference for Reflective Observation is characterised by the desire to watch and internally reflect on our feelings. The focus is on understanding the meaning of ideas and situations by carefully observing and filtering them through our own experience. Reflection is much more important here than practical application.

Figure 6.3 maps out the relationship between the two sets of polarities, *Sensing/Feeling* ⟷ *Thinking*, and *Doing* ⟷ *Watching*.[3] If we locate ourselves by making a mark, first on the grasping line, then on the transforming line, and finally draw a line at 90 degrees to each mark as in Figure 6.3 we shall then be able to identify which of the four learning

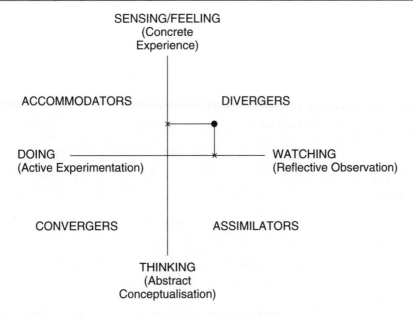

Figure 6.3 Kolb's model of Experiential Learning: identifying your own preferred learning style

styles we favour most strongly. Characteristics of each of the four learning styles based on the work of Kolb (Kolb 1976, 1985; Kolb and Fry 1975; Bell 1991) can be found in Appendix 1 to this chapter. Whilst none of us uses one style to the exclusion of all others – each of the four overlaps with its neighbours – many of us do have preferences and aversions with regard to our preferred way of learning.

It is particularly important that those preferences are not fossilised or used as an excuse for inaction or for heaping blame upon a teacher who asks us to work in uncongenial ways. The nature of certain tasks and the demands of particular situations and subject matter may require a method of working that we find difficult. Such situations can either tap into a learning style we seldom use and begin to stretch it or encourage us to develop learning strategies which enable us to cope more effectively.

To say that we should not use our preferred learning style as an excuse for inaction is not to say that teachers and students never have a case for being disheartened, bored or frustrated. It is to say that whilst teachers have a fundamental and enduring responsibility to their students, the nature of learning is fundamentally a partnership which takes learners' responsibility for their own learning as seriously as teachers' responsibility for teaching that leads to learning.

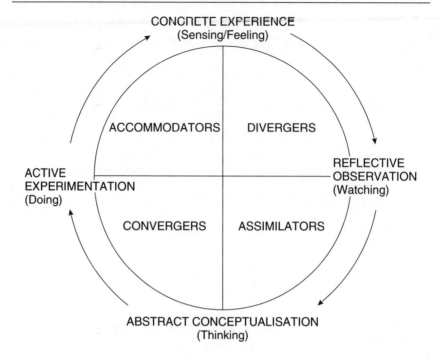

Figure 6.4 Kolb's model of Experiential Learning

Kolb's model of Experiential Learning

Whilst we all learn in different ways, Kolb argues that effective learning is likely to incorporate a particular sequence of processes. Kolb's model of Experiential Learning (see Figure 6.4) is cyclical and suggests that if learning is to be effective we need at the Concrete Experience stage to involve ourselves fully, openly and without bias in new experience.

Then, at the Reflective Observation stage, we need to reflect on and observe that experience from many perspectives before moving on to the third stage of Abstract Conceptualisation. Here we must be able to create concepts that integrate our observations into logically sound theories; we need to make sense of our experience from the standpoint of our existing understanding and be prepared, in the light of our reflections, to adapt or change those understandings as appropriate. Finally, the stage of Active Experimentation requires us to use these theories to make decisions and solve problems. Whilst we do not necessarily have to start at the beginning of the cycle and whilst it is perfectly possible, and indeed often the case, that we meander back and forth between different stages, for our learning to be really effective it needs to incorporate the demands and opportunities of each of the different phases.

The model is, of course, an ideal. Few of us have that steadfast evenness of approach and many would not wish to. Each of us favours particular stages of the learning cycle and these preferences reflect our dominant learning style. Thus Divergers typically enjoy the Concrete Experience stage, relishing exploratory questions, group interaction, discussion and the exploration of personal meaning, but are sometimes reluctant to be appropriately analytical, are easily distracted or wait too long before getting started. Assimilators feel at home between the Reflective Observation and Abstract Conceptualisation stages, and particularly enjoy the collection of data and detailed attention to facts. They are often skilled at analysing data and bringing different theoretical perspectives to bear, but are prone to getting bogged down in detail or theory and are often unwilling to form an opinion or take risks. Moving from the Abstract Conceptualisation stage to the Active Experimentation stage, Convergers share the Assimilators' delight in systematic working and the collection of data, but add a keenness for seeing the practical relevance of activity. That keenness to get things done and to see results often means that they pay too little attention to whether or not they should be doing the task in the first place or whether there might be alternative ways of doing it. Finally, Accommodators come into their own at the Active Experimentation stage where they demonstrate their willingness to take risks, work on hunches, and test things out in real situations, often with others whom they both lead and learn from. This emphasis on action and working intuitively in a broad brush way sometimes results in jumping in too quickly without thinking things through, lack of adequate planning and trying too many things at once.

Each learning style thus not only has its strengths and weaknesses but also has its own preferences with regard to particular stages of the learning cycle. Two consequences often arise from these propensities. First, it has led some writers like McCarthy (1987) to argue for a harnessing of the learning cycle to activities preferred by particular sorts of learners and to insist that each stage of the cycle is incorporated within a unit or sequence of work. This ensures that learners encounter experiences which they can relate to. Secondly, the use of the learning cycle as the basis of planned learning opportunities also requires students to extend and develop their particular learning style in stages of the work they find less congenial but which are nonetheless crucially important.

LEARNING MODALITIES: AUDITORY, VISUAL AND KINAESTHETIC LEARNERS

Although work on modality strengths does not appear to be particularly well known in Britain, many teachers find the understanding of auditory, visual and kinaesthetic preferences in learning very helpful. Barbe and Swassing (1979) suggest that

> A modality is any of the sensory channels through which an individual receives and retains information. . . . Sensation, perception and memory constitute what we are calling modality.
> (Barbe and Swassing 1979, quoted in Guild and Garger 1985 p. 63)

The most important sensory channels as far as the teacher is concerned are the auditory, the visual and the kinaesthetic. (See Appendix 2 to this chapter for examples of auditory, visual and kinaesthetic learner characteristics.)

Auditory students prefer to learn mainly through talking and hearing.[4] They tend to learn best when they are involved in discussion work or when the teacher explains something verbally. If they get into difficulty, talking it through is likely to be the most helpful response; the same applies to their enthusiasm, which is most satisfyingly expressed verbally. Noise is both a distraction, because they take particular notice of auditory events, and a relief, because they often find silence difficult to tolerate: being asked to work in silence for a sustained period can be very difficult and frustrating. When reading they will often do so aloud or by mumbling, and the same applies to their attempts to memorise something. If they tell you something they will assume you will remember it.

Visual learners are helped most when they can see a visual equivalent or encounter the thing or process itself in a visual way. Illustrations, charts, diagrams or pictures are important; so is seeing the word(s) written down. Handouts or overhead transparencies are much appreciated. Their physical environment is preferably stimulating or orderly. They love to organise and decorate their own materials or spaces. Revision is often done best by reading over old notes and by recopying and redoing them in outline.

Kinaesthetic learners have a need to touch and get physically involved in the learning process. They particularly enjoy and learn from situations in which they can make or do things; they are often busy learners who like to be as physically active as possible. Whilst they may take lots of notes, it is more as a physical process than anything else; they will often never look at their notes again. Their enthusiasm is often expressed by jumping up and down. Extended periods of silence are difficult to cope with and often fidgeting is the only relief. It is easy for kinaesthetic learners to be labelled as having behaviour problems.

INTRODUCING STAFF TO LEARNING STYLES

My experience of staff training days and INSET has been that, once introduced to thinking about different learning styles, teachers can usually see an immediate application to their own teaching and school settings, and find the frameworks useful in helping to generate new ideas. One way of opening up the discussion is to start by reminding colleagues of the national and college/school context and move quickly into focusing on participants' own learning, thus grounding their understanding and developmental work in the lived context of their own experience. This is often best done individually and privately before moving on to an introduction and explanation of the theoretical basis of Kolb's work. The first stage is thus primarily about answering the question 'Why learning styles?' before moving on to the second stage which seeks to address the question 'What are they?'

This second stage can be done by asking participants to locate themselves physically along the two axes of perception and processing prior to them arriving in a quadrant where they then compare particular aspects of their preferred approaches to learning with a nearby colleague. It is at this point I use a variety of ways to introduce staff to detailed descriptions of the four different learning styles prior to them identifying their own in more detail. Having done so I move on to individual and small group processing of theoretical and practical issues.

Immediately prior to the third stage, which focuses on the question 'How can learning styles be applied in the classroom context?', I introduce staff to the three learning modalities, again via an identification of their own modality preferences. I then divide staff into small groups and allocate each group a particular learning style. Having had more time to internalise the strengths and disadvantages of their allocated style they then apply it to headings such as Lesson Openings, Input/Encounter, Trying It Out, Homework, Assessment, Relationship with the Teacher, Classroom Environment, or whatever is thought to be a significant part of the teaching/learning encounter. At the end of the ensuing process staff have brainstormed an initial set of concrete ideas for harnessing the strengths of each of the seven learning styles which are of immediate relevance and application to their current work. (See Appendix 3 to this chapter for some examples.)

The final stage, responding to the question 'What if . . .?', involves a range of action planning which gives colleagues the opportunity to think through how they might carry forward aspects of the session on learning styles which they think may be of interest and benefit to themselves and their students.

Learning styles: enabling not labelling

As well as recognising possibilities opened up by learning styles theory, teachers also often express many reservations, which it is important to open up fully to discussion and debate. One issue which is likely to be raised by both staff and students is that of labelling and a concern that pigeon-holing learners is not only an appallingly crass blunt instrument, but also an excuse for inaction and a denial of learners' responsibility for their own learning.

There are a number of different aspects to the broad issue of labelling. First, there is the question of the degree to which learning styles are fixed or malleable. Whilst it is probably true that aspects of our preferred learning style(s), particularly those connected with our personality, remain firmly with us throughout our lives it is also true that our educational and employment experiences, our current role within the organisation and the demands of the tasks we frequently encounter exert a considerable influence on us. Learning styles are flexible structures, not immutable personality traits.

Secondly, there is a difference between a learning style and a learning strategy. Whilst it is true that each of us has preferences with regard to our own approach to learning, those preferences do not prevent, though they may affect, how we go about tackling the demands of a particular task in a particular situation. It is perfectly possible and, particularly from the teacher's standpoint, educationally essential that we develop the capacity and the motivation to extend the boundaries of our approach to, as much as the content of, our learning. As a diverger, it is often desirable in the context of certain aspects of my job that I adopt a learning strategy that is more typical of, say, a converger. I may not find it particularly easy or congenial, but the situation may demand it and in developing the capacities associated with this way of working I am more likely to appreciate and make use of a wider range of learning opportunities than I had hitherto been able to.

This last point reinforces the responsibility of learners as well as teachers for their own learning. Rather than shift the onus entirely on to the teacher, developing awareness in learners of their own preferred learning style(s) carries with it a concomitant responsibility for extending and deepening learning, not confining it behind the barricades of timidity, arrogance or indifference. Learning is about development, not stasis or dependency.

Undoubtedly a useful support in the process of developing students' responsibility for their own learning would be user-friendly materials on learning styles written especially for students. Prior to 1991, no considered attempt in the form of published materials or guidelines was made to help teachers to engage pupils or students with Kolb's work on learning styles.

with the honourable and pioneering exception of Barry Hopson and Mike Scally (1982). In contrast to the situation in the UK, US writers on learning styles such as Pat Guild have produced substantial material aimed at students themselves (Tobias and Guild 1986), and the work of the most influential and prolific of the Kolb-inspired writers, Bernice McCarthy (1982, 1987, 1990), has developed thorough wide-ranging material which engages knowledgeably with the daily reality of classrooms. There are also published accounts of teachers working through the McCarthy materials in a variety of ways with varying degrees of success (Hilgersom-Volk 1987). With regard to learning modalities I am not aware of any materials for students currently available in the UK.

THE LEARNING MAGNET

It is not really possible to articulate or explain what I see as the importance of an appreciation of learning styles in isolation from a wider consideration of the *human* dimension of learning. This is partly represented in what I have come to call the Learning Magnet, so named because it contains factors fundamental to successful learning to which teachers need to return constantly if their students' learning is to be as teachers would wish it. Learner motivation is significantly affected by the degree to which these factors are positively appropriate influences in the learning situation. In Figure 6.5 the eight different components of the Learning Magnet are shown, learning styles being one.

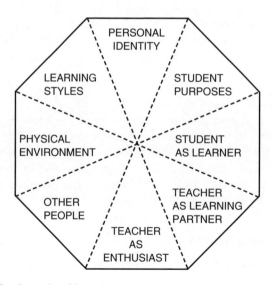

Figure 6.5 The Learning Magnet

The eight are separated by a dotted line which is intended to suggest that each of the factors is going to be of varying importance depending upon circumstances. A pie chart would be a useful way of making the point diagramatically. All are important and should be considered appropriately.

Personal identity

Learners' sense of who they are as a person is importantly affected by the communal context in which they have grown up. This will touch on issues to do with gender, race, culture, personal environment (relationships/ households), social class, age, religion, language, speech style and disability. Planned learning experiences need to be sensitive to those traditions, contexts and circumstances. This is not to say that students will not learn unless these issues are explicitly addressed. However, the violation or insensitive neglect of aspects of students' personal identity can destroy or seriously affect engagement with learners and the task in hand.

Student purposes

Important influencing factors in students' approaches to learning are often linked to their future aspirations, including qualifications. Also important is the degree to which the topic touches their existing enthusiasms. Whilst it is not always appropriate to key in specifically to issues of personal goals and job-related issues, and whilst it is not always possible to engender students' intrinsic motivation or enthusiasm for the topic itself, these areas need to remain on the periphery of a teacher's professional vision and be readily accessible as and when required.

Student as learner

For too many students past learning experiences have been less than positive. It is important to be aware of this, together with having a good professional grasp of individual strengths and weaknesses. Students' perception of their own ability often plays a key role in their approach to learning. Another very important factor which is often overlooked is the way our emotions deeply affect our readiness to learn.

Teacher as learning partner

A recurrent factor in conversations with students about quality learning is the positive influence of the teacher as someone who is caring, knowledgeable and challenging of them as learners and as people. What this draws attention to is the importance of the teacher listening, showing an interest in the individual learner, and being prepared to negotiate goals and tasks. In other words there is an insistent commitment to reciprocal responsibilities of teacher and learner. Learning is a partnership in which both voices are not only heard but also welcomed. This mutual care and respect provides the positive context of learning within which encouragement leads to challenge. Challenge without encouragement runs the risk of fearful inaction or retreat: encouragement without challenge runs the risk of cosy inaction or, if not conceit, then the kind of security that leaves the learner static rather than strong, content rather than curious.

Teacher as enthusiast

Also featuring strongly in conversations with students about quality learning is the importance of teachers being enthusiastic about learning, about the topic, and about its interconnectedness with other matters, other learning. Inspiration cannot be produced at the drop of a hat. Nonetheless we all recognise that students' interest is often caught by teacher enthusiasm. Learning can sometimes owe as much to the fire of enthusiasm as it can to the persistence and patience of a committed professional. A teacher's love of learning has many facets and is essentially about the teacher-as-learner; it is invariably about more than commitment to a particular subject or discipline; it is also about a delight in the process of learning; it is about the teacher-as-learner-about-learning.

Other people

Most learners are significantly affected in their confidence in themselves as learners and in the degree to which they are stimulated in their learning by the nature of the group of other learners. Teachers have substantial responsibilities in making the group work as a learning community. Students' confidence in their own ideas needs to be partnered by respect for the ideas of others. It is important that students are supportive of each other and learn to value difference and diversity. That diversity includes a range of working approaches as much as attitudes and aptitudes.

Physical environment

Where you learn matters. The extent to which the environment is welcoming, stimulating, positive and flexible is important. Poor environments, both physical and psychological, can be actual barriers to learning. Teachers need to do all they can to provide learning environments which are comfortable, accessible and non-threatening; enable different ways of working; are able to celebrate success and value difference; and are challenging and stimulating. Whilst many teachers do not have control over some of the key variables here, the imperative remains nonetheless. The fact is that the environmental context of learning is significant and there is much that can be done, despite physical constraints, that send important signals to students that their work is valued and the undertaking valuable.

THE CENTRALITY OF DIALOGUE

Susan Hart (1992b) has argued persuasively that we must be careful that a focus on differences does not divert our professional attention away from the key issue of whether or not the curriculum is responsive, imaginative and supportive of students' learning. The approach which she advocates focuses on the changing responses of students to their experience of the lived curriculum, rather than on the doubtfully 'fixed' aspects of their characteristics as learners. This emphasis on the dynamic, changing nature of learners and learning needs to inform an approach based on the use of learning styles and learning modalities, if this is not to become a further opportunity to categorise, discriminate and limit the circumstances and purposes of learning.

Central to such an approach must be the dialogic relationship between student and teacher. As John Macmurray reminds us:

> The first priority in education – if by education we mean learning to be human – is learning to live in personal relation to other people. Let us call it learning to live in community. I call this the first priority because failure in this is fundamental failure, which cannot be compensated for by success in other fields; because our ability to enter into fully personal relations with others is the measure of our humanity. For inhumanity is precisely the perversion of human relations. . . . Any kind of teaching involves establishing personal relations between teacher and pupil, and the success or failure of the teaching depends very largely on the character and quality of this relation.
>
> (Macmurray 1958 p. 6)

More recently, Mary Simpson's (1995) research on differentiation in secondary schools has pointed firmly in the same direction. Interestingly, what Stradling and Saunders (1993) called 'differentiation by dialogue' was perceived by students as being much more effective than the differentiation of resource materials or the allocation of students into particular streams, sets, or groups. Reflecting on her data, it became clear to Simpson and her colleagues that the good relationship with the teacher was not just a social nicety: it set the context for interactions to take place which were highly supportive of the learning process.

(Simpson 1995 p. 9)

The concluding section of her paper is both exhilarating and disappointing. It is exhilarating because she seeks to affirm the bankruptcy of technocratic processes:

> The pupils whom we interviewed were of the clear opinion that what helped them to learn – in all subjects and at all stages – was not an individualised scheme of work or set of resources, not a particular form or grouping or set of activities, but a TEACHER – a teacher who was readily available and approachable, who noticed when they had difficulties, who took time and trouble to give them explanations which they were able to understand, who paced the work appropriately, who set realistic goals for them both in the short term and the long term, and who gave them good quality and timeous feedback on their performance.

(Simpson 1995 p. 10)

It is disappointing because she is the victim of a language which betrays what she is striving to achieve. 'Feedback' and 'performance' have nothing to do with dialogue, with joy, with mutuality, or with the growing interdependence of learners; in this austere one-dimensional language (see Fielding 1994a) there is no sense of the students' voices or their part in exploring the direction or purpose of their own learning. We need to take seriously Michael Ignatieff's reminder that

> Our needs are made of words, and they can die for lack of expression. Without a public language to help us find our own words, our needs will dry up in silence

(Ignatieff 1984 p. 142)

The language and processes associated with learning styles have the potential to provide the confidence and the energy to begin the kind of conversations which enhance rather than diminish the possibility of learning and of education. For that to happen we need to be vigilant about the language we use to talk about both. It is too easy to trivialise a learning-styles approach. It is too easy to allow some of its language to misrepresent or mutilate the principle of equal value which provides its understanding and delight in difference with both its wisdom and its strength. Used with care, a knowledge and awareness of learning styles enable us to explore and negotiate emerging understandings in ways which help students and teachers to develop a richer and more co nplex sense of what learning is and what it might become. This is likely to be most successful when it is done together with appropriate sensitivity and with a tentativeness that is at times bold enough to be brave and hesitant enough to be wise. Learning is a shared undertaking in which students and teachers are at different times and simultaneously learners and teachers of themselves and each other.

We must insistently go beyond bullet points and inventories to the complexities and contestedness of negotiation, dialogue and discussion. That is where the learning will begin. It will be sustained only if we articulate and explore our sensibilities and emerging understandings with a language which captures delight as well as definition and nuance as well a number. Education is ultimately and immediately about being and becoming human; it is ill-served by the barren mechanics of a controlled and controlling instruction, however skilled and however various. Education is ultimately and immediately about teachers and students learning from and through each other in community. As learners/teachers and teachers/learners gain confidence in the sound and power of their own voice as persons, they realise that difference is not a precondition but a developing aspect of our shared, still forming humanity. Human development is an essentially reciprocal, interactive process in which diversity and commonality are interdependent. The richness of our difference depends on the richness of what we share; individuality is the product not the precursor of community. The richness of what we share depends on the richness of what makes us unique; the vibrancy of community depends on the degree to which it encourages and celebrates difference.

ACKNOWLEDGEMENTS

I should like to acknowledge my debt to a number of colleagues over the past few years who have helped me to get a clearer, though still partial, understanding of the nature and significance of Kolb's work and its application to education. They include Jo Faccenda and Sue Rawlinson with whom I worked on the FEU project RP661, Jen Andersen at CCDU, Matthew Baker at Trowbridge College, Colin Conner at Cambridge University Institute of Education, Pat Guild from Seattle University, Michael Eraut at Sussex University and David Burrell, also at Sussex University, who got me interested in the first place. Thanks, too, to Tim Everton at Homerton College, Cambridge, who invited me to contribute an earlier paper (Fielding 1994b) from which this current chapter draws substantially. My particular thanks to my colleague Susan Hart for her encouragement, her capacity to move our thinking forward and, last but not least, for her monumental patience.

NOTES

1 There is always a dilemma about how to refer to learners; teachers invariably have firm views about whether 'children', 'pupils' or 'students' is the most appropriate term to use. In this chapter I use the term 'student' to cover all three.

2 Material on learning styles based on writers other than Kolb is slowly infiltrating in-service work. Anthony Gregorc's work (Gregorc 1982; Gregorc and Butler 1984) has appeared in a number of LEAs, often via the universities of York and Cambridge, though, so far as I am aware, it has not gone on to focus on Gregorc's main protagonist, learning styles advocate and author in her own right, Kathleen Butler (1987). Like Pat Guild, Butler has also produced a booklet for students (Butler 1988) and for teachers wishing to support them (Butler 1989). In the last couple of years the Further Education Unit (FEU) has been supporting a growing interest in the FE sector in the Jungian-inspired work of Myers–Briggs (Myers 1962, 1980; Lawrence 1982) with a number of colleges developing interesting work involving both students and staff. As with Kolb, who incorporates Myers-Briggs's writing in his own work, the Myers-Briggs Type Indicator features on a number of management courses. However, Kolb's work, or work derived from it, is likely to remain at the centre of attempts to explore and develop the application of learning styles to the circumstance and context of education pre and post 16. The Technical and Vocational Educational Initiative (TVEI) flexible learning materials have raised many teachers' awareness of Kolb's work; references and examples are slowly beginning to creep into books (e.g. Harris and Bell 1990) and Gordon Bell's (1991) work for the RSA is becoming more widely known.

   In contrast to his relative neglect pre-16, Kolb's writing on experiential learning has had considerable influence on adult education and the understanding of how adults learn (e.g. Francis 1992; Francis et al. 1990; Gibbs 1988; Kolb and Lewis 1986; Krahe 1993; Weil and McGill 1989). In the FE sector the FEU ran Research Project RP661 Learning Styles in Further Education looking at the possible application and development of Kolb's learning styles in support of effective, flexible pedagogy (Fielding 1994a; Further Education Development Agency 1995). The Open University have incorporated a chapter from Kolb in a core reader (Thorpe et al. 1993) and used the work of Honey and Mumford (1986a, 1986b) in their imaginative 'Learning File' (Thorpe and Thompson 1993). Graham Gibbs's work for the CNAA-funded Improving Student Learning Project (Gibbs 1992) builds on his excellent earlier work in FE (Gibbs 1988), Bodi's use of Kolb with librarians (Bodi 1990), and the work of James Vondrell and John Michael Sweeney with independent study programmes (Vondrell and Sweeney 1989) provide other examples. In the initial teacher training sector the work of John Heywood and his colleagues at the University of Dublin has produced some interesting case studies and research (Carroll 1991; Fitzgibbon 1987; Heywood 1989; Heywood et al. 1991). Despite critiques of Kolb, Myers-Briggs, Gregorc and others (Sewall 1986), work on learning styles continues to have enough about it to feed growing interest and encourage developmental work. The situation in the UK would no doubt be improved if there were to be an equivalent to Pat Guild's accessible, wide-ranging overview of learning styles theory and practice within the context of education (Guild and Garger 1985). Nonetheless, experience running courses and small-scale projects suggests interest is growing rather than diminishing.

3 Readers new to Kolb may like to identify their own preferences at this point.
4 The following three paragraphs rest substantially on the account given by
   Guild and Garger (1985 ch. 8).

APPENDIX 1: KOLB'S LEARNING STYLE CHARACTERISTICS

Diverger

Strengths

- imaginative thinker
- uses own experience
- looks at situations from many different perspectives
- brings coherence to a mass of information
- sees relationships between things, grasps the whole picture
- wide-ranging interests
- good at listening and sharing
- likes to get involved in the experience/information directly and then
  reflect on it
- enjoys brainstorming and generation of ideas/alternatives
- likes social interaction/discussion/group work
- aware of people's feelings
- wants to see the whole picture before examining the parts

Disadvantages

- frustrated by action plans
- waits too long before getting started
- easily distracted
- can be too easy going
- sometimes indecisive
- cannot see the trees for the wood
- forgets important details
- only works in bursts of energy

Assimilator

Strengths

- precise
- good at creating theoretical models
- very thorough
- sets clear goals

- enjoys ideas and thinking them through
- analytical, logical
- interested in facts and details
- applies theories to problems/situations
- good at bringing different theoretical viewpoints to critique a situation
- examines facts carefully
- likes collecting data
- sequential thinker
- specialist interest
- avid reader
- uses past experience constructively
- sees links between ideas
- thinks things through
- well organised
- plans in advance
- enjoys didactic teaching
- happy to rework essays/notes
- works well alone

Disadvantages

- needs too much information before starting work or giving opinion
- reluctant to try anything new
- likes to do things in a set way, lets go of the past reluctantly
- gets bogged down in theory
- does not trust feelings, trusts only logic
- needs to know what the experts think
- overcautious, will not take risks
- not very comfortable in group discussion
- does not make use of friends/teachers as resources

Converger

Strengths

- practical application of ideas
- decisive
- integrates theory and practice
- enjoys solving problems in a common-sense way
- likes to try things out
- feels happiest when there is a correct answer/solution
- draws references from experience
- good at using skills and tinkering with things

- focuses clearly on specific problems
- able to see where theory has any practical relevance
- moves from parts to whole
- thorough
- works well alone
- goal setting and action plans
- strategic thinking
- knows how to find information
- gets things done on time
- not easily distracted
- organises time well
- systematic notes/files
- reads instructions carefully

Disadvantages

- intolerant of woolly ideas
- not always patient with other people's suggestions
- resents being given answers
- tends to think their way is the only way of doing something
- needs to control and do it alone
- details get in the way sometimes, cannot see the wood for the trees
- not good at suggesting alternatives/lacks imagination
- getting the job done sometimes overrides doing it well
- not concerned very much about presentation of work
- needs to know how things they are asked to do will help in real life

Accommodator

Strengths

- testing experience, trial and error
- committed to action
- very flexible
- wide-ranging interests
- enjoys change, variety
- willing to take risks
- looks for hidden possibilities and excitement
- not worried about getting it wrong by volunteering/asking questions
- gets others involved
- learns from others, quite prepared to ask for help
- gets involved in something which sparks their interest
- uses gut reactions
- often gets right answer without logical justification

- wants to see whole picture before examining the parts

Disadvantages

- tries too many things at once
- tends not to plan work
- poor time management, leaves things till the last minute
- not very interested in details
- does not check work or rework it
- jumps in too quickly without thinking things through
- sometimes seen as pushy.

APPENDIX 2: LEARNING MODALITY CHARACTERISTICS

Auditory	Visual	Kinaesthetic
Remember what they hear and say	Writing things down or drawing pictures helps	Remember what they do and experience
Talk aloud to themselves	Graphs and pictures help	Like physical rewards
Not always good with written directions	Difficulty in concentrating during verbal activities	Like to touch people when talking to them
Enjoy listening to others reading aloud	Watch rather than talk or act	Work through problems physically
Whisper whilst reading	Often well organised	Tap pencil/foot
Like class discussion	Remember what they see	Find ways to move around
Need to talk through new learning	Put information in visual forms	Often lose interest when not actively involved
Remember faces	Like reading/good speller	Poor speller
Hum/sing	Often quiet in nature	Outgoing in nature
Noise is distracting	Notice details	Cannot sit still for long

APPENDIX 3: PRACTICAL SUGGESTIONS FOR THE SEVEN LEARNING STYLES

Homework

Diverger

Open-ended
Lots of 'Why?'
Flexible, oral/visual
Related to personal/other experience
Reflective questioning
Reflection time allowed but *focused*
No worksheet
Interviews

Assimilator

Research
Reading
Worksheets
Independent work
Analysing data
Specific task
Written or diagrammatic
Give something to be marked

Converger

Relevant
Analytical
Problem solving
Regular homework
Set clear goals
Practical

Accommodator

Flexible/open
Multi-skilled
Multi-tasked
Group opportunities
Partnerships
Product without process

Auditory

Interviews
Watching TV programmes
Listening to radio
Reporting on tape
Research with a friend/teams

Research to report back verbally
Answer questions/do task on cassette

Visual

Topic web
Extended writing
Completion of maps/charts
Photos/models
Homework sheets with
     instructions
Rewriting notes
Clear deadlines

Kinaesthetic

Visits
Project
Making things
Survey
Map work

Read pictorially
Drawing activities
Collections/cuttings/evidence
Act out stories in books
Recording/tape

Relationship with the teacher

Diverger

'Friendly', close relationship
Role model, respect
Sensitivity
Informal
Noise tolerant
Imaginative
Personal interest
Time to talk and listen

Assimilator

Teacher knowledgeable
Teacher well prepared
Slight distance
Formal, clear cut
Cerebral/thinking relationship
Expect teacher to challenge
Respect rather than closeness

Converger

One-to-one
Organised teacher
Teacher encourage
Teacher as source of information
Business-like, down-to-earth teacher
Teacher who relates theory to practice
Specialist

Accommodator

One-to-one relationship
Trusting
Encouraging
'Personal', approachable
Supportive
Non-stereotyped teacher
Facilitator and resource for
pupils

Auditory

Verbal reassurance
Teacher as facilitator
Easy-going/informal
Adaptable/flexible
Emphasis on oral direction
High teacher input
Allowing time for talk/discussion

Visual

Warmth, approachable
Clear/directive
Appearance
Flexible
Keep attention
Repeat/reinforce
Patient/security

Kinaesthetic

Physical approach
Close relationship
Teacher involved in activities

Teacher offering tasks
Sympathetic approach
Positive appraisal

Chapter 7

'I felt wanted in the class'

Kiran Chopra

EDITOR'S INTRODUCTION

Chapters 7 and 8 describe ways in which teachers on the course chose to pursue theories about different learning styles in their work to develop differentiation in their own school contexts.

Kiran Chopra is a language support teacher. This chapter describes two linked initiatives undertaken, at one of the secondary schools where she works, with the intention of acknowledging different learning styles and providing equal opportunities for all pupils. She decided to pursue an approach to differentiation based on the three 'learning modalities', which linked up with her own personal interest in, and extensive use of 'mind mapping' as a technique for organising ideas visually. The first section of the chapter describes how this theory was used to inform, extend and enrich a programme to support the development of study skills with pupils about to embark on GCSE courses. The second shows how the same ideas about differing learning styles were incorporated in the planning and implementation of a language awareness project which aimed to celebrate and actively use the multilingual experience of the class group as a resource for the curriculum.

A strong feature of both initiatives was the involvement of pupils at every stage, explaining the thinking behind the activities and encouraging constructive dialogue about how people learn. The title of the chapter reflects the sentiments of one pupil, who suddenly discovered that she had something very valuable to contribute to the learning of the group.

Over the years, people develop personal learning styles that probably help them to benefit more from some experiences than from others. Some people prefer to listen to a tutor, while others prefer to obtain the same knowledge from a book or a video. Some people like to number everything, while others avoid numbers as much as possible. Some people learn by being told what to do, some need to be left alone to do something; some like to work with someone else, and for some people being tidy or organised helps their learning. Learners may not necessarily be in a position to negotiate what is learnt, or choose their books or tutor, but what they can do (the theory states) is to take control of their learning styles – visual, auditory or kinaesthetic.

How can we use awareness of preferred learning styles to support or promote effective learning? From the learner's point of view, if we understand about our preferred learning styles, then we can use this knowledge to aid our learning. From the teacher's point of view, if we appreciate differences in learning style and how our own preferred learning style affects our teaching, we have an important tool to help us review, evaluate and develop our teaching to foster more successful learning. For instance, in planning our teaching, we can bear in mind the following:

1 Visual learners benefit from visual aids, videos, pictures, colour and mind mapping.
2 Auditory learners benefit from oral practice, reading aloud, group discussions and use of tape recorders, talking through their mind map and working with helpful others.
3 Kinaesthetic learners would enjoy role plays, experiments, hands-on activities, drawing images on a mind map and field trips.

In this chapter, I describe two initiatives, carried out in a secondary school with sixty-two pupils and their fourteen teachers, aimed at enhancing learning through enhanced understanding of different learning styles.

LEARNING STYLES AND STUDY SKILLS

Following discussion on the course relating to different learning styles, I decided to explore the potential for using these ideas as part of our programme of study skills work helping to prepare pupils for their GCSE courses. The idea was that if we were to heighten pupils' awareness of their preferred learning styles, this would assist them in choosing methods of independent study that would be most effective for them. In addition, I was interested in introducing them to the technique of mind mapping (Buzan 1992), which I already used myself extensively as a note-taking and revision technique, since I saw its potential to accommodate all learning styles in different ways.

The first step was to encourage pupils to think about how they learn, and how they learn best, with the help of a broad set of questions (Figure 7.1) and then a more detailed questionnaire based on the ideas and materials Michael Fielding had introduced to us (explained in Chapter 6). We involved pupils in two Year 9 classes and their teachers. We wanted to see what patterns would emerge within classes regarding preferred modes of learning, and then compare these to the preferences expressed by teachers. We asked everyone to be as honest as possible, because there were no 'right' answers and the accuracy of the survey would depend

Myself as a learner

1. **Learning is most enjoyable for me when . . .**

2. **Things I'm skilled or good at as a learner include . . .**

3. **My favourite question is . . .**

4. **I get least out of learning when . . .**

5. **The thing I'd like to change about myself as a learner is . . .**

6. **The most recent thing I have learnt is . . .**

Figure 7.1 Myself as a learner questionnaire

upon how honest everyone was prepared to be.

All scores on the questionnaires were then collated and the information was then projected on graphs (Figures 7.2 to 7.4) by a pupil, Deepa Vakil, on the computer. These were made available to pupils and teachers and a full explanation of visual, auditory and kinaesthetic learning styles was provided. This stimulated further discussion about learning, as both pupils and teachers interpreted the information and checked it out against their perceptions of their own preferred ways of working.

Main findings

The graphs suggest a variation in each group's preferred learning style. In Class 9E, the pattern of responses suggested a preference for kinaesthetic learning, followed by visual and auditory. In Class 9F, the preferred learning style is more visual and auditory than kinaesthetic. All the teachers seemed to prefer a visual learning style.

These findings highlighted three things:

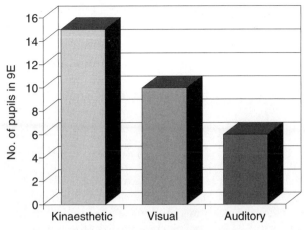

Figure 7.2 Preferred learning styles of pupils in 9E

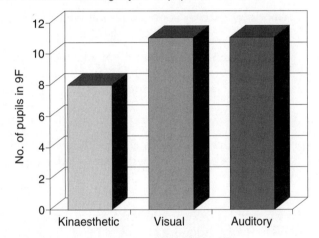

Figure 7.3 Preferred learning styles of pupils in 9F

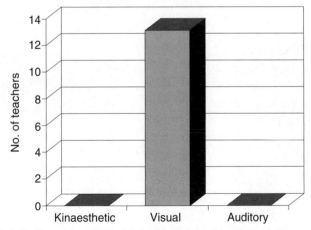

Figure 7.4 Preferred learning styles of teachers in 9E and 9F

1 The preferred learning styles vary within a class.
2 The overall preferred learning styles of pupils can vary from class to class.
3 There may be differences between pupils' and teachers' preferred learning styles.

The survey gave us insight into individual pupils' as well as class learning styles. We found considerable variation between individuals, ranging from pupils who had the same or similar scores in all areas to those who were more skilled in one learning style. We matched up the open-ended comments that pupils had written about their own learning with the results on the 'learning preference' questionnaire, to see if they appeared to confirm each other. In many cases, the two did seem to be closely related.

These views were expressed by some pupils identified as strong visual learners:

As a learner I need confidence, dreams of the future, knowledge, understanding, self-esteem, support from friends and family, and learning favourite subjects. Worrying about exams hinders my learning.

(Angela Pathmanathan)

Mind mapping [see Appendix to this chapter] helps me to revise my work quickly and I have easier notes with me to read. However, being ill reduces my capability to learn.

(Sima Patel)

Learning for me is most enjoyable when I am in a tidy, comfortable atmosphere with no one around. I also need to be able to write down everything. If it is hot, or there is music playing, it hinders my learning.

(Olivia Bright)

I like writing down and I enjoy mind mapping. I tend to learn little when I read through and do not write down.

(Stephanie Feldman)

These views were expressed by some pupils identified as strong auditory learners:

When I listen to tapes and music I enjoy learning. I wish to increase my speed of learning.

(Natalie Jackson)

Learning for me is most enjoyable when I can discuss it and not when I am all by myself reading from notes.

(Noreen Zareef)

I find it easier when my friends understand and explain to me. I get least out of learning when I day dream on other activities.

(Elizabeth Cook)

These views were expressed by some identified as 'strong kinaesthetic learners':

Learning for me is most enjoyable when there is practical work. I wish to improve my skills at remembering things better.

(Caroline Clifford)

Things I am skilled at are doing practicals and drawings. I enjoy highlighting and mind mapping.

(Sheena McKay)

The things I am good at as a learner include Art, Physical Education and Technology. I learn little if it gets boring and hard.

(Laura Tilbury)

Teachers' views on 'myself as a learner' indicated that they were all very strong visual learners absorbing information through visualising pictures in the head; understanding maps, charts and graphs; and remembering by writing down most of the time.

Apart from the specific study skills programme we were seeking to develop, evidence of these differences in learning styles seemed to confirm the need to review the range of learning opportunities provided across the curriculum, so that pupils can enjoy greater success and teachers can experience greater satisfaction from the raising of standards that this process engenders.

Introducing mind mapping

We asked the children to identify the tools they used in the process of learning. The pupils we worked with were all familiar with the following tools:

Visual

- linear learning
- underlining key words
- highlighting key words

Auditory

- using cassette recorders
- talking with helpful others
- reading aloud.

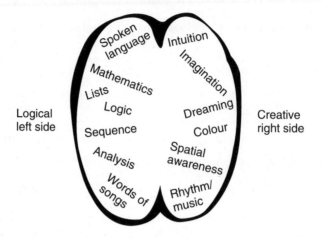

Figure 7.5 Logical and creative sides of the brain

Kinaesthetic

- doing practical work
- pacing up and down while studying
- drawing flow diagrams.

Mind mapping

We then went on to introduce mind mapping; this technique was invented by Tony Buzan in the 1970s. It is a spatial approach to learning which brings all the different areas of the brain – from the logical left side and the creative right side – into the process of learning (Figure 7.5). The rules, advantages and uses of mind mapping are described in the appendix to this chapter.

The logical left side is thought to deal with more academic and structured activities and the creative right side is thought to process more artistic activities.

Mind map is a visual or pictorial representation of information which directly affects the way the brain works. Making notes and trying to learn in a linear way from lines across the page is not a natural way for humans to learn. We are used to seeing an overall picture rather than a two-dimensional reference. With mind mapping one creates a picture, with branches off a central image for different topics and further branches for sub-topics. Colours, pictures and images are included in the map, but only key words (nouns and verbs) link the different connections. In this way a whole lesson, a chapter, evaluation, a lecture, a book review, project, or even a year's revision or syllabus or study skills can be contained on one sheet of paper (Figures 7.6 and 7.8). The size of the brain does not influence intelligence, but using it does. Each cell can make thousands of connections; together, they are responsible for human learning.

Although mind mapping might seem best adapted to visual learning, in fact it has characteristics which enable it to cater for all styles of learning. Auditory learners find that it helps to make a mind map with a partner, using the mind map as a focus for discussion and debate. For kinaesthetic learners, mind mapping provides opportunities for actively doing and making something that helps sustain concentration.

Our aim in the study skills programme was to help pupils exercise more control over their learning and learn more effectively at home and at school. Teaching them mind mapping was a way of adding to their repertoire, and in the process encouraging them to review that repertoire and become more consciously aware of the choices available to them. The success of this aspect of the project is reflected in pupils' comments about how they find mind mapping helpful in project work and revision:

> I enjoyed looking at the finished project and knowing how much work I had put into it. I enjoyed setting out the work in not only just boring left to right lines but filling up the page with colours, pictures and key words to make it look more interesting
>
> (Caroline Clifford)

> I find mind mapping a helpful way to revise.
>
> (Menaz Akhtar)

> Doing the language project taught me to mind map and as a result has benefited me in other subjects as you will see by my environmental mind map [Figure 7.8].
>
> (Georgina Whiteley)

> I am finding this method is helping me. I find it a more enjoyable way of revising and I can stick to it without having too many breaks.
>
> (Lucy White)

> I find mind mapping helps me to remember key facts that I have forgotten.
>
> (Alice Robins)

> I have found mind mapping very interesting and helpful. It helps my revising as I have found my best point is visual. The mind maps are stimulating and help me to get an inside view of work. While I am working, it is also very interesting to do as well; it's not boring like revising from books.
>
> (Angela Pathmanathan)

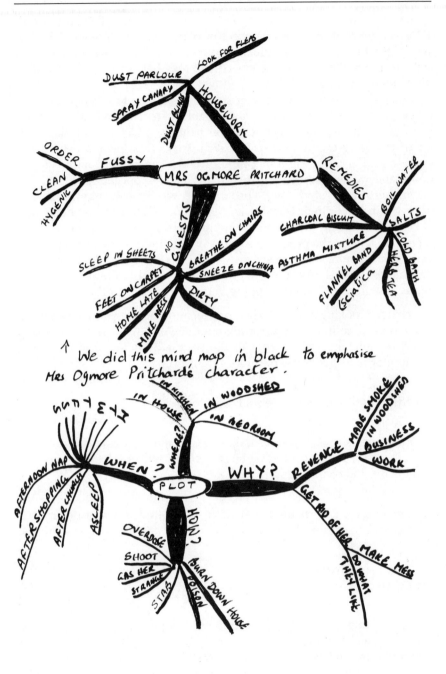

Figure 7.6 Under Milk Wood mind map

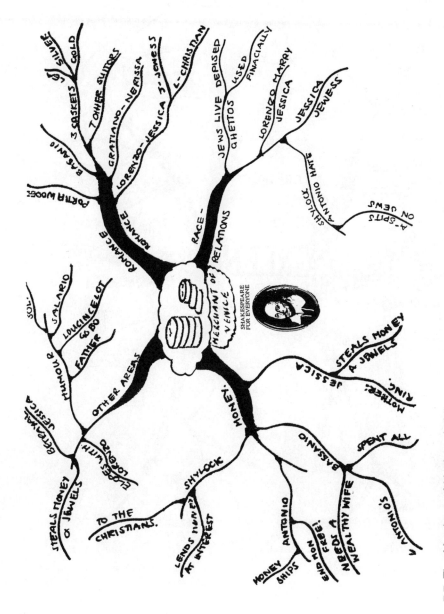

Figure 7.7 The Merchant of Venice mind map

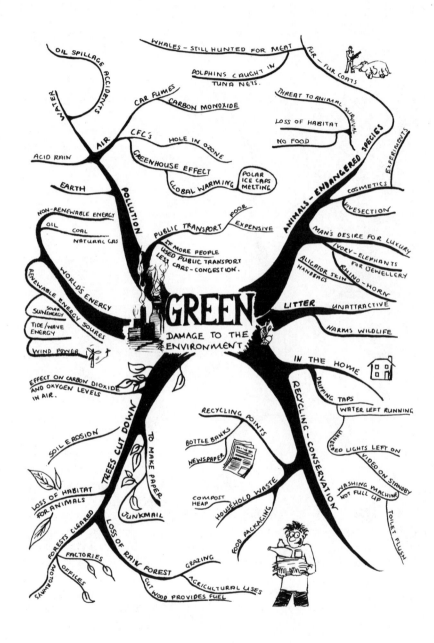

Figure 7.8 Environmental mind map

Mind maps have helped me in a big way. I just write down my information and it's so easy to read when I go over it. I use them for
everything.

(Anoushka Craig)

LANGUAGE PROJECT

As these comments indicate, we also built opportunities to use mind
maps into the second of our initiatives, the Language Project. By doing
this, we hoped not only to enhance learning within the project itself,
but also to offer pupils an added tool to help with their learning
generally.

The purpose of the Language Project is to help students understand
how we acquire, learn, present and use language. It provides a
wealth of material on English languages and world languages. It is cross-
curricular, drawing on aspects of English, maths, science, history,
geography, information technology and art.

Our aim in developing this project was to pursue the study of
language by drawing directly upon the diverse linguistic experience
of the whole group. At the same time, we tried to develop the project
in a way that would reflect acknowledgement of different learning styles,
and encourage children to make choices about ways of working
that reflected an awareness of their strengths and preferences. Hence,
the project involved presenting information in charts, graphs and
pictographs; talking and writing from experience; reading and writing
information; selecting from a range of reference materials; using different
tools of learning including mind mapping. In these different ways, we
hoped to key into visual, auditory and kinaesthetic ways of learning.

We began the project with an activity designed to encourage learners
to think about similarities and differences between people as individuals
and as learners (adapted from a sheet in Visser (1993); see appendix (pp.
133/7) on INSET material and additional reading). This was intended to
help raise awareness that the similarities of the human race are greater
than any differences. The pupils were then given some handouts on the
different languages spoken in Britain followed by the spread of English
throughout the world. The pupils were asked to collect information about
languages they were in contact with through the family, languages spoken
in the class, and so on. This was to be expressed in such forms as tables,
pie charts and block graphs. We discovered, for example, that tables and
block graphs were a better way of expressing this information than pie
charts because everybody speaks English – taking up 100 per cent of the
pie chart. This we concluded does not work.

We allowed the project to expand, partly through its own momen-
tum as individuals pursued particular interests, and partly through

Table 7.1 Language Project topics

1   Language
2   Language development
3   Languages spoken
    • by my ancestors
    • in my class
    • in my school
4   Languages spoken around us – shopping areas, library and other places
5   Tree of Languages
6   Languages spoken in Britain
7   The English speaking world
8   The future of English
9   Languages spoken in the world
10 Top languages of the world
11 A poster in different languages
12 Different language scripts
13 Numerical guide of scripts
14 Chart of 'borrowed words'
15 Map of history of a word
16 What do languages have in common?
17 What are the uses of learning a language?

introducing different topics on language use, for example – how do babies learn language? What happens if you go to a country where you cannot speak the language – how do you cope? What are the languages spoken in Britain – and in the world?

We looked at different source material (e.g. the English dictionary) to show how words change their meaning (semantics); we looked at words coming into the language from different countries (France, Germany, Italy, the Netherlands, Greece, India and the United States of America). We also discussed the history of a word (e.g. father to the Sanskrit word 'pitar'), why and how words have been added to the English language (the Norman conquest, the British Raj, and through trade and travel) as well as many other topics (Table 7.1).

The project was to be completed over half term. It included one double English lesson a week for six weeks and some homework assignments. The pupils were shown the topics that could be covered in the project through a mind map (Figure 7.9). We observed that this gave the pupils an insight into the different areas that could be covered in the project. It gave some pupils an indication of the sort of material they could be gathering to refer to, in their research, and the resources they could tap into both in school and outside school. It also provided the means of stretching pupils of all abilities: for the able pupils it provided open-ended tasks that would meet the demand for enrichment within the curriculum, for the average pupils it provided an overall plan to work to at

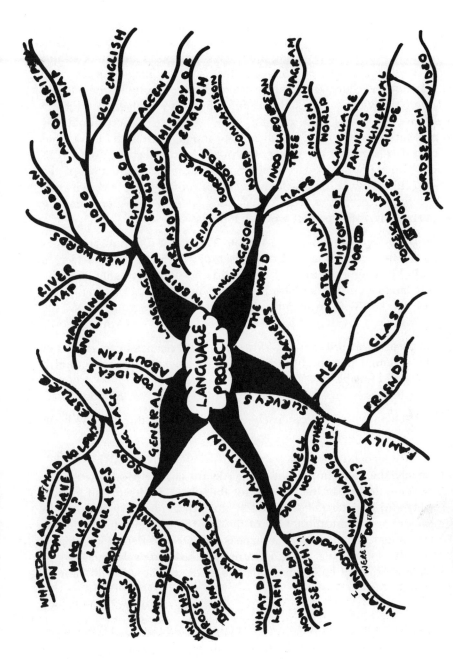

Figure 7.9 Language Project mind map

their individual pace and for the less able pupils it provided a selection of areas of interest that they could work on.

We also found that the visually strong learners made strong reference to books, encyclopedias, language dictionaries, newspapers and other printed material. The kinaesthetically strong learners produced excellent mind maps, enjoyed conducting interviews with peers and other adults, doing language word puzzles and the class language survey, and constructing pie charts and graphs. The auditorily strong learners found watching the videos especially useful. They also enjoyed conducting interviews in school and outside school and discussion about the progress of their project helped them to formulate their own ideas better.

Towards the end of the project the pupils were asked to do an evaluation. Some pupils used a mind map to do their evaluation of the project. This allowed for alternative ways of representing and reflecting on learning, according to preferred learning styles. Pupils' comments on the evaluation of the project were as follows:

> I learnt a lot from this project about the many different languages around the world. Before I did this project I thought there were a handful of languages around the world and that they came from the same language. I worked around my friends in school and at home. I also worked with my family asking and answering questions.
>
> (Amy Clifford)

> This project was brilliant *as I felt wanted in the class* as I can speak not only the languages taught in the school, English and French, but also Urdu and Punjabi.
>
> (Samira Afsar)

> I enjoyed this project immensely. I found looking through the book with three languages I speak fascinating.
>
> (Carla Danesh)

> Probably the most important thing I learnt is how special language is not only for the individual but for the whole framework of human society and how terrible it would be if we didn't have such a diverse means of communication. One of the most interesting thing I found out was that people in my class speak seventeen different languages. The only unfortunate thing I learnt was how some languages e.g. Latin and Sanskrit have fallen out. We must not allow this to happen to Welsh.
>
> (Georgina Whiteley)

> I have learnt from many books and people of my class that it is important to respect all types of religions and languages.
>
> (Zarina Yeoh)

The best bit in the whole project was doing the bilingual books. This was quite easy for me as I knew the language very well and I had a Hindi dictionary.

(Tulika Pandey)

I especially enjoyed the section on language development. I learnt that language is nearly the most important thing in the world.

(Kristina Flemming)

This project contained a lot of information I had never come across. It has been the most valuable and stimulating project I have ever done. One of the most obvious things this project taught me is that, the human race is united by its dependence on languages. Wars could not be stopped, business deals could not be made and a day to day life could not be carried out without languages.

(Deepa Vakil)

I realised that schools would not be able to develop as teachers would not be able to instruct pupils – so how could the pupils learn as they do. I will be able to carry the information I have learnt throughout the project for the rest of my life.

(Leanne Walker)

Teachers' comments on the evaluation of the project included the following:

The substantial amount of material and variety of topics allowed pupils to choose what they were interested in; we allowed them to survey their classmates and to build up the project at their own pace thus catering for differentiation and equal opportunities. Another benefit of the project was the amount of independent learning and the fact that the pupils took responsibility of their own learning. The result was extremely pleasing. All pupils, from the weakest to the most able, seem to have stretched themselves and everybody produced a respectable – rising to impressive – piece of work. We felt that as well as learning facts, pupils had learned how to commu-nicate in a variety of forms.

(Elizabeth Cicolini)

All pupils were motivated to produce a worthwhile project but for some it extended outside the classroom – bringing in information, colour photocopies, and using information technology. I liked the way the girls shared information and the way work was displayed around the room for them to refer to. There was a happy working atmos-phere created in the classroom. It gave me an opportunity to give the pupils one to one support and encouragement at greater length than is usually possible. The project was effective in raising the self-esteem of those who speak a language as well as English. These pupils became prized possessions within the class, and were much in demand. I felt all girls produced lovely projects but some who are middling in most work really excelled themselves which was really pleasing.

(Julia Draper)

Gardner (1993) argues that schools can deliberately collect and make available resources – human and technological – that fit comfortably with the disparate learning styles and cultural backgrounds that exist in any student body. Although time and resources are inevitably limited, this project showed that there is no need to be limited by them.

The approach adopted in the Language Project acknowledges that learning does not just take place at school or college, in a classroom with a tutor. It provides an example of how the home, school and community can jointly foster the learning opportunities of a child. It is an example, too, of how the school curriculum can acknowledge and use the diverse resources of a multicultural, multilingual learning group to enrich one another's learning. In Samira's words, everyone can 'feel wanted' because everyone has something unique to contribute to the work of the group (Figure 7.10).

CONCLUSION

In summarising it is important to remember two key issues. First, that we need to expose pupils to differentiated learning styles and through our teaching styles allow pupils to use a strategy that sharpens their dominant learning style or strengthens their weaker one.

Second, we need to draw on pupils' interests and experience at home and in the community, as well as in school, if we are to enhance their opportunities and motivation to appreciate differences in society and culture. At the same time, we must continue to emphasise that the similarities of all members of the human race are greater than any differences.

ACKNOWLEDGEMENTS

I should like to express my thanks and appreciation to the staff and pupils of Watford Girls' Grammar School, and particularly to all those who supported and worked with me on these initiatives: Hugh South, Head of South West Herts Section 11 Project; Head of the school, Helen Hyde; Deputy Head of the school, Steve Johnson; Head of English, Elizabeth Cicolini; Julia Draper; fourteen other teachers, and sixty-two Year 9 pupils.

Figure 7.10 Students' response to working on the Language Project

APPENDIX: MIND MAPPING

Rules

- start with a coloured *image* in the centre
- words should be printed
- printed words should be on lines
- one word on each branch
- use colours, use images.

Advantages

- centre with *main idea* is clearly defined
- importance of *each idea* is clearly stated
- *links* between *key concepts* are easily recognisable
- *recall* and *review* are more *effective* and *rapid*
- *easy* to *add* new information
- each map is *different* and therefore *easier to recall*.

Uses of mind mapping

- taking notes in a lesson or a lecture
- as an aid to storytelling
- doing a book review
- planning project work, coursework and schemes of work
- working on a syllabus
- brainstorming
- memorising
- revising, recalling and preparing for exams
- conducting and delivering GCSE orals
- organising events
- drawing up a problem-solving format
- setting agenda and minutes for meetings
- holding discussions and getting group consensus
- making presentations
- making decisions.

Chapter 8

Teaching and learning styles as a starting point for INSET

Nicola Hancock

EDITOR'S INTRODUCTION

This chapter describes how classroom research designed to explore the value of learning styles theory was used as a stimulus for opening up staff discussion around the topic of 'differentiation'. It is by no means easy to organise training days for staff that people will feel to have been genuinely valuable, as experience has repeatedly demonstrated. Should an outside speaker be brought in, to stimulate discussion through presentation of fresh ideas? Should existing expertise within the school be used? What combination of activities and groupings are most likely to lead to productive debate and discussion?

Nicola Hancock was invited to help plan and lead two INSET days on differentiation, which would then lead on to further development work in different curriculum areas. She decided to draw upon the research which she had undertaken, as part of course work, trying to apply learning styles theory in her own English teaching. In this chapter, she describes her research and what she learnt from it that was of relevance to her own work with children. She also shows how, in collaboration with colleagues, she built successful staff development activities around these ideas, and identifies some of the principles which helped to make the experience a worthwhile one for colleagues.

'Differentiation' is a single word with enormous implications. How do we define it, let alone put it into practice, let alone relax in the knowledge that it is working, convinced that the needs of each and every student in each and every classroom are being met? It is at this point that I began my study, intending to seek some means of challenging and, in some way, overcoming the huge obstacles surrounding the issue of differentiation.

The task of defining the term is an awesome one since everyone carries with them into the classroom their own ideas and preconceptions. I began from the basis that successful differentiation is the process by which we attempt to maximise the potential of all students and create equal access and opportunity regardless of race, class, gender, 'ability'. The National Curriculum Council (1991) suggests the following definition:

Differentiation is the process by which curriculum objectives, teaching methods, assessment methods, resources and learning activities are planned to cater for the needs of individual pupils.

Whilst a range of definitions are in circulation, however, there remains no guarantee that they are widely understood or, more to the point, actually translated into classroom practice within our schools. Having questioned and surveyed a cross-section of colleagues in my own secondary, comprehensive school, I soon discovered that concerns centred around a number of areas:

- lack of time, money and resources
- ambiguity and uncertainty about the definition of differentiation
- practical means of successfully executing appropriate differentiated classroom activities and provision of resources
- uncertainty as to whether differentiation was an issue only for mixed-ability classrooms.

This survey unearthed an interesting range of understanding and interpretation. Having identified their initial response, staff were then asked to give some indication of which techniques they employed within their classroom practice in order to cater for the various needs confronting them. It appeared that most staff relied upon 'differentiation by outcome', namely, using the same stimulus and set of activities with the whole class, leading to differences in nature, quality and quantity of response on the part of learners. Few made use of 'differentiation by task or input', where learners choose or are set different stimulus materials, activities or tasks, according to different interests, needs or preferences. Very few responses contained detail of actual classroom activity and teaching style, probably not due to neglect but largely because these were not recognised as making a contribution to differentiation.

Clearly, there was a case for opening up discussion and sharing ideas among the staff at my school since my prior investigation had highlighted so many concerns and doubts and such a vast range of interpretation. I felt that this could be exploited as a basis for the pursuit of a more coherent whole-school definition or understanding. Ours is a school in which subject departments tend to maintain a strong sense of identity and independence, so a balance had to be sought in terms of providing INSET activities which would be received as appropriate to everyone. An overarching, relevant theme was necessary to which all members of staff, regardless of subject expertise, could make connections with their own classroom experience. Hostility and resentment had been evident in the past among some members of staff when apparently 'impractical' and 'inappropriate' educational theory had been presented with little opportunity to make connections with real classroom practice.

I considered, then, that the balance might be redressed by using the outcomes of my own research into students' learning styles, showing how I had used theory to explore and think about the 'child's experience' and the implications for organising and planning teaching. The common theme would be created by focusing on the student as a learner who enters each lesson equipped with the same skills and preferences regardless of subject. Actual, working examples of recent classroom practice at the school would, it was hoped, make the INSET activities more pertinent.

I would use my research as the basis for a range of activities designed to raise awareness of the variety of needs represented by students throughout the school and encourage more widespread attention to the issue of 'differentiation'. Having concluded, from my initial survey, that consideration of teaching and learning styles was a largely neglected area, I felt that this might be presented as a feasible method or starting point. The outcomes of my own research suggested that this could offer an economical approach in terms of time, money and energy. It also would hopefully help to alleviate some of the nagging concerns about 'finding the right worksheet', lack of knowledge of individual needs and uncertainty about how to accommodate them.

CLASSROOM RESEARCH

I shall first describe the research into teaching and learning styles which I undertook with a mixed-ability Year 7 class, and the useful insights which it yielded for my own teaching. I shall then explain how I used this for INSET purposes, and describe the activities actually used on the INSET day and some of the ideas which were developed as a result.

I was intrigued by the ideas of Kolb and McCarthy (outlined by Michael Fielding in Chapter 6) and wanted to explore their possible application in my own teaching, using and adapting the methodology proposed in their work. I was interested to see whether providing students themselves with information about the many different ways in which we learn and absorb information might serve to empower them with a greater knowledge and understanding of the advantages of learning in a variety of ways and exploiting the range of their own personal learning styles.

I began by conducting a series of classroom-based activities in which students were given the opportunity to investigate the four learning styles identified by Kolb's inventory and attempt to discover more about their own preferred learning style. This was carried out with the use of a previously prepared set of questionnaires. The activity involved the children moving around the room to locations which were dependent on the result of their own questionnaires and my more detailed explanations delivered orally (areas of the classroom represented the various learning styles).

I made some personal predictions about the preferred learning style of a randomly selected number of students from this class which were based on my own awareness of their abilities and personalities. I attempted to predict the outcome of their own attempt to identify a preferred learning style in order to examine the extent to which this matched with the actual outcome. I planned to follow this up by observing the same four girls (Rita, Moshana, Helen and Rebecca) throughout a day's lessons, in order to see how well their learning needs were catered for across the curriculum. The results of this particular exercise were more interesting than useful since my predictions were inaccurate in most cases, highlighting the point that one cannot make assumptions about students and that any attempt to label a child as a specific type of learner is both misleading and unhelpful.

The whole process was somewhat chaotic and inconclusive but it did serve to illustrate that the four learning styles were all represented and that many students found that they recognised something in themselves within each category, highlighting the conclusion that variety existed in individuals as well as the class as a whole. It was interesting that the children were able to evaluate the activity with great clarity and insight and draw valid conclusions. Follow-up discussion was vital to this activity in order to encourage the students to think and talk about what they had learnt about themselves. They were keen to participate in further investigation based on their own learning styles and I felt that this might enable them to capitalise on their now greater understanding of learning and greater awareness of themselves as learners.

My original objective had been to identify the individual learning style of the pupils in this class in order to accurately establish the variety of need represented. I thought that I would then follow this up by investigating the extent to which this range of need is catered for during an average school day. I had recognised that an initial danger inherent in this process lay in the tendency for myself and the student to seek a conclusive result, resulting in the labelling of students as one, distinct type of learner. Clearly, this would have been misleading and inaccurate, and I came to an early and emphatic conclusion that exact identification of individual learning styles is not only difficult but also unnecessary. Indeed, the most satisfying outcome of my own research was that it was inconclusive in terms of labelling individuals but served rather to illustrate and recognise the diversity within this representative class. Variety exists not only within classes but also within individuals, and failure to recognise and accommodate this variety through a corresponding variety in teaching and learning styles would deny access to the curriculum for members of this class.

This conclusion was confirmed by my observations, during the time that I spent shadowing the class. I noticed that the majority of students responded best in those lessons that offered a variety of tasks, a choice and a sense of flexibility. Fewer children appeared comfortable and enthusiastic in those lessons where only one distinct teaching style (e.g. didactic) was evident. I also realised that my initial investigation into individual learning styles bore little relation to the ways in which individuals responded in lessons. Subsequent discussions with pupils regarding their own learning brought some fascinating results. Many pupils, with a keen and unexpected insight into their own learning requirements, expressed a sense of frustration at being deprived in some lessons of opportunities to learn in the way that suited them most.

I wouldn't remember it tomorrow because it wouldn't go into my head the way (the teacher) was doing it.

(Moshana)

For example, some resentment was evident when the opportunity to learn through talk was denied in all lessons of one particular subject:

The teachers have to listen to me in order for me to learn. I learn much better from group work and working with my friend, discussing.

(Rita)

Rita's particular awareness of her own learning requirements was extremely refreshing and positive and led to problems when she would clearly 'switch off' in a lesson in which she was not given the opportunity to exploit her preferred methods of learning (i.e. talk, interaction, movement, visual aids).

The period of time that I had spent shadowing this class heightened my appreciation of the difficulties and challenges that they faced in adapting to very specific teaching styles in certain lessons during a school day. Discomfort and frustration was evident among the class when they switched from a very relaxed, collaborative teaching approach to a formal, didactic approach in the space of one hour. A more positive feedback was received in response to those lessons in which a choice was offered in terms of input and expected outcome. I felt satisfied, at the conclusion of the process, that adjustment and variation of teaching styles and an awareness of learning styles is indeed a valid and useful (though not comprehensive) means of effective differentiation.

IN-SERVICE TRAINING

These were the insights, then, that I planned to share with colleagues and make the basis for discussion and further development, starting with two INSET days. The main issues of the INSET days were to be based around:

- definitions of differentiation
- sharing methods of differentiation and good practice (not subject specific)
- a presentation of my case study
- subject specific differentiation, definitions and establishing effective techniques
- practical means of ensuring that a degree of differentiation exists in every class through teaching and learning styles.

During preparation for the INSET days we were heavily concerned with creating a variety of interesting and accessible tasks which might stimulate interest and enthusiasm and help us to substantiate the message that this is exactly the kind of planning and practice we were promoting for use in the classroom.

As a relative newcomer to the school, I felt a sense of trepidation since I was aware of the negative attitude which had been displayed by many members of staff during past internal INSET days. Also, conscious of my 'new-girl' status, I was tentative about creating hostility by appearing to criticise existing practice in the school rather than celebrate, exploit and develop existing good practice. In an attempt to inject some humour into the proceedings at the outset, I had prepared a video entitled 'The Reluctant Teacher Learner' using the drama staff as my actors. This was a satirical presentation of the typical, negative reaction to INSET days, showing teachers displaying the very worse traits of the disgruntled and reluctant teenage student. The message came across that preparing activities for staff was equally or more challenging than preparing lessons for the most difficult of classes. Though it did show an exaggerated response, this video did serve to make us laugh at ourselves; those of us responsible for organising the day were quick to include ourselves! This initial 'ice-breaking' activity did appear to lighten and relax the general atmosphere and served to deflect some of the resentment and hostility that I had feared.

A senior member of staff then introduced the theme and content of the forthcoming sessions and provided an explanation of the purpose and rationale behind them. This was extremely useful in creating a focus and meaningful objective since it was made clear that everything on offer was appropriate for everyone.

Initially, the staff were divided into pre-arranged groups of three or four for a discussion activity. I had drawn from my research material a selection of anonymous quotations from members of staff when requested to give their reaction to the term 'differentiation' and these were presented to staff alongside a leading question to help stimulate discussion.

---

1 'I find the word a little threatening as I feel people will bandy the word around and not actually get on with the task of teaching.'
   How can we ensure that differentiation is not a huge barrier to overcome but becomes a natural part of our planning and teaching?

---

2 'I rarely set different tasks because it would be like subversive streaming.'
   What strategies can we employ to ensure that differentiation allows for differences but does not discriminate?

---

3 'How do I know what each student's preferred learning style is, let alone meet it?'
   How can we allow for the various styles of learners within our classrooms?

---

4 'It is a way of giving students equal opportunities and respecting them as individuals not a group . . . it stops competition and therefore cuts out the "losers"; we can all be winners in the right category!'
   What strategies can we employ to allow for differences within the classroom?

---

5 'One tries but it is difficult at times.'
   'Desirable but difficult.'
   How can we overcome the difficulties of differentiating within the classroom?

---

6 'Differentiation has something to do with mixed ability teaching which doesn't really work in mathematics.'
   How can we ensure that all classes, mixed ability or otherwise, receive a differentiated curriculum?

These were presented in colourful, laminated form and the intention was that, by concentrating on one specific quotation or viewpoint, discussion would be more focused. Subsequent feedback as a whole group was considered rather too impractical and time consuming. We therefore introduced a competition that required each group to devise a ten word slogan that most effectively summarised the outcome of their discussion on differentiation. 'Entry forms' were distributed.

THE SLOGAN THAT BEST DESCRIBES OUR REACTION TO
DIFFERENTIATION IS . . .
(in no more than 10 words)

_____

_____

_____

_____

The results proved to be interesting and incisive and were displayed
for all staff:

Respect the 'process' rather than the outcome.

Constant, caring evaluation of response to a variety of tasks.

Giving ownership to pupils / access to a variety of resources.

Varied, open-ended, self-selected learning opportunities.

Create happy equal opportunity ethos enabling personal
esteem and success.

Encourage / enable / inform / cherish / assess / monitor /
support / involve / value.

'Must, should, could' philosophy vital (simple to complex, etc.).
Flexibility.

All students need individual negotiated teaching and learning
programmes.

Variety of tasks allowing everyone to work at optimum levels.

Is a way of ensuring that every student understands what we
wanted to teach and they need to learn.

Confidence, flexibility, providing variety of tasks, diversity of
teaching style.

I then presented my own research to the staff group, explaining the process from the beginning and the purpose behind it, illustrating my ideas and conclusions by a description of the case study. I was surprised and pleased by the positive and genuinely interested reaction that I received from the majority of my colleagues and felt that this was due to the fact that they were presented with concrete evidence from actual classroom practice within the school rather than general theory.

ENGLISH DEPARTMENT INSET

The staff were then organised according to department or faculty in order to pursue a range of activities that would complement and develop those ideas discussed and referred to in the previous sessions.

Our departmental day began with general discussion about 'Differentiating the English Curriculum', reflecting on the issues that had arisen on the previous day and deciding how they best applied to our own work within the department. We developed some ideas about the 'definition' of differentiation within the context of English. One of our objectives was to work towards a Departmental Differentiation Policy that would work within an overarching departmental scheme of work. Matters arising from our discussion included concerns about the practicality of implementing workable differentiation within truly mixed-ability classrooms and the need for greater sharing of good practice that might serve to increase the variety of tasks within all units of work.

We then focused on the subject of 'Teaching and Learning Styles' as a suggested way forward for the department in terms of the way in which we differentiate. Reflecting once again on the events of the previous day, we looked at the different learning styles as a means of establishing the variety that exists within our classrooms. Inventories of various learning styles were distributed in order for all members of the department to discover more about what type of learner they are. Having analysed the variety represented by the staff, we were then able to conclude that similar variety will inevitably exist within each class. Having established that such a variety exists, how then do we make decisions about what these differences are and how do we accommodate them? It was necessary to establish with everyone from the beginning that we should be working from the assumption that equality of opportunity within the classroom means catering for differences rather than treating everyone the same.

The next practical task was 'Putting it into Practice' whereby each member of the department became involved in the creation of a new unit of work incorporating existing good practice and fresh ideas that was differentiated through teaching and learning styles. Since war poetry is taught at Key Stages 3 and 4, it was deemed an appropriate topic, being common to us all. Each member of staff then became responsible for a specific type of learner and was asked to brainstorm ideas for lessons on war poetry that would best suit this particular type of learner. Once collated, the combination of ideas, tasks, activities and resources would form a comprehensive and differentiated unit of work on war poetry. Use of the unit would be left to the discretion of the individual class teacher since appropriate selection of activities could ensure that a wide range of need among different types of learners was being met. (See materials produced in the appendix to this chapter.)

A similar technique was then employed as we turned to broader topics such as 'Teaching a Novel'. This method of planning proved to be successful and satisfactory due to its collaborative nature and because it provided our department with a means of sharing and recording good practice.

CONCLUSION

On reflection, I had failed to anticipate one of the inherent dangers of this process which was highlighted as I collated the information gathered from colleagues, that there are many preconceptions related to ability. It became clear that at least one member of staff was making a clear connection between learning style, ability and intelligence. For example, her written feedback clearly contained the assumption that the 'analytical' learner who might respond best to the formal, traditional teaching style was the 'most able' in contrast to the 'imaginative' learner who might prefer active, collaborative, interactive tasks. The latter was perceived in this instance as 'less able'. With this in mind, I reflected on my original research and became aware that in making predictions about the preferred learning styles of individuals, I had predicted that the student who had previously illustrated the highest ability in terms of written work and response to reading (Helen) was an assimilator, an 'analytical' learner. This further convinced me that seeking and providing information about the preferred learning style of individuals is littered with pitfalls and should be avoided, leaving us to work from the assumption that all styles will exist within a given class, regardless of individual preferences.

The experience of organising INSET for colleagues had been both daunting and challenging but was generally successful in terms of the response received. The initial injection of humour and satire had served to eliminate some hostility and the use of actual classroom research enhanced the general interest since the experience became more relevant for many staff at this point. The departmental sessions relied heavily on the interest and enthusiasm of those involved and success was more difficult to evaluate though the feedback that I received on reflection showed a positive response to the progression from whole-school to departmental issues. If nothing else, I would hope that the training days at least raised awareness and created some questions and ideas in the minds of us all which might serve to enhance and improve the general curriculum provision for our students.

APPENDIX: DEVELOPMENT OF A UNIT OF WORK USING TEACHING AND LEARNING STYLES

The following unit of work was developed as a direct result of work done by the English department during the internal INSET day on differentiation through teaching and learning styles.

Activities were used to introduce and emphasise the variety of learning styles among our students. We then took a central topic within the overarching schemes of work for Key Stages 3 and 4, war poetry, and planned a unit of work which was differentiated since it provided for a range of learning styles. In order to achieve this, the staff present were divided into groups and each group became responsible for a specific learning style. For the purpose of this exercise, we used three styles:

- Kinaesthetic learning
- Auditory learning
- Visual learning.

Using the resources available within the department, the groups brainstormed their ideas for tasks which would most suit their given learning style during a study of war poetry.

Once the ideas were collated, a unit of work was put into place which provided a whole range of tasks from which a teacher could select during a study of war poetry. In order to differentiate successfully in the intended way, the teacher would have to select from all three sections and only then could the teacher feel that a range of learning styles was being catered for and a variety of teaching styles was on offer.

Clearly, the unit as it stands has much room for improvement but it represented a start for us and introduced a new way of planning and thinking. This technique gave everyone a sense of ownership and served to raise awareness of the importance of teaching and learning styles as an aid to effective differentiation.

The worksheet (see p. 137) was devised as a direct result of the unit and could be distributed to all students during a study of war poetry. The intention here is to allow for student choice. All students can select from a range of tasks suitable for all three learning styles and can, in this way, select a task which is most suited to their preferred learning style thereby allowing them to exploit their individual skills to the full without having to depend on teacher input.

Tasks suitable for kinaesthetic learning

Use games, role play, experiments, and other active strategies. Provide activity and variety. Provide materials, i.e. large paper and markers. Hands-on activities and field trips. Group activities and movement around the classroom.

Suggested tasks

Resources required: audio or video tapes with war songs, tape recorders, scissors and glue, video reorder and microphone, relevant pictures and postcards.

1 Class provided with range of poems. Produce collage to illustrate the various attitudes to war revealed in the poems. Look at posters; devise own propaganda poster, pro- or anti-war. Active discussion about the reasons for war and possible justification. Make it topical by intro-ducing discussion and asking for research into the war in Croatia. Also look at conscientious objectors and link with Wilfred Owen. Invite a guest speaker.
2 Experience songs of the period – rhythm poems or those used to raise morale. Class produce a dramatic presentation of the songs (in collab-oration with music).
3 Read/act sections of *Journey's end*. Role play in trenches; voice over about feelings.
4 Drama: 'Life in the Trenches'. Voice over reading a Wilfred Owen poem. Dramatic presentation to illustrate contrast of 'rosy' image of the war portrayed by morale-boosting propaganda on the home front with the reality of life in the trenches. Use posters as additional material and clips from pro-war films and news footage.
5 *Dulce et decorum est*: present with some softly chanting the Latin, one on a soap box reciting *at* us with the rest in line miming in slow motion.
6 Role play of life in trenches. Voice over section of *Testament of youth*. Or groups use the poetry of Owen or Sassoon to produce a TV news report of 'Life in the Trenches' in documentary style.

Commentary

Active lessons in which the students are able to move around will best suit this learning style, therefore the inclusion of role play is appropriate. Putting life and meaning into the war poems will make them real and allow the kinaesthetic learner to learn through action and hands-on experience. An opportunity to look at posters from the time will appeal to this learner because the events and the era will become more 'real'. The kinaesthetic learner benefits from active participation and group work therefore flexible activities like performing the poems for the class will help.

Tasks suitable for auditory learning

Emphasise directions and important information verbally; let students repeat in own words; encourage them to study aloud. Provide opportunities for discussion and group work. Have quiet work space, allow use of earphones. Encourage verbal feedback and discussion of work in progress. Oral practice and evaluation.

Suggested tasks

Resources required: radio plays, audio tapes of war poetry, speeches and video material, tape recorders and microphones.

1 Read poems out loud with partner or group. Discuss meaning, tone. Pick out words or images that sound effective or significant. 'Telegram' exercise – in small groups the class 'converts' stanzas of a given poem (e.g. 'Exposure' by Owen) into a telegram. This allows for focus on key words and leads to discussion.
2 Listen to audio tapes of the poems. Class prepares own readings. Listen to radio plays (extracts). In groups, prepare their own radio play on a war theme.
3 Watch videos of original news footage/war scenes/films/TV programmes. In groups, prepare radio news broadcast from the front line, using the poems as evidence. *Or* produce a radio 'chat show' with an interviewer discussing poetry with one war poet. Questions prepared to explore style, content and viewpoint.
4 Present a role play/TV type interview of e.g. soldiers returning after a battle or interview medical staff caring for the wounded.
5 Interview relatives/friends who have memories of their time in the war or of their relatives involved. Tape the conversations if possible. Write up the interview in style of feature article or other.
6 Write poem or account of the time using the information collected. Present to a group reading/performing aloud.

Commentary

Auditory learners respond to activities which require them to listen or communicate orally. Use of complementary materials with a class such as tape recorders and microphones is therefore appropriate. Hearing the poems read aloud will allow this type of learner to absorb their meaning more thoroughly. Allowing flexibility in terms of the way that tasks can be carried out will allow auditory learners to learn by interviewing, listening to others and participating in active performance of the poetry which will avoid the restrictive and limiting understanding that they would gain from merely reading them from a page.

Tasks suitable for visual learning

Use visual aids, models and demonstration. Encourage visual strategies (webs, pictures, highlights). Write important information on board or overhead projector. Visual practice and evaluation.

Suggested tasks

Resources required: war paintings, war videos (including original footage), photographs and slides, artefacts, war posters (recruitment, propaganda), coloured pens, historical background.

1 Study an account of the outbreak of the First World War. Produce picture strip of main events of the war.
2 Colour coding. Highlight poems in various colours to reflect the mood/tone of the words or the poet, e.g. black/red/green. Explain reasons for colour code.
3 Role play. Acting out poems. Illustrating stereotype, way of life, e.g. day in the trenches, important battles, day before or after, etc.
4 Re-assembling poem from separate sections. Sequencing using pictures as visual aid.
5 Interview a war veteran or ask someone to give a talk about life and times of war. Interview older member of staff about childhood during the Second World War. Make use of photographs and artefacts. Devise a question-answer game in which students investigate the origin of these.
6 Life on the home front. Use film such as *Home and Glory* to support study of relevant poems from the Second World War.

Commentary

The visual learner responds best in lessons which promote the use of visual aids and resources such as TV and video. Drawing and studying pictures will allow the visual learner to relate more clearly to a particular era and gain a more thorough understanding of the poems being studied. This type of learner will enjoy and benefit from use of colour which is why a colour-coding task might aid this student to explore the tone and language more successfully. Active tasks such as role play will create a more visual and realistic picture and use of film and TV will help to bring the poems to life and lift them from the page.

War poetry: class worksheet

Select one task from the following list. In order to complete the task you must plan carefully and collect together the appropriate materials which are available from your teacher. Select the task which most appeals to you and will help you to understand the poetry that you are studying.

1 Carefully study the war posters and decide which ones are pro-war and which are anti-war. Carry out some research into propaganda and the reasons why this was used during the First and Second World Wars. In some cases, posters were used to raise morale and, in others, to persuade people to fight. Design your own war poster which uses a theme from the posters you have studied and included words and phrases from the war poems that you have studied.

2 Select one of the war poems that you have studied. Using a range of different colour highlighter pens, go through the poem and highlight words and phrases with a colour which reflects the mood or tone. For example, red could represent morbid thought of death and blood, yellow might reflect optimism, blue could be patriotism. You can decide on your own colour code. When you have done this, write about your poem, saying why you chose it and why how you have used colour-coding. You must explain reasons for your choice of colours.

3 Listen to a range of audio tapes on which you will hear readings of some of the war poems set for study. Select any war poem that you have looked at and prepare your own reading which you should record on audio tape. You should use appropriate sound effects and a commentary (written or recorded orally) to explain the reasons for your choice of poem and an explanation of your reading. Think about the tone of your voice, the speed of your reading, include any appropriate music which would complement your poem. You will be expected to play your tape to the class.

Differentiation through support

Chapter 9

Finding the right worksheet?

Barbara Parry

EDITOR'S INTRODUCTION

In this fourth part of the book, we turn to the work of support teachers and support services to consider the part that they have to play in ensuring that all children have the opportunity to participate as fully as possible in the range of learning experiences to which they are entitled, and to use and develop their existing resources as fully as possible in the context of school learning. The 'duty to integrate' clause of the Education Act 1981 is still a statutory obligation upon all schools and local authorities under the Education Act 1993. This means that children are entitled by law to be educated in mainstream schools, and to have appropriate provision made for them to allow them to learn alongside their peers, unless it can be demonstrated that this is incompatible with their interests, with the interests of other children, or with the effective use of resources.

Partly as a result of legislation, and partly as a result of heightened aware-ness of the importance of external influences shaping children's learning and behaviour, it became the norm during the 1980s for special schools and support services to work in much closer collaboration with mainstream colleagues. The aim was to try to create conditions in which children could be successfully enabled to learn in their mainstream classes rather than removed to be taught in segregated provision. Partnership work between special needs teachers and mainstream teachers, with in-class support rather than withdrawal or teaching in special units, became accepted practice rather than the exception. Outreach work from special schools began to be set up to try to create conditions that would make re-integration possible.

The advent of the National Curriculum, testing, league tables, OFSTED (Office for Standards in Education) and market-place philosophies linked to parental choice have had the effect, in some cases, of dampening schools' enthusiasm for such initiatives. However, there are also many schools and teachers who remain committed to such developments. This chapter looks at the work of two such teachers as they attempt to understand and respond to the needs of a 14-year-old girl with a statement for emotional and behavioural difficulties, with a view to fostering her successful participation and learning in a mainstream context. Barbara Parry explains how her thinking developed in the course of this work, from an initial expectation that all would be well only if she could 'find the right worksheet' for Kelly, to a much more complex understanding of what 'differentiation' entails and what might need to be done to help Kelly learn more successfully.

The chapter illustrates the complexity of the task of trying to understand and respond to the 'needs' of all learners, even when two teachers are working together to pool ideas and resources. Definitions of 'differentiation' which refer to 'meeting individual needs' often gloss over these complexities, making it more difficult for teachers to admit uncertainties. It is important to look closely at the processes through which we arrive at these judgements. What exactly do we mean by 'individual needs' and how can we ascertain what can or should be done in a particular situation to enhance children's learning?

◆ ◆ ◆

When I carried out the work described in this chapter, I was working for a special school for students with emotional and behavioural difficulties (EBD). I worked as a specialist teacher with an outreach team, supporting students with recognised emotional and behavioural difficulties in mainstream schools.

In one secondary school I have been supporting two Year 7 students, whom I shall call Kelly and Michelle, who have statements for behavioural difficulties and learning difficulties. Both of these students had spent a number of years at the special school. My brief has been to support their return to mainstream school through individual counselling, also to liaise and advise the teaching and support staff who work with these girls.

The teachers were concerned because there seemed to be little work that these students could or would do. We were using behaviour modification programmes with both of them. I was using my time with them to teach social skills, and raise their self-esteem. The combination of this support had lessened their difficult, acting-out behaviour and brought about some cooperation. There continued to be a concern about Kelly and Michelle not doing much work and understanding very little. I hoped that the course would teach me how to prepare worksheets which would be exactly right for these students, thus solving our problems. As it turned out I came to understand differentiation as being much more than just 'providing the right worksheet'. Rather it involves a whole range of activities which enable all students to access the curriculum in their own way and at their own level. This study details the process by which this new understanding emerged, and the implications specifically for my work to support re-integration.

SCHOOL CONTEXT

The Year 7 timetable in this school is organised differently from many secondary schools. These students spend fifteen of their twenty-five lessons in a special block, taught by their tutor. This facility is an important feature in the transition between primary and secondary school. It is intended to help the new students to feel secure. This was one reason why this school has been chosen as the mainstream school for Kelly and Michelle. It was felt that spending 60 per cent of the week with one teacher would help them to settle.

Kelly had been put into 7P with Ms Pounds, a very experienced teacher and Head of Year 7. Michelle had been put into 7E with Ms Edwards, also a very experienced teacher and long-standing member of the Year Seven Team (YST). Because of initial difficulties in settling in, a special welfare assistant (Maxine) from the special school came to work with Michelle and 7E for eight hours a week. Ms Pounds is a friend and colleague whom I have known for many years. Because of this, and because 7E already had extra support, I decided to concentrate my work with 7P. The class was composed of twenty-three students of mixed ability. There were three bilingual students who were new to Britain, who knew very little English.

Over a period of six weeks, I spent two hours a week observing and supporting the class as a whole and Kelly in particular. I tried to gain a sense of the range of activities undertaken by the whole group and the kinds of differentiation that were made possible within this overall framework. I observed in different ways. I did one formal class observation noting down every minute the range of activities taking place in the classroom. I also made many less formal observations, noting when and how new activities were used, and how Ms Pounds made adjustments to match work to individual abilities. Through my observations of Kelly, I tried to build up a picture of her responses to different kinds of activities and groupings, noting what her teacher and I did in order to try to accommodate her needs, and how she responded to these interventions. When working with her as a support teacher I was able to talk to her about the classwork. I was also able to draw in other students to lessen Kelly's isolation.

Through my observations I was able to reach a new appreciation of what 'differentiation' means: how the learning environment was organised and activities varied to create flexibility and allow for differences, and the many ways in which Ms Pounds skilfully responded to the needs of individual pupils, as she perceived them, including Kelly's. Yet at the same time I realised that many of the activities which were so successful with other students did not work so well for Kelly. I began to see a pattern emerging in Kelly's behaviour and responses in class which suggested to me that these were above all ways of coping with the enormous pressures, both social and academic, which the situation created for her. She was unable to participate fully in the range of group activities because she found them too threatening. I was able to appreciate in a new way just how much 'progress' had been achieved already, and begin to see ways forward that would build on these achievements and, with my support, make wider range of learning opportunities accessible and acceptable to Kelly.

DIFFERENTIATION WITHIN THE WHOLE-CLASS GROUP

The YST work is taught as integrated programmes of study, based on the National Curriculum. Students will work at one integrated programme until it is finished, rather than move hourly to separate subjects. All the activities are carefully planned. One module which I worked on began as a project about healthy eating, then went on to look at advertising and the media, to plan and record jingles as group work. The final part was to design and make up a box to contain muesli. This was made according to the individual's recipe.

A second project on the medieval world started with the Normans, had clear enlargements of the Bayeux Tapestry and went on to look in detail at William's invasion and establishment as king. A visit to a Norman castle was part of this module.

The programme of study is developed as a booklet, which works through a series of activities giving lots of information. Each student has a photocopy of each booklet. All the Year 7 tutors teach the same modules at the same time. They work collaboratively to plan and produce each module. For most lessons some computers are available in the Learning Library and Resource Centre (LLRC). On a rotational basis students can go to the library to use computers or research from books. These resources are well used. There are some books available in the classrooms.

Although the text of the booklets was too difficult for some students to handle independently, many of the larger tasks were broken down into more accessible units by Ms Pounds, through the following strategies:

1 Often she used discussion to review information and pick out key points.
2 Key words were put on the board as a reinforcement to the work in the module.
3 There were simplified materials available for all students.
4 Many of the key pictures were enlarged and simplified.
5 Other graphic work was supplied which could be used, traced or copied.
6 Each module contained a wide variety of activities.

It appeared that differentiation was taking place on two levels. At one level there were the planned range of class activities which were allowing for differentiation by pace, level and outcome. These included:

- brainstorming
- drama
- paired work
- small group work
- using discussion to review and progress.

Another layer of differentiation was supplied by Ms Pounds who was very well aware of individual needs. I saw her

- allow students to work at their own pace, by developing and extending activities which caught an interest
- intervene with individuals at appropriate times to simplify/clarify tasks
- scribe for individuals whilst they spoke
- draw parallels with students' own experience and interest.

Using the framework provided by Lewis (1992) to assist my observations, I saw clear examples of differentiation by:

1 Pace: students could take varying amounts of time to finish a task.
2 Level: Ms Pounds used easier resources and language with students who needed these.
3 Interest: students made muesli according to their individual favourite ingredients.
4 Access: when working on a newspaper 'front page' individuals had a different starting point.
5 Teacher time: varying time spent with individuals according to need (e.g. scribing).
6 Grouping: groups changed; some were self-selected, e.g. for drama, activity, some were teacher selected, e.g. for paired activity.
7 Structure: some students worked through a 'chunk' of material as set out in a study booklet. For others this chunk was broken down by the teacher using supplementary materials, into much smaller targets of work.

I also saw Ms Pounds continuously provide other vital aspects of differentiation, as outlined by Lewis (1992).

> Other features of effective teaching include clear and immediate feedback, children taking some responsibility for their own learning and the development of children's reflectivity about their learning.

Using oral reviews to enhance learning was a common short activity in 7P. Ms Pounds also used humour and empathy successfully along with a great sensitivity to individual needs. As Lewis notes:

> There are also personal qualities about the teacher herself. The effective teacher has qualities such as empathy and humour which are vital to her broader role.

(Lewis 1992)

To sum up, I realised that in setting out originally to look for the 'right worksheet' I had a far too narrow view of differentiation. It is really about giving all children access to the curriculum, and this is done by offering a range of activities. A variety of differentiated activities were being used daily in Year 7 classrooms at the school. An important factor was that the tasks did not rely *only* on writing, or reading or talking, but included much more. The mix of different activities catered for all learning styles: students could see, hear, touch, talk about or use drama to learn and understand about a task. Good use of group work meant students could learn from each other. The constant use of talk to review and move on meant students with low reading and writing abilities were less disadvantaged. The situation was further enhanced by the sensitive and skilful way Ms Pounds understood each individual's ability and matched learning tasks to individual needs.

KELLY

How did Kelly fare in this context? Over the period of six weeks' observations and support, I gradually built up the following picture, both positive and negative, of Kelly's learning, behaviour and needs, and began to see how it made sense from Kelly's point of view.

In the classroom, Kelly seemed isolated. She sat at a desk on her own, facing away from the board. Various other arrangements had been tried: for example, sitting with other students, sitting facing the board, but these had not worked well. Kelly made inappropriate remarks when she sat at tables with other students. When she was forced to face the board she became very uncooperative to the point of leaving the room. The arrangement that I observed had been arrived at through trial and error and seemed to work better than any other. Kelly had chosen not to stay in any of the other seats. By moving away, she chose to sit on her own. She could sit and look out of the window or turn her chair to face inward if she chose. That way she was in control. With this arrangement, she sat adjacent to Ms Pounds which she also preferred.

Whole-class work

I discovered that in order to become involved in any whole-class learning experience Kelly had to be allowed to be doing something active. If she stayed still, she became 'switched off'. The one time she was still, she sat with her coat over her head which seemed to be a way of her controlling her behaviour, preventing herself from 'acting out'. Kelly particularly liked colouring in things and tidying things. Ms Pounds found that if she allowed Kelly to occupy herself in this way while a class activity was in progress, it did not distract Kelly's attention. On the contrary, doing something made it possible for her to concentrate and answer questions which were part of a class discussion, showing she was accurately comprehending. When she sat still Kelly did not contribute to discussions. Ms Pound managed this well, but knew other staff found it difficult to tolerate Kelly's movement whilst they were talking. The solution was to provide activities which did not disrupt the class activity.

Individual work

Kelly also had fixed ideas about schoolwork. Her favourite activity was copying, and she would copy out whole books at home, and bring in copied work as homework she had set herself. Kelly copied without much comprehension. There was little indication that she was reading for meaning. To enable her to answer simple questions, it needed an adult to intervene and make her look for meaning in the task. It helped Kelly to control her behaviour if she could negotiate tasks, for example 'Can I copy this?' Her work did not have to be the same as everyone else's.

Kelly could write independently but at a low level: simple words not in proper sentences with numerous spelling mistakes. Maybe she was self-conscious about the standard of her independent work, so she preferred the safety of copied work. Kelly was not the only student who produced independent work of a low standard and I never heard any adverse comment about any piece of work.

To write independently Kelly needed a reward, such as being able to collate some work for her teacher (which she did quickly and well) or some time on a computer, etc. It seemed that Kelly did not move her mind on to understanding the purpose behind the task, a process necessary to help her learn (Ainscow 1989). Kelly seemed to make no effort to glean meaning from the information she was given. Perhaps previously she had been given more difficult work that she had not understood so now lacked confidence in trying anything new.

Confidence was certainly an issue in relation to drawing. Kelly would not draw in class, although she would draw in one-to-one sessions with me. Kelly would colour inside an outline, or go over a pencil guideline, but do this very quickly and roughly. Both writing and colouring were completed at high speed, so Kelly needed many activities in quick succession to keep her occupied.

Groupwork

There was anxiety about Kelly taking part in group work. She was not able to initiate or offer herself to a group. The group might be persuaded to take her. This was achieved subtly by Ms Pounds who settled for a larger than ideal group, say six instead of four. This supported the other students in the group. Kelly would shout constantly, and often say inappropriate things to other students, such as 'move your f—— paper'. She had some understanding when she should be working, but was not able to make contributions to the task. She might understand the task but did not have the skills to contribute well. If forced into a group then she would opt out completely by moving away to sit on her own. This is different from others who, although challenged academically, are able to fit in socially. Much of Kelly's isolation seemed to stem from her initial poor behaviour which was characterised by a lot of 'acting out' and of swearing and rudeness to teachers and peers. This had not happened recently but was remembered by her peer group. Ms Pounds saw it as Kelly 'remaining isolated at the bottom of the pecking order', because of her initial behaviour, and her low level of social skills.

I tried to understand this behaviour in context, and appreciate what the experience of integration into mainstream education might be like for children whose previous educational experience has been very different, recalling the impressions of one support teacher who noted:

> After spending many years in the safe haven of a special school, venturing into a mainstream primary school to offer support I was immediately struck by the hustle and bustle which accompanies large numbers of children actively engaged in the business of learning. There is little wonder that children who have received a prolonged special education often find it very difficult to leave their protected environment and re-integrate into the ordinary school.
>
> (Baker and Bovair 1990)

Kelly had been at the special school since she was 4 years old. In her last year there, Year 6, she had some time in a mainstream school. That year all her acting out took place at the special school. In Year 7 she became full time at the mainstream secondary school without a bolt to let out her frustrations and feelings of anger, confusion and failure. Support from myself and Ms Pounds had now helped Kelly to modify her behaviour, but the class had not forgotten the initial acting out which Kelly had shown them.

Pair work

I observed one example of a successful piece of paired work: a mosaic. This was produced by negotiation between Kelly and her partner, structured by Ms Pounds. It was unusual. My understanding of Kelly is that she can operate in a pair provided that she does not feel dominated by the other person. For some time Kelly worked with Zulekha, who is a

Tamil refugee, new to England, with very little knowledge of English. Kelly would swamp Zulekha to the point of doing her writing. Kelly could sustain this help for an hour or even a whole morning. Once Zulekha had some understanding, she began to reject Kelly's over-whelming help. Kelly then became quite hostile and nasty, making Zulekha cry. At this point the pairing no longer worked.

Drama

This demanded much more of Kelly. She needed to be able to discuss a subject, and come to an agreement with other students. Discussion was very difficult for Kelly, but she could be involved at some level. If asked a direct question, she might give an anecdotal response, but other-wise would rarely contribute. Kelly could follow and understand discus-sions, showing this through laughing or grimacing appropriately at comments from others.

Attendance

Kelly now consistently attended all lessons with Ms Pounds, although she absented herself from other lessons, using a variety of excuses. She would spend time with the caretaker or tidying the library. Initially, she had avoided Ms Pounds's lessons, but now she wanted to be there. Kelly's response to Ms Pounds's lessons became clear in conversation. Kelly said Ms Pounds was her favourite teacher, and that she 'liked her lessons'.

Summary

My observations revealed both positive and negative features of Kelly's current patterns of learning and behaviour. I saw that she was some-times isolated because of the difficulties she had cooperating with others. I also saw that she did not often understand the meaning behind her work, but merely copied out. Her increasing ability to control her temper was certainly a real success and was vital if she was to remain at the school. At first it had led to a series of exclusions. Kelly had not been excluded for the previous two terms.

I could see other areas of success:

1 There had been tremendous improvement in Kelly's behaviour since her starting at the school.
2 Kelly enjoyed being with Ms Pounds and enjoyed her lessons.
3 Ms Pounds had found many strategies which worked well with Kelly.
4 At a low level Kelly was engaged in many of the differentiated activities.

5 Kelly could now negotiate instead of 'act out'.
6 Kelly was gradually widening the range of activities she was prepared
   to participate in.

Outcomes

I concluded that Kelly was not yet able to benefit from many of the
activities which gave other students access to the curriculum, such as
the oral work, drama, paired work and group work because these were
too threatening for her, socially and academically. Yet this sense of threat
was entirely understandable, given the enormous change which Kelly
was having to cope with after spending most of her education in a special
school. It was important to acknowledge how far she had come in quite
a short time. Moreover, the patterns of work and behaviour which I had
observed were all comprehensible when understood as ways of coping
with these pressures.

It seemed that the change had been brought about by Ms Pounds's
support. Her approach was similar to that proposed by Ainscow and
Tweddle (1988) who suggest that:

> Learning difficulties are context bound. . . . In seeking ways of helping
> all pupils to experience success in the classroom we should focus our
> attention on those factors over which we have significant influence
> particularly those classroom factors associated with the planning and
> implementation of the curriculum. Our aim as teachers must be to
> improve our own practice, particularly by taking account of the indi-
> viduality of pupils within our classes and finding ways to help pupils
> understand the nature and purpose of the tasks and activities in which
> they are engaged.

Ms Pounds had been very flexible in responding to Kelly, willing to
try all sorts of approaches and negotiate with Kelly in order to
learn what conditions would bring about the most favourable responses.
She did not insist on Kelly accommodating to a particular set of
norms, but was prepared to discover what Kelly seemed to need and
try to accommodate that within her overall approach. Each of these
individual negotiations and accommodations were like stepping stones
for Kelly. They were the means by which Kelly would be enabled to
move forward, slowing and tentatively, from her current set of self-
protective needs, preferences and choices. With the right support
and encouragement, she would gradually become increasingly able to
participate in the many learning opportunities which the environment
provided but which she was not yet able to benefit from. A priority now
was to find ways of encouraging more active involvement in her own
learning.

Through this study, my perception of Kelly's 'needs' and their implications for my own input changed completely. I came to appreciate that what was needed was not to find, or devise, 'the right worksheet', but rather to provide help in cooperating with other students, so that she would be able to take part more successfully in the many activities involving interaction with peers. Looking back at my teaching experience at the special school, I realised that Kelly would have had little experience of the kind of collaborative group activity that she was expected to be able to contribute to at her secondary school. The situations where groups were expected to work together positively towards a negotiated task may have been a new and incomprehensible experience to Kelly. I noticed that Kelly used language to make remarks which 'wound up' or put down other students, but she found it very difficult to express an opinion. This lack of skill in communication prevented her joining in discussions. Providing experience of discussion and shared activity in a small group would become a priority for future work.

As a result of this study, Ms Pounds and myself had a clearer understanding of activities and strategies which work with Kelly. We were able to pass this information to other staff who worked with her. This has enabled Kelly to build good relationships with other staff. Ms Pounds and I met weekly to discuss areas of progress and difficulty for Kelly. We were confident now that the most important question, for our work with Kelly, was to keep asking ourselves 'How is what I am doing helping to give the work meaning for Kelly?' (Ainscow and Tweddle 1988).

CONCLUSION

I was able to transfer much of what I had learnt to other students whom I observed operating in the same way. Leading an INSET session at the special school, I stressed the importance not only of using supplementary materials, but also of building in pair, group and oral activities. I have used the points below as a guide (Ainscow 1989). These encapsulate everything I have learnt about good differentiation:

- an emphasis on what the pupil knows, understands and can do
- the encouragement of self-esteem by giving the pupil more responsibility
- the involvement of pupils in self-assessment that is both formative and summative
- the establishment of clearly understood short-term as well as long-term goals
- the development of thinking skills through research and problem solving

- a teaching situation that makes use of practical work and active participation by the pupils
- group work, which shows an ability to work cooperatively and to communicate with others
- the encouragement of oral expression through discussion and explanation
- the use of tape, video, computer, word processor, etc., particularly as an alternative means of recording.

Chapter 10

Integration or differentiation?
The case of bilingual learners

Jean Mayala

EDITOR'S INTRODUCTION

The development of language support for bilingual and multilingual children has followed a pattern broadly similar to the development of support for special educational needs. Until the 1980s, the predominant pattern was for children deemed to be in need of additional support in learning English to receive that support through withdrawal from mainstream teaching for specialist help in small groups, or through attendance at a language centre. Initially, this was seen as a form of positive discrimination: a vital and necessary resource to address a specific need affecting a small minority of children. Gradually, however, there was a groundswell of opinion amongst language teachers that the mainstream classroom might provide richer, more productive contexts for learning language by using language for the purposes of other learning.

> In mainstream lessons, if they were of the 'right' kind, 'our' students might have even wider, more productive access to a range of language and a range of opportunity to develop a repertoire of skills than we were able to construct in the 'special' language situation where everyone was in the process of learning to use English.
>
> (Levine 1989 p. 22)

Observations of children's responses, in special language classes, when teachers experimented with deriving the language syllabus from the subject content and activities of mainstream lessons suggested that, in such situations, pupils' use of English increased in power 'almost naturally' (Levine 1989 p. 21). There was good reason to suppose, then, that if rich language environments could be created within mainstream classrooms, this would not only provide a more empowering environment for learning English but also overcome many of the other problems associated with the provision of support through separate provision. The Swann Report (DES 1985c) summed up the case for providing more inclusive forms of support in the following six points:

- the limitations on the breadth of curriculum which a language centre or unit can offer and the inherent injustice of denying any pupil access to other subjects until he or she has mastered English
- the absence in many cases of direct links between the language centre or unit and the mainstream of school life which means that the work being done does not mirror that of the school and that the language needs perceived by class teachers are not necessarily met by E2L specialists

- the possibly negative effect on a pupil's progress in learning English of mixing primarily or even solely with children for whom English is not a first language
- the possible effects on a child's socialisation and developing maturity of being separated from his or her peers and away from the 'social reality' of the school
- the inevitable trauma for a child of entering the English-speaking environment of the mainstream school is merely postponed and in no way avoided
- mainstream school teachers are discouraged from regarding ethnic minority pupils' language needs as their concern and are indeed encouraged to regard E2L work as of low status.

(DES 1985c pp. 391–2)

The report's recommendations were firmly in favour of a move away from provision through withdrawal towards more integrated forms of provision *within* the mainstream schools, and 'as part of a comprehensive programme of language education for all children' (p. 426). In line with this recommendation, the 1990s have certainly seen some exciting and innovative work in mainstream classrooms, much of it through Section 11 funded projects, where language support teachers and classroom teachers have been working together to develop the kind of multilingual classroom environment in which all pupils' language and learning can flourish (Bourne and McPake 1991; Enfield Language and Curriculum Access Service 1995).

However, the Committee also qualified this general principle with respect to older pupils, acknowledging that 'in the case of pupils of secondary school age arriving in this country with no English some form of withdrawal may at first be necessary' (DES 1985c p. 392). The report recognises that the long-term vision of providing language support in a wholly integrated way has to be set against the urgent, immediate needs of pupils entering the system now whose educational opportunities are determined by what is available *now* rather than how things *might be* in the future. The situation is particularly acute for young people of GCSE age arriving in the UK with very little knowledge of English. The pressures upon teachers of this age group, the linguistic demands of subject teaching and current levels of support make it very difficult, for the time being, to cater effectively for the needs of such pupils initially except through the provision of at least part-time specialist, separate support. The authors of Chapters 10 and 11 offer different perspectives to help explore the question of how the needs of bilingual learners, and indeed all who live in more than one language (Hall 1995) can be most equitably and fully met within the education service.

Jean Mayala works in an LEA where part-time provision in an 'induction class' is made for all young people newly arrived in the UK who are in the early stages of learning English. The class is based at a secondary school, and provides language tuition for all beginners, concentrating on English, including literacy skills, maths and science. Pupils attend every day, for half a day, for a period of up to six months. They attend their own school when not at the induction class, where support is provided either through collaborative work with subject teachers (drawing up a programme of work together) or through advice and provision of resources to subject teachers on a weekly basis. In this chapter, Jean Mayala draws on his own experience, that of colleagues and conversations with the young people themselves to explore the contribution that an induction class can make, as part of a wider structure of support, in facilitating access to learning in the mainstream.

❖ ❖ ❖

Children with no or minimal knowledge of English who newly arrive in the United Kingdom are likely to face many types of difficulties in settling into schools. In this study, I examine what kind of learning environment is needed to support the learning of these young people in these initial stages, and the part that an induction class can play in facilitating the settling-in process.

I draw on an example of my own practice to explore how time in the induction class can be used to help develop the confidence and learning skills that will support pupils' learning in the mainstream. I then go on to describe briefly the other part of my work supporting pupils and colleagues in mainstream contexts, and consider what might be done to enhance and develop the collaborative dimension of our work with mainstream colleagues.

THE CONTRIBUTION OF THE INDUCTION CLASS

An induction class constitutes a response to the needs of bilingual pupils with no or little experience in English. The borough policy makes it clear that the ESL (English as a second language) class has to be understood as the newly arrived children's stepping stone into the education system of the UK. In the induction class, the needs of the individual bilingual learner are always central to the concerns of the curriculum and of the teachers who provide the language support. This is one setting where the students' bilingual or multilingual resources are always recognised and appreciated, and given status as part of each individual's identity. The teacher–pupil ratio makes it possible for each student to feel known and valued individually, which may be vitally necessary to psychological security in the early days of coping with life in a large secondary school, where pupils cannot yet express their identity or communicate their needs through language. The induction class is one place where no one feels marginal, where there is common experience to unite all participants as members of one group. The class provides a ready-made reference group which offers support and acceptance to all, irrespective of what other relationships they may be able to form with their wider peer group in the mainstream.

It is possible to envisage that secondary schools of the future might be able to offer such a secure and immediately affirming environment for bilingual pupils with little or no English, some of whom may recently have undergone quite traumatic and disorienting experiences in their personal lives. For the time being, however, there are limits to the support that mainstream teachers and schools are able to provide, within existing resources and at the present stage of development of more integrated forms of provision. Fending for oneself, for much of the time, in the unfamiliar situation of a large secondary school may be overwhelming, particularly if there is no one on hand who speaks the same first language to offer help and reassurance.

This is why I believe that the opportunity to attend an induction class has an important part to play in the social and psychological well-being of newly arrived bilingual pupils. It offers young people with little or no English the opportunity to build up confidence in themselves as learners and as people in a new situation, while helping to reduce the impact of culture shock. The fact that the class is composed exclusively of bilingual learners reminds any newcomer that she or he is not alone in the struggle to achieve success. Individualised help is necessary, and the induction class is staffed in such a way as to make this possible.

How, then, can time spent in an induction class be used to best effect if it is to maximise the potential of the withdrawal situation?

FOSTERING ACHIEVEMENT IN THE INDUCTION CLASS

One way in which the induction class can help to prepare students to be successful in the mainstream is to help them to realise that they can work independently through the medium of English, even though they have only a very limited command of English as yet. In this section, I describe an activity used in the induction class that was developed with a specific view to giving pupils the experience of working independently, and exercising control and choice in their own learning when working through the medium of English. I hoped that giving them a successful experience of this independence and control would help them to develop the confidence to transfer these abilities to the mainstream classroom. My aim was to try to raise students' expectations of what they could achieve, already, with the English they had so far acquired, while at the same time creating a corporate activity in which pupils' prior experience could be acknowledged and, where appropriate, shared within the whole group.

The activity described was thus developed with this general aim, and the following questions in mind:

1 What types of learning activities will best help the students improve their English while giving them the opportunity to be in control of their own learning?
2 How does one succeed in developing learning activities for pupils from different linguistic and cultural backgrounds? How can bilingual pupils' previous experiences and interest be explored to help improve learning opportunities?
3 What activities could offer pupils an opportunity to work in a group while allowing them to be in control of their own learning? And what

Table 10.1 Pupils in the induction class

Name	Age	Sex	Country
A. R.	16	M	Somali
F. K.	14	F	Cyprus
H. R.	15	F	Sierra Leone
J. M.	11	M	Bangladesh
K. A.	16	M	Somali
K. V.	16	F	Georgia
N. M.	14	F	Zaire
N. P.	15	M	Thailand
R. B.	15	F	Bangladesh
T. V.	13	M	Georgia

skills may be learned from such activities and how will they prove useful in the mainstream classroom?

4   What kind of activity will be appropriate to the age and maturity of the pupils, yet capable of being carried out by them independently within the limits of their available language?

The pupils involved in this study were all secondary school children (see Table 10.1). They attended the induction class each morning and the mainstream in the afternoons.

In the next section I give an outline of the activity that pupils were asked to carry out. I first describe the activity itself and its outcomes, and then examine the various responses to these questions which it incorporated.

Making a class magazine

Dealing with pupils of different abilities and from different cultural backgrounds, one has to find ways of making pupils display their potentials, and maybe reveal what they can achieve. Pupils were asked to write short stories based on their own experiences which could be included in a class magazine intended to introduce the induction class to newcomers. Pupils were told that they were free to draw, use colour or stick pictures where they felt appropriate. Detailed instructions were provided (see appendix to this chapter), so that pupils could organise the pacing of their own work, while having a sense of how they would progress through to achieving a completed piece of work.

Objectives

The activity had three main objectives: first, to allow pupils to work according to their levels or abilities. The activity was open-ended, so that it could be equally well suited both to complete beginners and to those who were already gaining confidence and competence in using English. The activity would be appropriate in its maturity level, whatever learners' level of competence, because it drew on real-life experience. The second objective was to encourage pupils to take responsibility for what they do and therefore be in control of their own learning; to give each learner the opportunity to make a personal contribution to group work. The third objective was to give students an opportunity to make full use of their capabilities, by drawing as much as possible on previous learning. In particular, the activity aimed to promote accurate spelling, reinforce the use of known lexical items while creating a purposeful context for learning new items, and to stimulate the use of complete and meaningful sentences. The task was thus intended to offer to all pupils an opportunity to work in an interesting, challenging and a motivating way.

Organisation

The classroom had to be set in a way that would create an appropriate atmosphere for work. In view of the fact that pupils have no or limited English, my prime concern was to present the task in a way that would be understood by all. It was important, as De Vesey (1990 p. 16) points out, that pupils 'understood exactly what was involved in doing the task and they were able to explain this back to us'. Such an overall understanding was vital although every group was expected to produce something slightly different: suggesting different titles and drawing material for their writing from personal experiences and perspectives.

Breaking with the habit of keeping the desks in rows, my class was organised in a workstation layout with sufficient space to move around, an easy access to resources and freedom to use the equipment available. In many ways the classroom was set to offer flexibility of movement and free access to resources. In order to stimulate discussion among pupils more fluent pupils were mixed with less fluent ones. The aim was to ensure that every pupil was given the opportunity to contribute to the decision making in the production of the magazine.

To help the pupils keep up interest in the task, they were encouraged to write about their own experiences: about friends, family members, the schools they first went to, etc. They were also encouraged to use a language style they themselves could write as well as read. To make sure the pupils worked according to the instructions, I took every opportunity to check, question or get them explain to me what they were doing.

For the purpose of this task I brought to the classroom twenty-five different magazines. Pupils were requested to look at and pass them round so that everybody was given the opportunity to see as many different magazines as possible. Writing about their own experiences appeared an enjoyable activity for the pupils.

In short, the classroom was organised in a way that enabled pupils not only to work in a more relaxed atmosphere but also to make a better use of the materials provided. Furthermore, the activity offered to pupils an opportunity to decide for themselves what to write about, how and where to put it in the magazine, whether the text should be typed or handwritten, whether to use pictures with the text, and more important what language structures were appropriate for their stories.

What happened

I have focused on three areas: ability to work collaboratively, making reference to personal experience and ability to work independently.

Ability to work collaboratively

This aspect of learning requires a lot of negotiation when introduced for the first time. For various reasons, some pupils did not want to work in the same group with some other pupils from other parts of the world. Some refusals seemed to be based on colour alone. Such prejudices are not easily dealt with. They need to be seriously addressed by schools. In the context of this lesson, however, it seemed to have an effect when I responded that 'we form a big family, and as in any family, we may be different in attitude, size, etc. Colour should not divide us. We are all human beings'. Although working together proved difficult at the beginning of the activity, the need to come out with a title of their magazine put the pupils in a situation where talk was vital.

I moved from one group to another encouraging them to talk. The class took more than half an hour before the first group came out with some sort of title despite the suggestions made in the instruction sheet. The pupils' tendency was to talk to me rather than to their classmates. It was observed that after a title had been found for the group, more and more interactions between members of the same group started to take place. One may argue that the process of sorting out ideas, that is agreeing and disagreeing, questions and answers and cross-fertilisation of ideas, is inevitably a slow one, particularly for those struggling to express meanings in English.

Making reference to personal experience

Reference to pupils' lives and personal experiences seems to be an exceptionally powerful way of getting children to learn. All my pupils, without exception, found it easier to write stories on their own experiences. Those who wrote about their families or friends produced particularly interesting pieces of writing. This is one example:

> My name is ... I am 16 years old. I come from Georgia. When I came here, I had nobody except my family. I never forget my Georgia friends. My friends always stay in my heart. I will never forget these good times.
>
> When I came here I went to school. At this school I did not have friends. This time I was not speaking English very well and now I have friends. I've lost my friends in my country. I don't know if I will see my friends again or not.

This text was contributed by a girl who had been at the induction class for five months. In a few brief sentences, the pupil manages to convey her feelings of loss, regret and disorientation with considerable power.

Ability to work independently

There is evidence in this study that pupils were not only actively involved in the task, but also working independently. This is reflected in various ways:

1 In the outcome product: pupils' compositions clearly show writing in which pupils refer either to their personal friends or to members of their families.
2 In the choice of content/ideas: there are individual differences in the way they describe events they experienced and the way personal feelings are expressed.
3 In the use of personal pronouns 'I' and 'we': the use of these pronouns suggests pupils' own involvement in the stories.
4 In the presentation of work: the way the different texts were presented, their choice of stickers or pictures to go with the texts, or even the choice of colours in writing up the texts illustrate the exercise of independent judgement in the pupils' approach to learning.

When pupils can take responsibility for what they are doing, this for me is evidence that they are becoming independent learners. The activity selected was meant to offer an opportunity to pupils to make a personal contribution to a group task. The outcomes of pupils' texts show that almost every pupil worked from their own perspective and thus produced differentiated writing levels (as evidenced in the range of vocabulary and structures employed).

Summary of the activity

The activity used in this study was set up to encourage interaction between pupils in accordance with the principle that:

writing with other children on paper or on word processor enables them [pupils] to pool their knowledge of the writing system and produce more ambitious texts than they might undertake alone. This will be a good context for young bilingual children with little experience of English, who can be supported by teachers or peers. The collaborative activities, and their parallel experiences of readings, are the foundation of their writing development.

(Barrs *et al*. 1990 p. 24)

The choice of the activity was based on the view that open-ended activities may be designed to take account of differences in pupils' abilities and personal experiences. Such activities can provide a great deal of insight into pupils' ways of learning. In fact, it was observed that:

1 Pupils were improving their confidence and started to ask more questions on what they were doing. For instance, I received an impressive number of requests on 'How do you spell . . .?' and 'What does . . . mean?'
2 Pupils' references to personal linguistic and cultural experiences in their writing were spontaneous, as may be seen through the use of names of people and places and that of 'I' and 'we'.
3 A 'growing pleasure and involvement in writing leads to growing confidence in writing, so that they can begin to operate more independently' (Barrs *et al*. 1990 p. 26). Such an active involvement gave the pupils a greater freedom in the choice of lexical items, context and presentation of texts.

It follows from these learning behaviours that pupils' performance (discussing, writing, sticking, etc.) and the appropriateness of the task demands offered them an opportunity to master skills which are vital for learning in the mainstream classroom. Three of those skills may be summed up as follows:

1 Working collaboratively: by agreeing to work in a group, each pupil was mentally prepared to learn from others' experience through comparing, revising, asking and responding, explaining, checking maps, etc. Such skills help develop oral language.
2 Decision making: every pupil became aware of the fact that they had to write stories of their own making, not what a friend or a classmate was doing. For instance, the decision to use the computer to type rather than handwrite the text was a personal decision.
3 Ability to organise work: how the writing had to be presented or whether such a picture would be suitable for the magazine depended on individual sense of organisation.

These skills and many others help to demonstrate and reinforce pupils' belief that they can take responsibility for their own learning when working through the medium of English.

SUPPORTING LEARNING IN THE MAINSTREAM

I have explored what I feel an induction class has to offer in principle and described an activity developed to explore ways of exploiting its potential further. However, pupils' experience in the induction class is obviously only one part of their total educational experience. What happens the rest of the time is equally vital. I shall now explain the other part of my work, which involves working with colleagues to support the learning of bilingual students in mainstream schools. I draw upon conversations with individual pupils to help highlight areas for further development of this collaborative dimension of our work.

I work in two schools for six hours per week. During this time, I support three bilingual pupils. Each pupil is seen twice a week for English and maths. While two pupils are supported within the mainstream classroom, one pupil is supported outside the mainstream classroom in order to offer specific help with literacy difficulties.

At the beginning of every term the subject teachers and I plan the work with regard to every pupil concerned. The planning agreements need to specify the number of pupils to be supported in a given classroom, the area(s) of difficulties, the general needs of the pupils, the specific targets to be achieved, the resources to be used and the discussion time.

During lessons, depending on the activity, my role is basically to ensure that:

- the pupil understands what is going on in the classroom
- the instructions are clear enough to allow pupils to work on their own
- appropriate exemplification is given to illustrate what is to be done
- a complex text is simplified for better understanding
- key concepts are explained and, where necessary, translated into mother tongue.

The aim of this work is to help ensure that bilingual learners are able to participate fully in lessons, and that as far as possible the curriculum acknowledges and builds on the diverse academic and socio-cultural experiences that are reflected in the pupil population generally. In building a supportive learning environment, we are trying to encourage the development of approaches which are sensitive to a variety of prior experiences. These may include:

- differences in the nature of previous education

- limited experience of using English for academic/social purposes
- varied cultural and linguistic background
- diverse personal and social experiences.

The time I spend supporting pupils in the mainstream allows me to discuss pupils' needs both with teachers and pupils themselves. Pupils' comments on their experiences in the mainstream can be quite revealing. Aweis, a Year 9 pupil who was recently transferred to the mainstream summarises his feelings: 'I enjoy Science and English because I can understand what's happening. I like my English teacher, and I like to play football. I don't enjoy PSE [personal and social education] because I don't know what's happening and all the other students understand the work except me. Sometimes the students treat me like I am not there.'

From his comments, it seems that Aweis is well catered for in some subjects and is able not only to participate but also actively to enjoy lessons. Nevertheless, he is clearly still facing some significant problems. He manages to find words which convey with considerable poignancy his experience of marginalisation in the PSE lesson. This seems to be a particularly unfortunate missed opportunity, since PSE is one area where pupils' own personal experiences, needs and relationships can and should be the central concern of the curriculum.

Aweis's experience is by no means unique. Other pupils also express concern on how they cope with lessons in the mainstream. Patrick's experience in the mainstream gives us a different insight into school life. As he puts it:

> I like my friends because they sometimes help me in English. They explain to me how to say things. I also like some teachers who help me [about] with my lessons. I don't like some teachers because they are bad to me if I don't understand some work. If he gives you a text and you can't do because you don't understand he does not believe you. He will say you must do your work. Yes, but if I don't understand what can I do?

Patrick feels that not all the teachers are willing to help when he has problems. His peers seem to play an important role in his education, probably because his peers try to sympathise with his situation. I worked with Patrick once a week. He told me that he felt very secure every time I was in his classroom. But one visit a week was not enough to give him the hope and confidence that he needed. Patrick had spent six months before joining the mainstream education full time. The challenge for all teachers of recently arrived older bilingual learners is how to make the content and language demands of Key Stage 4 of the National Curriculum accessible to young people who still are still in the early stages of learning English.

CONCLUSION

My experience of working with bilingual pupils both in a withdrawal context and in the mainstream system shows that many schools still consider provision for bilingual pupils as the responsibility of some other external or specialised body, not theirs. This attitude has no doubt been reinforced by the new demands and pressures on schools in recent years. I believe that it is a recipe for marginalisation rather than the full integration which should be every school's objective *vis-à-vis* bilingual pupils.

The early learning environment which newly arrived children come into contact with is vital to their psychological well-being and future development. For the time being, the induction class has an important role to play in minimising frustration and ensuring that each child feels known and recognised as an individual with a unique personality and prior experience. It should be emphasised that pupils are only partially withdrawn as they attend the mainstream classroom in the afternoons.

At the same time, schools should be aiming at providing a learning environment that is appropriate for both monolingual and bilingual pupils where multilingual and multicultural resources are made readily available. It is only under these conditions that withdrawal of newly arrived pupils – even a partial one – will become redundant.

APPENDIX: THE INDUCTION CLASS MAGAZINE

Instructions

PLEASE READ THESE INSTRUCTIONS CAREFULLY.

1 Today we are going to make a magazine on our classroom, the Induction Class. We will work in groups. Every group is going to produce a six-page document with interesting short stories of your choice.
2 To help you understand what a magazine looks like, the teacher has brought 25 copies of different types of magazine for you to see and refer to as models. Most of those magazines are on *education, schools, languages, science, holiday resorts, public services, etc.*
3 You may need some of these words and phrases for your magazine: OUR LANGUAGE CLASS, LEARN ENGLISH WITH US!, INDUCTION CLASS, EASTBURY UPPER, BARKING, . . .
4. You are expected to make your magazine look *colourful, interesting, important and useful.* Remember, you want people with little or no English to come to your class.

TIMING

Thursday	9.15–9.20	Teacher explains instructions
	9.20–9.35	Students go through magazines
	9.35–10.05	Students plan what to do
	10.05–10.35	Students work on magazine cover
Friday	9.15–10.15	Students work on stories
	10.15–10.35	Students work on layout
	10.50–11.30	Students write down stories
	11.30–11.50	Final checks

Please use the time effectively and productively.
Whenever you need help, don't hesitate to ask the teacher.

Chapter 11

'I belong here . . . they speak my kind of language'

Neil Parr

EDITOR'S INTRODUCTION

This chapter takes up some of the issues raised in the conclusion to the case study in Chapter 10. It looks at developments already being undertaken in mainstream schools to create for bilingual learners, as for all learners, a supportive and stimulating learning environment. Neil Parr is Head of the Language and Curriculum Access Service in another London borough. Neil was not a participant on the course, but was invited to make a contribution to this section of the book in order to expand on the potential for development to meet the needs of bilingual learners within mainstream education. He explains what, in his view, helps to make a school a genuinely multilingual establishment, and describes some innovative work currently being undertaken by schools to take account of the cultural and linguistic diversity of their pupils.

Yasmin sat wearily gazing through the window. Last period before lunch. Geography. Before her lay the textbook, open at page 28, 'Erosion'. Around her, the other pupils were in various states of activity. Most were writing, some talking to each other, some were working with the teacher who was talking them through the task. Others were anticipating lunch and the weekend having completed their task. Yasmin had assumed the task was to produce a written text, and had spent some time making a reasonable copy of a few paragraphs from the book. Her teacher had given the instructions and she had attempted to perform what she understood by them.

Her teacher approached her, 'Let's see what you've been doing, Yasmin . . . yes . . . well done. You must try to find the main factors affecting the erosion of sedimentary rocks in the region described in the passage. Try to find them from the writing. Do you see what is needed? . . . Hasan, can you help Yasmin with what she is supposed to do?'

This was to be Yasmin's first and only direct contact with her teacher this lesson. He thought she did not know much English. He thought often about why she seemed so unwilling to speak to him in any of the lessons, and could not answer his questions however simple. He thought that she might have some learning difficulties. He thought about how he lacked the skills to enable her to complete his lessons, and that she would benefit from work in a withdrawal group where she would learn English and then be able to get on with work like the rest of the class.

Yasmin sat back. She thought her teacher would probably not approach her again. She thought he was unwilling to communicate with her and did not want her to communicate with him as he rarely asked her opinion even when she had her hand up to give an answer. She thought he was not really interested in her, as the other pupils seemed to have more of his attention than she did.

After lunch, Yasmin sat watching her teacher. Science. Her teacher caught her eye frequently. Her teacher demonstrated what was going on. Her teacher encouraged the pupils to give their views and share their involvement. Her teacher gave short tasks for a few pupils to do together, which led to further tasks which eventually 'told the story' of the lesson.

Yasmin was writing, talking with other pupils near her, working with the teacher as she talked her through the tasks. Yasmin anticipated the end of the day with the pupils next to her and discussed the weekend when her task was completed.

Yasmin's geography teacher says Yasmin does not speak much English. Yasmin's science teacher says Yasmin is a keen and alert student willing to participate in the lesson and making good progress with her science.

Naturally, this 'case study' is fictitious, as are the teachers and the pupil. This situation for bilingual pupils is familiar enough. Why is it that the same student can appear to perform so differently in these different situations? How does the learning environment affect, facilitate, or hinder their performance as learners in the classroom?

Work with bilingual pupils throughout Britain finds itself, in general, placed on a continuum within two extremes. At one end there is a focus on individuals and the need for bilingual pupils to acquire English, assuming that a structured English course will provide what is necessary for bilingual pupils to integrate with the English-speaking peer group. There is a genuinely held view that curriculum presentation is most effective when delivered as discrete simplified tasks where the English language demands are reduced. 'Problems' of communication are viewed only from the perspective of the teacher: pupils need to learn how to understand the language of the classroom. A great deal of work is put in to develop additional teaching programmes, work packs and extra support classes to include bilingual pupils. The school itself, though, is unaffected. It remains a monolingual establishment.

At the other end of this spectrum, pupils are seen within a wider institutional and social context. The issue of access is addressed and communication within the classroom is viewed as a two-way process: the pupils and teachers learn how to understand each other. The school recognises that it is a multilingual establishment and adapts its procedures and approaches to take account of the nature of its population, and becomes fundamentally affected by it. It is this dynamic view which is explored here.

THE MULTILINGUAL SCHOOL

Responding positively to the diversity of a multilingual school requires that staff work to develop a full awareness of the linguistic, cultural and experiential differences between pupils. Bilingual pupils are not a homogeneous group. They have background experience of different languages which they may speak to varying degrees of proficiency and in differently focused situations. They may have a widely different experience of using English. Many of the bilingual pupils in a class will speak very fluent English in all situations and attend community schools to bring their own community language to the same standard. Many bilingual pupils in a class will be members of different religious communities, and where their religions are similar, their local mosque, temple or church may interpret its teachings in different ways. They will have different experiences of what tradition means, and interpret the world from different perspectives and standpoints.

Knowing the pupils

The best way of gaining an awareness of diversity is if, as teachers, we have the means of knowing our pupils well. Without this positive approach, it is all too easy to make assumptions about pupils that may be false and lead us to treat pupils in an inappropriate way. For instance, simply knowing that a pupil is bilingual gives only a partial picture. We need to be aware that often pupils have a knowledge and experience of several languages which they use or hear in different situations. Knowing what languages they speak to whom and when becomes as important as knowing the educational background of pupils. Here it is equally important to remember that education is world-wide and broader than simply formal schooling in the UK. Information about culture and religious belief needs to be known and, most importantly of all, information from parents and carers should be sought, as they know their children best and care most about them.

Regular conferencing with parents is increasingly the norm in schools. If the teaching process is seen as a partnership between parents/carers, teachers and pupils, then a shared understanding between the school and home is vital. This understanding can be achieved only through a genuine two-way communication, when members of the school listen to carers as well as giving information.

Knowing the pupils to this extent provides a vital background to decisions about how we organise a class to enable all pupils to feel it is theirs. Teaching within such a class will automatically be inclusive.

WHOLE-SCHOOL RESPONSES

Clearly, inclusive classes cannot operate effectively in isolation in an institution. The whole school needs to be organised and managed to this end. A multilingual school recognises and records the range of languages known to its pupils, and tries to be actively involved in making this apparent through its resourcing policies. Books and other teaching material may appear in a dual language format. Resources, signs and other information will appear in the different languages of the school. Pupils will be encouraged to use their own first language, when appropriate, not only in the playground but also in group work in the classroom when discussing curriculum content and learning tasks. This not only affirms the recognition of pupils' identities but also ensures that they have additional opportunities to gain a clearer understanding of lesson content.

A multilingual school will not only reflect language recognition at the superficial level of display or resources, but also actively support its diversity through overt policy statements which are implemented in practice. There would be a clearly understood and specific approach to curriculum delivery which will ensure a learning environment that supports the confident learning of all pupils and bilingual pupils in particular. Children learn a great deal from one another. Thus policies that withdraw bilingual pupils from the peer group in order to learn English and that remove bilingual children from their own classroom are disadvantaging those pupils. Where a student's classroom is supportive, then a withdrawal room is second-rate.

AN ASSESSABLE, ACCESSIBLE CURRICULUM

There is a common misconception that students need to have learned English before they are able to engage with the curriculum content, and that the two are in some way separate. This could not be further from the truth:

1 To learn a language pupils need to use it to communicate (talk and write about something).
2 To learn about the curriculum content, pupils need to discuss and communicate about it to each other and the teacher (something needs to be talked and written about).
3 Therefore the curriculum content is the subject matter of language learning, and the language acquired is the medium for curriculum communication.

Accepting that curriculum learning and language learning can proceed together puts the teacher in the multilingual classroom in a very powerful position to ensure success and progress for bilingual pupils.

Planning can ensure that the curriculum is accessible by the careful staging of presentation, by building in a range of group support (pupils learn and gain a lot of confidence from peer group support), by making available a range of resources – visual, taped, video and translated. Careful planning and presentation through progressive steps can also ensure that no false assumptions are made about the range of knowledge and experience that all pupils bring to the class.

All pupils, whatever their age or experience, are involved in learning the language of the curriculum, so a dynamic, structured learning environment in the classroom which exhibits at least the following items, creates the right conditions for successful learning, including language learning:

1 Identity:	does the pupil feel valued as an individual with a home language, culture, life experience and intellect?
2 Classroom management:	does the classroom ensure the confident involvement of bilingual pupils? Can pupils work in different groupings to ensure social cohesion?
3 Curriculum planning:	is planning geared to clearly defined and staged tasks that are purposeful, practical and related to the pupil's experience? Is collaborative work with visual and contextual support included? Are there opportunities for talk, and time for listening?
4 Resourcing:	are pupils' languages, cultures and experiences reflected in the resources?
5 Teacher–pupil interactions:	are interactions effective in promoting learning, and is there a process for monitoring this?

This challenging approach, which experienced teachers strive to establish, provides the necessary context for bilingual pupils to make progress and will benefit all pupils in the multilingual classroom – bilingual and monolingual alike.

SCAFFOLDED LEARNING

Within such a context – a well-recognised and explicit support for diversity – do we really need more differentiation? Or should we now be looking for the means of building a common route to learning, within the National Curriculum framework, that all pupils, with their different linguistic, cultural and educational experiences can travel together?

A developmental project coordinated by our Language and Curriculum Access Service has been exploring the second of these two options. The Service, in conjunction with eight teachers, and supported by the Exeter University EXEL (extending literacy) project, has been investigating the many different ways that teachers can *scaffold* the learning of their subject content, and curriculum outcomes.[1] The main focus for this work has been within the humanities (history and geography) curriculum, where the most effective and inclusive means of enabling pupils to research history or geography topics through factual texts has been explored. The principles underlying work already undertaken will be used to develop strategies across Key Stages 3 and 4 over the coming year.

A humanities development project

There is little room here for a detailed description of the work (which will be the subject of a forthcoming publication). An outline of the process adopted to support pupils in researching a particular topic can, however, serve to illustrate the points being made here.

The guiding principle is that task structuring is targeted on the learning process and the strategies for achieving outcomes, and not on the content alone. The focus is one of facilitating participation and involvement, based on the assumption that learning is a process of linking new knowledge to what is already known. In this example, the research task was supported – or 'scaffolded' – in the five following ways.

Modelling

First, this is a way of ensuring that all learners know what they are required to do. A traditional approach often relies on an initial explanation of a task requirement and the task implementation itself then becomes a testing activity whereby those who are familiar with the task design can do it and those who are less familiar may struggle. A modelling approach – where the class or group undertake a task with the teacher as participant who models with the pupils an example of the task – ensures that all have been 'apprenticed' and therefore have experience of what is required. This process defines a common approach for all, and makes no assumptions about pupils' prior experience.

Put directly, this approach simply shows the pupils what needs to be done and how to do it.

Activating prior knowledge

Secondly, strategies were used to encourage pupils to recognise, use and build on their existing knowledge. A class with a very diverse background has members who are able to bring knowledge from a wide range of standpoints. In this research task, focused on Victorian Britain, 'expert' groups of pupils were engaged in researching aspects of life: education, homes, health, work, crime and punishment. Some members of the class had very specific knowledge to contribute, whereas others who brought detailed knowledge of other cultures, histories, traditions and opinions found themselves in new territory. Despite this lack of specific knowledge, it was recognised that all pupils had generic knowledge and opinions about all these aspects of life through their own experience, either in Britain or in other countries of the world, which could be tapped as a route to understanding and exploring further the particular topics identified for research in Victorian times. It was important to capture this as a foundation for the work.

In this case, the strategy of concept mapping was employed to help pupils make an effective representation of their existing knowledge. Through the teacher modelling the organisation of information from a 'brainstorm' into a concept map for the whole class, the 'expert' groups were enabled to repeat this process, and build a common picture of what was already known by the members.

The concept map shown in Figure 11.1 was produced with one class. At the beginning of the project, the whole class declared that they knew nothing about Victorian Britain. The brainstorming activity and the resultant organisation of the information served to demonstrate to the class the extent of the information they already possessed. Through making their existing knowledge explicit in this way, the pupils were able to define not only gaps in their knowledge, but also the information and ideas that class members felt they would like to verify or research further. All pupils (and their teacher as well) were surprised at just how much of their own experience they were able to bring to bear on the task. The display also served to alert the teacher to those areas where pupils had misconceptions and were making false assumptions.

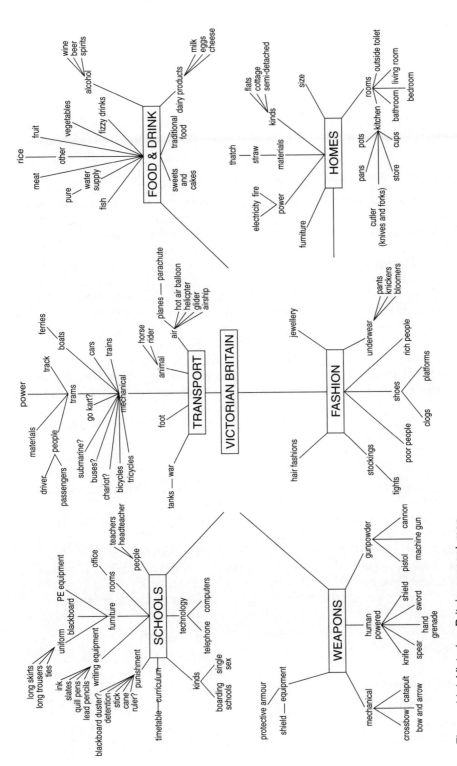

Figure 11.1 Victorian Britain concept map

This concept map was produced as a large wall poster which remained on display throughout the topic. Pupils were able to track how information, acquired by different groups during the research, built a larger picture, and contributed to their collective knowledge. Foregrounding the pupils' prior knowledge in this way helped to enhance self-esteem, generated interest and encouraged a sense of ownership.

What do I want to know?

Thirdly, strategies were used to help pupils take control of, and manage successfully, the search for information, including the use of printed material. Pupils were given responsibility for generating their own questions, and so were able to set their own goals in information gathering. This process is one which intimately links what they already know to what they want to know. The process of building on current understanding also involved the use of visual texts – media, photographs, engravings – as a means of augmenting existing knowledge. In this way, past and present learning provided a means of building up pupil prediction prior to using written texts. This we know to be a vital element in the ability to extract meaning from information texts.

Different strategies for supporting pupils in being able to pose appropriate questions and record them have been developed through this and other work, and it is this central role that the teacher undertakes in guiding and structuring the pupils' passage through their learning.

How do I find the information?

Fourthly, strategies were devised, to support the search for and selection of information, and to aid pupils in recording relevant material without verbatim copying. Equipped with an understanding of what they want to know, and with a high level of prediction, the pupils were better able to engage with a range of sources, including original texts. These were scanned for key words, phrases or blocks of information relating to their research, before they undertook a more detailed exploration.

Different recording sheets and grids were devised to help pupils set out and evaluate the information they found, and the process of using them 'modelled', so that all pupils were able to gain a sense of how the outcome would 'look'.

Working together

Throughout, the emphasis was on pupils working together, sharing their knowledge and supporting the research for their group, based on modelled processes that the teacher as acknowledged 'expert' also shares.

The challenge for the teacher was in devising appropriate support or scaffolds to give effective and successful routes through the process, rather than the provision of individualised and simplified content.

CONCLUSION

Much of the current work on scaffolding learning for the multilingual classroom is still in development (although most experienced teachers will recognise strategies that they already use in what has been said above). It is therefore difficult to know how to end this chapter. Perhaps, by revisiting Yasmin, we may find it possible to select an ending.

What of Yasmin?

Either

Yasmin's geography teacher became so concerned at her lack of progress in geography, and so frustrated with his own sense of failure in teaching her that he registered his concern. Yasmin reached Stage 2 in the assessment of her special needs as she was increasingly unable to read her geography texts. Her own frustration affected her behaviour in the classroom.

The special needs department was able to arrange a reading skills programme (set against science) which she followed for most of the year. She is now more comfortable with some of the reading demands of geography, and is provided with an alternative but complementary set of worksheets in her class.

Or

Yasmin's geography teacher contacted his head of department who arranged, with the INSET coordinator, for departmental training on bilingualism, and curriculum responses to ensure access for all pupils. After implementing the three session course, Yasmin's geography teacher wrote: 'Yasmin is a keen and alert student willing to participate in the lesson and making good progress with her geography.'

Or

Perhaps you may be able to supply an ending from your own experience.

NOTE

1 The work of the EXEL project led by David Wray and Maureen Lewis is to be published in 1996. Similarly a detailed evaluation of strategies for the multilingual classroom is in preparation by Kathy Coulthard, the Enfield project coordinator, and is to be published by London Borough of Enfield.

Part V

Differentiation at a whole-school level

Chapter 12

Developing school policy

Susanna Pickstock

EDITOR'S INTRODUCTION

In this final part of the book we move to a consideration of whole-school policy and management issues relating to the development of differentiation. Since 1975, when the Bullock Report (DES 1975) proposed that all schools should have a policy on 'language across the curriculum', we have been acutely aware that there is a great deal more to developing a 'whole-school' policy on any aspect of practice than writing a policy document. If documents have not been produced as part of a process involving all colleagues at some level, and reflecting their values, understandings and practices, then they are unlikely to make a significant difference to children's experience in the classroom. How, then, might schools best proceed?

Experience has demonstrated that, when schools are embarking on policy development, it is as important to think about the processes to be undergone as it is to think about the content to be included. In a large secondary school, it is not possible to involve all staff actively in every stage of development of each policy needed. Nevertheless, there must be consultation and discussion with the whole staff, and eventual agreement about common aims and principles that are to inform future practice. All schools are different, and therefore processes that are appropriate in one context may not be helpful in another. Each school has to establish its own processes, in the knowledge of the needs, interests and other urgent priorities on its current agenda.

In this chapter, Susanna Pickstock describes the way in which her school set about developing a whole-school policy on 'differentiation'. This is not presented as a blueprint for other schools, but as an example of the kinds of decisions that were made and what the process entailed in one particular school setting. Her account includes a breakdown of the different sections of the policy document itself, explaining how each was intended to contribute to the whole, and how the policy itself was intended to support and promote the development of practice in her school.

♦ ♦ ♦

In November 1993, Suffolk County Council produced a leaflet 'The Suffolk Education Promise'. In this, they stated 'our aim, first and foremost, is to provide people in Suffolk with educational services which match their needs, entitlements and interests.' As a school in Suffolk and with our own motto 'a community committed to success', the staff at our school are committed to ensuring that each pupil has equal access to, and opportunity to benefit from, the National Curriculum as a basic entitlement. Previous to this statement and concerned to fulfil such aims, the staff became involved in September 1992 in a collaborative research enquiry aiming to determine what counts as quality of learning. One of the outcomes of our research was the decision to establish a differentiation working group in September 1993.

The task group was charged with the writing of a paper (eventually to become the whole-school policy document) which would articulate the entitlement of all pupils to learning experiences clearly differentiated to enable each pupil to fulfil his or her potential. To achieve this, several targets were set out for the group to address:

1 The process of differentiation should be fully researched and a paper written which could be used as a tool by departments to begin to plan lesson activities which are differentiated in a number of ways.
2 The team should identify the professional development needs of the staff, in relation to differentiation, and make recommendations to the professional development officer.
3 The team should identify library resources which should be purchased to develop staff understanding of the process of differentiation.
4 The team should identify physical and human resources which will be required to ensure quality implementation of the whole-school policy for differentiation.

The group was to set its own programme to accomplish the targets set but the central method of working should be that of action-research enquiry: evidence gathering, consultation and collaboration to ensure whole-staff involvement. The group was also given criteria by which the success of the policy would be measured:

1 Success will be evidenced by the manner in which departments are enabled through the use of the policy document and the paper to translate theory into practice in schemes of work and detailed lesson planning.
2 Success will be evidenced by the manner in which staff need is clearly identified in order for activities to then be designed which will have maximum impact on the quality of learning in the classroom.
3 Success will be evidenced by the production of a recommended reading and video list which is the result of reading and staff evaluation. A brief evaluation of these resources written by the staff should accompany the list.
4 Success will be evidenced by the manner in which the recommendations pre-empt difficulties and potential problems that may be

encountered as the whole staff move towards differentiation on a much larger scale.

WRITING THE DIFFERENTIATION PAPER

A definition is only the start of a policy statement but it is vitally important that the team has a common framework to adhere to. Everybody has their own concept of what differentiation is about and what it really means to put it into practice. A few people may have no real idea at all. It is therefore necessary that a team working on a policy, agrees through collaboration, their own definition that they feel comfortable with, can work to, and covers the needs of the school as stated in the School Development Plan. It is also important that the definition allows staff to have a common understanding in order to set a standard of expectation throughout the whole school when the policy is introduced.

In our own task group, this was achieved in the preliminary meetings by reading and discussing. Several of the articles read were taken from a NASEN (National Association for Special Educational Needs) publication *Differentiation: Ways forward* (Peter 1992). From this we were able to decide:

- our own definition
- a justification for differentiation based on statements in the 1988 Education Act, National Curriculum documents and the Warnock Report (DES 1978b)
- how to relate school aims to our developing aims for differentiation.

The definition of differentiated teaching that we eventually came up with was as follows:

> Meeting every child's learning needs so that each can share access to the same curriculum in the same school at the same time. It should allow all pupils to demonstrate what they know, understand and are able to do. Differentiation should be used to ensure that pupils achieve success and feel that their learning experiences have been worthwhile.

It made sense to place the definition at the start of the policy as this was the basis of the rest. Included in this first section we also expressed our view that differentiation can manifest itself in the form of content, resources, tasks, outcomes and responses and that any policy on differentiation should consider and embrace the following:

1 There will be a wide range of ability within any group of pupils.
2 There will be a wide range of experience within any group of pupils.
3 The pace at which pupils learn varies considerably.

OUR RESEARCH ENQUIRY

In order to make recommendations for a policy on differentiation, we wanted to build on current good practice. Staff responses were elicited to a questionnaire which enabled us to assess our present position and determine progress and change that would need to be made. In each department the head of department and one other member were asked the following questions:

1 What does your department understand by 'differentiation'?
2 How far do you believe that your department delivers effective differentiation?
3 What difficulties are you encountering/will you encounter in trying to deliver differentiation?
4 What do you want to see re. differentiation at this school?

A variety of responses were received from the departments, but once the answers were collated, a number of common factors were identified. The team's survey showed that teachers had a good general understanding of the term 'differentiation':

A range of learning opportunities with each class, so that different abilities are catered for.

Meeting the educational needs of individuals through the use of a variety of materials and strategies.

Differentiation is necessary to identify and meet the needs of every individual pupil.

The majority of staff took differentiation to mean that the 'individual needs of the child are met'. It was accepted, however, that much of the present practice was rooted in differentiation by outcome:

We do the best that can be done in the circumstances – differentiation mainly by outcome.

Pupils achieve to their own ability level.

Further differentiation was achieved by some departments using a flexible approach in teaching, learning styles and resources to allow pupils to negotiate with the teacher the level at which they work. It was also generally accepted, though, that the issue of differentiation was not being satisfactorily addressed and that the key areas of planning, resourcing and teaching styles need to be recognised. Most departments requested that any principles for differentiation should be flexible enough to allow teachers to select and interpret them in line with the demands and nature of their own subject.

PRINCIPLES FOR DIFFERENTIATION

Using this enquiry, and having recognised existing expertise, we were now able to draw up a set of principles upon which to base our school approach to differentiation. These were obviously not all written at once, but modified and expanded during the course of several meetings.

The task group initially came up with a list of thirteen principles. These were re-ordered and modified to form the eight principles which finally became the 'Policy for Differentiation' in the draft policy document:

1 The school is committed to both breadth and significance in its curricular experience and to providing access to the whole curriculum for all pupils, from the less able through to the gifted child. The school seeks to ensure equal opportunity and access to all educational experiences regardless of gender, ethnic origin, physical, mental or social disadvantage.

2 Pupils are entitled to experience a variety of teaching strategies in their learning. Resource-based learning and student focused work in particular are recognised as important in the provision of differentiated learning.

3 There should be the greatest access for teachers and learners to a wide variety of resources, both physical and human that the school can make available to support differentiated learning styles.

4 Where differentiation is successful, it is accepted that different forms of learning outcomes are valued.

5 It is recognised that a key element of effective differentiation is the participation by learners in the selection of effective strategies for achieving agreed targets.

6 All pupils, where possible, should be taught within the mainstream classroom. There should be no regular withdrawal of pupils. Occasional withdrawal should take place where it is recognised as necessary by subject departments and the Learning Development Department. This approach aims to ensure that all pupils have equal access to the same curriculum and a variety of learning experiences, without suffering the low self-esteem which can arise from normal lessons.

7 The school embraces a variety of approaches for the organisation of children into groups, i.e. mixed ability, broad banding and setting. As far as possible, and in order to facilitate differentiation, it is school policy that the timetable is and will be structured to deliver what departments consider to be the most suitable system of grouping for their subject. However, forms of organisation should not unnecessarily separate pupils from the year group appropriate to their age.

8 In addressing the issue of differentiation, the school will give consideration to:

- the ability of its pupils
- the pace at which children learn
- individual children's interests and experience
- the curriculum offered
- teaching strategies followed.

IMPLICATIONS AND CONSTRAINTS

As the principles evolved, their implications were identified and discussed. These became significant both in terms of resources and the organisation of the school. They highlighted departmental concerns and possible constraints likely to influence the process of differentiation. The aim of this section was to use the research data already collected from departments and the points raised by the task group to give an appreciation of possible constraints that could hinder the successful implementation of the differentiation policy.

Points raised included the following:

- requirements of examination syllabi
- the length of lessons in particular subject areas
- transfer of information from middle schools to Year 9 and from Key Stage 3 to GCSE
- size of classes
- classroom support
- timetabling of subjects and flexibility within groupings
- availability of resources for both staff and pupils.

Finally, we stated 'there is a danger that in pursuing differentiated learning, we account for pupils' learning difficulties purely by reference to their individual attributes'. At the heart of the group's proposal was a desire to see a broad definition of differentiation embraced, one alert to the possibility that a child's 'poor concentration' or a 'slow pace of working' might reflect teaching strategies or a curriculum which has so far not tapped the child's curiosity, interest and imagination (Hart 1992a, 1992b).

A PROGRAMME FOR THE DEVELOPMENT

Finally, we come to the section intended for the senior management team and accountability group structure. Having arrived at the eight statements of principle which would form the basis of our policy for differentiation and identified constraints, we now had to visualise how the recommendations could be put into practice. To help us with this process we asked ourselves three questions:

1 What suggestions for action can we make?
2 What time scale do we envisage?
3 Can we prioritise our suggestions into short-term and long-term objectives?

From ten brief initial suggestions, this ultimately became five sides. These covered issues such as the availability of support staff, suites of rooms for each department each with its own resource centre, departmental requirements for the timetable, pupil profiling, pupil study skills, and teacher awareness of how pupils learn. Also, proposals were made for whole-staff INSET on aspects of differentiated learning to underpin the whole-school development that we expect in this next year. Some of these suggestions are naturally easier to achieve than others. The key, however, is that we now have a policy from which development can be planned. INSET for staff is essential to introduce this policy in an acceptable way without it being seen as yet another load to be taken on board. Some of our suggestions will take planning in the budget to accommodate them and others will occur naturally as the policy is put into practice.

Most of the above issues can be applied generally to any school but the details within each one would have to be specific to the needs and requirements of each individual school. This final section brought to an end the two and a half terms of collaborative meetings at fortnightly intervals. The team was then provided with a day's INSET time to write the departmental guidelines. Our aim here was to provide departments with information in the following areas:

- the role of support within curriculum implementation
- resources
- learning styles and teaching methods
- classroom organisation.

Material used included:

- *Differentiating the secondary curriculum* (Wiltshire LEA 1992)
- *Guidelines for secondary schools for effective differentiation in the classroom* (Essex County Council 1993).

The guidelines are by necessity of a general nature. To try to impose rigid ideas upon widely different departments would be inappropriate and unwelcome. The group tried to gather together materials which would highlight common areas of concern and make suggestions which departments may wish to pursue or adapt to their own subjects. What the guidelines suggest is a balanced approach to teaching and learning. Without balance, there is the teacher at one extreme who allows no independence at all, with no elements of variety and choice built into their work. At the other extreme, there are teachers who give pupils so much freedom and choice that they may receive inadequate preparation or instruction. Using a broad range of teaching styles as an approach to differentiation recognises the differences between pupils as learners and should enhance the teaching and learning experiences for everyone.

Two sections were added to complete the paper.

Monitoring and evaluation

This is a complex area and we felt that much work will have to be done in the future before we can arrive at effective strategies to monitor the success of the school at delivering differentiated learning. As a starting point for discussion we used the guidelines on performance indicators from Essex County Council (1993). They list three types of performance indicators that can analyse the differentiated approaches being undertaken by a school:

- Enabling indicators: evidence of things put in place to enable something to happen.
- Process indicators: evidence of what is actually happening.
- Outcome indicators: evidence that what is happening is producing results.

These may be used as a useful base from which to start from but eventually we hope to 'develop our own indicators to ensure that the stated objectives are our own'.

Suggested reading list

This was compiled by one member of the team. Useful material was listed with a brief summary outlining the content of each piece. All material will be held in the school library for reference for members of staff.

THE DRAFT SCHOOL POLICY STATEMENT

The final draft policy was presented in three sections followed by eleven detailed appendices:

1 A definition of differentiation
2 The policy
3 Recommendations
4 Appendices:

- the brief
- a justification for differentiation (this sets out the rationale and philosophy for the policy)

- the aims of the school as they relate to differentiation
- implications and constraints
- the learning development department
- classroom resourcing: a proposed model
- differentiation and professional development
- next steps: phased school priority
- departmental guidelines
- monitoring and evaluation
- suggested reading list.

The paper was completed and reviewed in October 1994 by the senior management team prior to its consideration as the 'Draft Policy for Differentiation' by the school accountability group structure, and ultimately all the staff so that their views may be built into the final recommendations. The school development plan intends that the policy should now be introduced into whole school practice.

It can be seen that the time taken to develop such a policy is not a short one. Careful consideration for the criteria of a policy has to be followed by detailed research and discussion. If the policy is to have the impact in the classroom that we intend, the change must be brought about with care and sensitivity for both staff and pupils. Implementing the policy will therefore have to be a gradual but defined process: a process that will be managed through clear development planning and supporting professional development.

THE NEXT STEP: INSET

The next step was to introduce the policy to the whole staff in a way in which they could see that it is possible to achieve a direct impact in the classroom. As part of my responsibility within the science department, I had already led a Differentiation and Learning Styles INSET workshop the previous September, so it was decided to use this in a carousel of three sessions on the Professional Development Day in January 1995 for the whole staff. Department teams were grouped according to accountability structure and each attended, in rotation, a session lasting one and a half hours.

The aim of the session was to reinforce the policy not only by emphasising that differentiation is not something new, but also by stimulating staff to look at differentiation from the angle of learning styles by first considering their own preferred learning style. Using this information, we hoped staff would start thinking of how to work collaboratively to include some of the ideas and activities in the classroom.

The session began with a reminder of the differentiation policy definition emphasising in particular that 'differentiation should be used to ensure that pupils achieve success and feel that their learning experiences have been worthwhile'. We then went on to brainstorm and produce a spidergram of how children differ. Using this information, we then considered the advantages and disadvantages of grouping pupils with perceived common characteristics together: this involved much discussion! Ideas for this were based on material taken from *Differentiation: Making it work* (Visser 1992).

As few people in our survey had made reference to the way in which children learn, we spent the rest of the session on learning styles based on Michael Fielding's work (see Chapter 6). The important point to be drawn out from this work is that teachers as well as students need to consider their own learning styles.

Each member of staff was presented with a pack of material to work through, based on Michael Fielding's session that we participated in during the course at Cambridge. It started with a few questions on 'Myself as a learner' (see Figure 7.1, p. 106), an excellent sheet to use with students showing how they learn and in trying to identify their own strengths and weaknesses. When presented to the staff, what was surprising was the fact that many of us rarely contemplate these questions ourselves and a few assumed that the questions were not relevant because, as teachers, they felt that they were not at a learning stage in their life.

Finally, we looked at pupils' learning styles through the slightly easier to understand modalities of visual, auditory and kinaesthetic. We discussed ways in which children could identify their particular learning modality through a list of characteristics and then improve their learning in those areas they felt weakest in. One method of helping pupils in the future is to perhaps update our current study skills package which the students do in tutor time and allow departments to have access to the information so that the skills are reinforced across curriculum areas.

Staff left the session with examples of material that incorporated learning styles into work schemes, plus suggestions under a number of headings (e.g. tasks set, homeworks, classroom environment, etc.) for each type of learner. Time now needs to be given to staff to put some of these thoughts into practice, perhaps by working to produce ideas and activities that can be applied to a variety of work schemes rather than writing separate work schemes with differentiated ideas.

CONCLUSION

It is important to acknowledge that the task of 'writing a policy' is never complete. Thoughts and ideas are continually evolving. Also, as policy is put into practice and the ease of implementation is considered by all staff, parts may need to be modified. This is when it truly becomes a whole-school policy. To be effective, staff need to feel comfortable with its implementation.

Since taking part in the differentiation working party, I have also been part of the equality assurance policy team. This is a huge area to be tackled. It has made us realise that you have to concentrate on small areas at a time and plan steps of action carefully. It is all too easy to think and write about the ideal, and to overlook the very real constraints of putting ideas into practice. However, we should not be put off by the constraints, no matter how difficult they may seem, but use the whole staff to evaluate ways of getting round them. The more people have been involved, the more workable the final product becomes. The aim is to try to create a team of people working together.

Chapter 13

Equality: what else is there to consider?

Judy Erwin

EDITOR'S INTRODUCTION

It is widely argued that 'differentiation' has a central part to play in achieving equal opportunities for all children within the common framework of the National Curriculum. But what exactly is meant by 'equal opportunities' and what is the link between school policies on differentiation and the broader work that needs to be undertaken in order to foster equal opportunities for all?

Judy Erwin is an advisory teacher for equal opportunities. One of our course members attended a series of workshop sessions which she regularly runs on equal opportunities and, as a result of this contact, we invited Judy to make a contribution to the book to help set our own discussion of 'differentiation' in this wider context. In this chapter, she argues that if we are to work towards creating school environments in which all have an equal chance to learn and develop their individual capabilities, this work needs to be informed by an understanding of the nature and sources of inequalities in education and in society more generally. She explains her own understanding of these complex issues and offers some specific practical ideas to help schools open up constructive discussion and support teachers in their continuing search to provide a motivating, high quality school environment.

In this chapter, I examine some aspects of equality in education that have not so far been addressed in detail in earlier chapters. My aim is to provide some thoughts and suggestions on what else we need to consider if schools are genuinely to offer equality of opportunity to their students. In doing this I shall be drawing extensively on the work that I have done as an advisory teacher in a local education authority and on my own developing understanding of what we are attempting to deal with when we raise the head of equal opportunities above the parapet.

In this chapter I attempt to:

- set a context by summarising various perceptions of the importance of equality issues in schools, including some references to official requirements

- explain my understanding of why we need to address equality issues in a broad sense
- demonstrate that the effects of inequality are detrimental to everyone
- describe some approaches and activities used to raise awareness with staff in schools and develop policy and practice.

SETTING THE CONTEXT

There is no wide consensus in Britain on the term or phrase 'equality' or 'equality of opportunity'. Just as the word 'differentiation' will have different connotations for teachers so will the words 'equal opportunities'. For example, for some it may mean addressing the needs of pupils with learning difficulties; for others it may mean ensuring that girls and boys get equal chances to participate and succeed in all areas of the curriculum.

I use these terms in this chapter to reflect a moral stance that all people are of equal worth and have a right to equal chances, access and opportunities. This does not mean the same treatment if we take 'same' to mean 'identical'. The authors of previous chapters in this book have explored, in a number of challenging ways, the notion that equality needs to accommodate difference if we are to truly acknowledge the value of each individual in an equitable way.

In my experience, the issue of equality often raises powerful emotions when the subject is opened up for discussion in staff groups. These understandings and emotions range on a continuum from passionate concern, commitment and awareness to outspoken hostility and dismissal. The acceptance of or the denial of the importance of examining our practice through an equality lens will reflect an individual's perspective. These various perceptions will be an outcome of the messages each person has received about how society functions and the interpretations each one of us uses to make sense of our world. If issues of power and self-esteem are fundamental to an understanding of equality, which I shall argue is the case, then it is not surprising that to examine the issues can be a very uncomfortable business. Some would take the view that to discuss equality is to stir a hornets' nest that is too hazardous to tamper with. Others might argue that there is not a problem in their school. After all, achievement, fair play, caring and a sense of justice are the cornerstone of what a school stands for. Yet others believe something should be done but are overwhelmed by the apparent enormity of the task and the pressure to get on with clearer, approved objectives.

It is not uncommon for teachers to equate the relevance of equality issues with types of school intake. The view often expressed as 'no problem here' usually means, in my experience, that the school has a 'business as usual' approach. The diversity within the school population is perceived as being minimal or equality issues are seen to be largely about difference in ethnic background. 'We haven't got any of them here' has been used as a reason for not needing to address equal opportunities. The assumed normality of the curriculum and the way it is taught means that pupils are expected to 'fit in' or be in need of extra, usually outside support. It is increasingly accepted, and supported by legislation and requirements, that being a single-sex school or an 'all white' school does not mean that issues of sexism and racism for example are not vital parts of pupils' education. If we believe in the importance of a just and equitable future society for everyone then it is the business of all schools to address the issues. We are all affected in negative ways by injustice whether we are the recipients, the perpetrators or the silent onlookers.

So the task of assuring equality in schools is not one that can be left to the enthusiastic few. Official documents and national legislation since the mid-1980s have made reference to the importance of the principles and practice of equality in educating all pupils for life into the twenty-first century. The National Curriculum Council (1990a) guidance document on *The whole curriculum* states that 'A commitment to providing equal opportunities for all pupils, and a recognition that preparation for life in a multicultural society is relevant to all pupils, should permeate every aspect of the curriculum.' This document, along with others – for example, *From policy into practice* (DES 1989), guidance for schools and the National Curriculum Council (1990b) guidance on *Education for citizenship* – confirmed the importance of the whole curriculum in conveying the ethos of a school. It is clear that the ethos or spirit that the various documents refer to is one where pupils are encouraged to question prejudice, to develop an understanding of different perspectives and to view diversity as an asset. The new OFSTED Handbook *Guidance of the Inspection of Secondary Schools* makes reference to equal opportunities throughout the inspection schedule and guidance. Inspectors will, for example, wish to examine 'the effectiveness of the school's leadership and management in overseeing the creation and implementation of policies to promote equality of opportunity and high achievements for all pupils' (Part III). Equality issues permeate each section of the inspection schedule, highlighting the importance of questions such as:

- Does the school have effective measures to eliminate oppressive behaviour including all forms of harassment and bullying?
- To what extent does teaching meet the needs of all pupils, in particular, pupils who have special educational needs or for whom English is an additional language?

- Does the school teach pupils to appreciate their own cu tions and the diversity and richness of other cultures?
- Are there significant variations in attainment amor different gender, ethnicity or background?

The Education Reform Act 1988, and subsequent supporting guidance, identifies access for all pupils to equal opportunities and education for life in a multicultural society as a right and not a matter of chance. There is not, however, any clear articulation of the relationship between principles and practice and there remains a gap between intention and implementation which individual teachers and schools either ignore or attempt to address with varying degrees of success. Some aspects of new legislation may in effect work against equality.

> In practice the national curriculum may fail to be inclusive and common to all. Pupils who have been disadvantaged in the past may not be enabled to achieve higher standards and qualifications, or to gain improved access to further and higher education. Indeed, they may be even more disadvantaged than before. Some communities and parents continue to have insufficient influence and involvement in education. New structures, measures and arrangements may actually increase inequality in schools and society.
>
> (Runnymede Trust 1993)

Currently it is left largely to teachers to find their own way forward. Legislation requires all 'educators' to contribute to the development of a society free from discrimination, prejudice and inequality on grounds of race, gender, disability and social circumstance. Yet the National Curriculum fails to help teachers understand, interpret and enact that responsibility in their work in schools. I believe that one important way forward is to broaden our understanding of what we are talking about. Reading, discussing, training sessions, gathering information all contribute to our awareness raising. In the next two sections I give the arguments and reasons that I see forming the basis of the need for action in schools.

WHY LOOK AT THE ISSUE OF EQUALITY?

It may be true that we are sometimes motivated only by the crack of the whip of legislation. My professional and personal work has led me to a view that there are other powerful reasons why every teacher needs to examine her or his understanding of equality and the consequent practices in the classroom and wider school community that underpin our principles or ideals. The words of the black American writer, Alice Walker, summarise the importance of keeping equality at the centre of all school policy:

Keep in mind always the present you are constructing.
It should be the future you want.

(Walker 1989)

An ongoing challenge for anyone motivated to provide a more equitable society is how to engage the interest and commitment of others. Our own understanding of how inequality manifests itself, and its effects, helps us to speak with conviction, clarity and sensitivity. This will put into context any practical suggestions for change in schools and form the basis of the debate for awareness raising. My current understanding of the issues includes the following three areas.

First, I believe that inequality pervades our actions, our relationships and our institutions, and that to deny that inequality is an issue for all schools is likely to indicate a lack of awareness or resistance to change. If I extend the analogy for a moment to likening the pervasiveness of inequality to toxins in the air that we breathe in from birth, largely unconscious of what we are inhaling, it may help us to accept that it is unproductive to wag the finger of blame at ourselves or others for the attitudes we hold. I believe attitudes are learned, they are being formed from birth and are the product of our total life experience. Unfortunately, many of the attitudes we form about people, situations and ideas will be negative, involving false assumptions, prejudices and stereotyping. Our behaviour is likely to reflect these attitudes often at an unconscious and unintentional level. If what we have learned is called into question, is shown to be limiting, negative, contributing to conflict, then there is potential for unlearning or relearning.

Research shows that children are absorbing the prevailing negative stereotypes about themselves and others by the age of 2 to 3 years old (Milner 1983). These understandings of the world about them are being formed by what they see and hear and from what is absent in their lives. We are conditioned by the world around us and the messages can come in subtle forms. Attitudes towards race and gender are becoming entrenched by the age of nine unless important events or major input cause us to question how things are.

Where does this leave secondary schools? Here is a big challenge for us. How do teachers identify the attitudes with regard to equality we wish to change? How are our own actions and messages bound up with these attitudes? What actions and messages do we want to put in their place? How do we do that? If we take the view that the damage is already done we underestimate the power we have to provide the 'event' that can reshape attitude.

Secondly, I believe that many teachers agree with the importance of equality of opportunity and do, on the whole, wish to align themselves with principles of equality. However, it is understandable and likely in any one staff group that there will be a range of views and experiences in terms of how equality or inequality operates in practice. For example, if we belong to a group that is regularly discriminated against in our society, it may be that we are more likely to feel passionately about that particular form of injustice and to be motivated to change things in relation to how society treats the group we belong to. This urge for change may not be experienced by someone who is a member of a powerful group and/or where the status quo seems normal and comfortable. It is not always easy to 'walk in other people's moccasins'. Most of the time, though, positions are by no means so clear-cut. Many of us have complex backgrounds and experiences where we identify with a number of groups and can move from the position of 'oppressed' to 'oppressor' in the space of a few hours or less. We also need to understand that people who belong to a minority group or groups may have internalised many of the limiting views that society at large holds about them. Disabled people may, for example, hold a view of themselves that they are to be pitied or that they are unproductive. This sad effect of oppression can lead to inadvertent collusion with injustice by the recipients of inequality. It can be a very painful process to examine in oneself the effects of being discriminated against or having discriminated against another. Encouraging people to do this requires skill and sensitivity. We need to work on acknowledging our common experience of how injustice perpetuates lack of humanity and lowers self-esteem.

One route to empathy with oppressed groups is to invite colleagues to recall an injustice perpetrated against them and to recall the feelings associated with that occasion. What emerges from this sort of activity and discussion is that everyone has been on the receiving end of injustice at some point in their lives.

It is very important to follow this kind of activity with a clear analysis of the different degrees of injustice and discrimination experienced by some people on the basis, not of who they are as individuals, but of the group they are perceived to belong to. For some people their experiences of discrimination or injustice are likely to have been relatively mild and infrequent. They may have had to delve back into childhood to recall such an event. Other people's experience of discrimination will reach the opposite end of the continuum and can be constant, even life threatening.

It is crucial that we make the difficult step of accepting that particular groups in our society (I am referring to British society although what I am advocating will apply elsewhere) experience discrimination based on false notions or theories that still permeate our belief systems, our institutions and organisational structures and are manifest in our behaviours. These theories, while they are being eroded through the struggles of those committed to developing an equitable society, still operate powerfully through the media, through the language we use, through our economic, health, housing, employment and education systems. They are based on relationships of power held by one group over another over very long periods of time and are internalised, at least to some degree, by everyone.

The 'isms' created by these notions of superiority and inferiority have become familiar labels to many of us. I am talking about racism, sexism, ablism, heterosexism (or homophobia), classism, ageism. By definition racism describes the set of behaviours and institutional practices that disadvantages black and minority ethnic groups. The deeply conditioned beliefs that lie behind racist behaviour and institutional practices come from a legacy that tells us, in crude terms, that to be white is superior to being black. This legacy has its roots in history and grew, to a large extent, out of the justifications for imposing slavery. As a society I believe we carry similar legacies rooted in history, religious belief and 'common sense' understandings that tell us it is 'better' to be a man than a woman, it is 'better' to be able-bodied than disabled, it is 'better' to be heterosexual than gay or lesbian. We convey these messages in a myriad of subtle and largely unconscious ways hence my earlier reference to toxins in the air.

When we have the power to act – and as teachers we are inherently in a position of power – this value system will lead to discrimination. Discrimination is always negative in the sense of who it leaves out. Legislation defines discrimination and clarifies what is unlawful with regard to race and sex (Sex Discrimination Act 1975 and Race Relations Act 1976 – see Appendix 1). Negative attitudes plus power plus the application of the theories of superiority (usually operating at an institutional level) compound to produce a potent concoction which I choose to call oppression.

This leads to my third belief. This is that there is no inherently hierarchical order to the various forms of discrimination in our society. What I mean by this is that no particular form of discrimination is more important to address and deal with than any other. The existence of each is connected to the others. Each form of discrimination contributes in a particular way to the divisions between people. When people claim that their particular oppression is worse or more important than another person's oppression this is in itself divisive and pits one group against another. This stance usually indicates that that person's particular oppression is not being addressed (or that the person believes that it is not).

However, there is also a real danger that if we accept that there is no order of importance for tackling equality issues, this will allow leeway to focus on those areas that we feel more comfortable about tackling and avoid the issues that we find most difficult to face. Society – and schools as a microcosms of our society – have dealt with different forms of oppression in a piecemeal and ad-hoc way. This is reflected in legislation or the lack of it. For example, the law prevents discrimination on grounds of race, gender and disability, yet lesbians and gay men are not afforded the same rights. It is often the case, then, that we do impose an implicit order of importance on equality issues and bring different sets of beliefs and conditionings to the way we view groups individually and collectively. It may for example be far easier to discuss gender in the staffroom than lesbian and gay issues despite the irony of their connection.

The complexity of this phenomenon is complicated further by each person's emotional involvement with the issue which may cause them to react in unhelpful ways, such as denial or aggression. I have noticed how teachers nod with passion when age discrimination is cited as a example of oppression, perhaps thinking with some discomfort how this has affected, or is likely to affect, them sooner or later personally. In predominantly white, middle-class, heterosexual communities it may be difficult for members of those groups to feel with the same intensity the oppression of racism, classism and homophobia. If empathy is not sufficiently forceful to bring about a commitment to positive action in these areas, it will be important for managers in schools to take a lead in clarifying and developing appropriate codes of behaviour.

THE EFFECTS OF INEQUALITY

It is relatively easy to monitor and record the detrimental effects of oppression at an institutional level. For example black men and women in British society generally have jobs of low status and pay, higher unemployment rates than whites, poorer housing conditions and are visibly absent from the important decision-making roles in Britain today. The same is true of disabled people and similar lists indicating disempowerment will apply to women, lesbians and gay men, and on the basis of people's class, age and cultural background. In addition our institutions are generally organised to cater, usually at an unaware level, for the majority or powerful groups in our society (i.e. white and male) in ways which make access to the rewards of the organisation more difficult for other groups (for example, promotion, career development, and identification with the curriculum in the case of schools). This is not to imply that men and boys are not also oppressed, for instance by society's messages that tell men that their prime function is to be wage earners and soldiers. Boys and men are discouraged from expressing feelings of tenderness and sadness or from admitting weakness, particularly in public. Various forms of pressure, including ridicule, threats and violence operate in a way that leads many males in our society to relate to one another, and to women and children in fairly well-defined, limiting and often oppressive ways. One Year 6 pupil expressed his understanding of some of these limitations as follows:

> The worst thing about being a boy is that, if you cry in front of boys, they think you are a girl.
>
> (Hertfordshire County Council 1992)

As teachers, we will have observed at first hand the detrimental effects of inequality. We may not make the connections that I argue are there and it is tempting to go along with a view that propounds the inevitability of things expressed as 'Boys will be boys', 'They have natural rhythm', and (far less often now) 'Girls are no good at science'. I referred earlier to research that has demonstrated that young children absorb messages about the way the world around them views people, situations and ideas. Children will look at the world with the 'spectacles' they are given. These will be issued as 'standard' spectacles and will reflect back to the child what we select as important for them to know and experience. Parents and teachers play a large part in what is selected but a lot of what children absorb is beyond our immediate control, that is we cannot prevent children (nor would we wish to) from receiving information from a far wider source than home and school. However, we need to take conscious, planned and well thought out steps to counter some of the negative views that prevail.

People who are the targets of negative bias are more likely to

- absorb negative messages about themselves, believe in their own inferiority and develop low self-esteem
- be affected by adult expectations linked to race, gender, ability and other stereotypes
- have limited choice of learning experiences (including self-limiting of choices)
- experience an unsafe learning environment (e.g. where concentration is affected by harassment or fear of harassment)
- experience stress symptoms which can manifest in illness, aggressive behaviour, withdrawal or absence from school.

Since the late 1960s there has been concern over the achievement and behaviour of Afro-Caribbean boys in particular. However, this concern has not been sustained at a high level nor have the aspirations of Afro-Caribbean parents and young people been seriously listened to and incorporated into our education systems. When this issue is examined, there is a recognition that teacher expectations, the relevance of curriculum content, teaching styles and gender stereotypes all play a part in the dynamics which lead to unacceptably high levels of exclusion, and low levels of achievement, amongst this group.

As already noted briefly, a group of pupils who so far have received serious lack of attention are lesbian and gay pupils. The assumption that heterosexuality is superior to homosexuality currently has implicit and explicit support in legislation. The directive not to 'intentionally promote homosexuality' in Section 28 of the Local Government Act 1988 does not prevent local authorities and schools from including reference to lesbians and gay boys/men, among other groups, in their equal opportunities policies. Nor does Section 28 prevent teachers from discussing lesbian and gay sexuality with pupils, from giving affirmative counselling to pupils concerned about their sexuality, or from challenging homophobic name-calling and 'teasing'. Teachers have a positive duty to protect all pupils from being bullied. However, the directive has in many cases had the effect of frightening some into silence and confirming the prejudices of others. The force of this legislation has been more symbolic than real. It has influenced public perceptions and compounded prejudice. It is likely to have had a 'chilling' effect on discussions of gay and lesbian issues in schools. The guidelines on sex education in schools (Department for Education 1994) compel teachers to inform parents if they advise lesbian, gay or bisexual pupils about sexual relations or safety. They face disciplinary procedures or criminal sanctions if they fail to do so. This adds to the chill.

If our aim is to create a school environment in which every child can feel accepted and valued, free from harassment and discrimination, we need to be aware of the damage that homophobia does. While we may struggle to adopt an approach that gives equal credence to different sexual identities we may have no difficulty in supporting measures that prevent bullying, loneliness and suicide. No matter how embarrassing, disturbing or shocking the notion that on average one in ten of us will prefer to express our sexuality with someone of the same sex as ourselves, the effects of sidelining gay and lesbian issues can be devastating. Two quotes from *Something to tell you* (Trenchard and Warren 1984) express a common experience amongst gay and lesbian young people.

> I really did think I was the only young gay. That's what made me take the tablets, attempt suicide.

> I found it very difficult at school, being surrounded by male class-mates who all had girlfriends. I often felt there must be something wrong with me. It might have helped if we were told simply that not everyone's sexuality is the same.

I have given space to these specific issues both as an example and because they are perhaps those that we find most difficult to address, they may present the greatest challenge to us as individuals and as insti-tutions. This is not to imply that they are inherently more important than racism, and so on. What I wish to emphasise is the unfairness of a lopsided focus.

To estimate the damaging effects of inequality is not a straightforward equation. Some people will be affected by more than one form of oppression. For example, a black, disabled woman will be affected in complex and interconnecting ways by racism, sexism and ablism. Unfortunately one of the features of oppression is that it encourages pecking orders. Belonging to one group does not mean automatic empathy and understanding of the position of other groups. For example, a group of disabled people are likely to have and express a range of prejudices and negative attitudes about black people, gay people and women. Sometimes we are in positions of power and sometimes we are the powerless; it will depend on the context.

There are detrimental effects, too, of oppression on people who consider themselves in a position of superiority at a conscious or unconscious level. I suggest that they are as follows:

1 Self-concepts are based on a false sense of superiority and normality, so the maintenance of self-esteem has a vested interest in the maintenance of prejudice and stereotype.
2 Double standards are learned and these lead to hypocrisy and pupils' ethical development is affected (i.e. the explicit adult message that we are all equal and that everyone needs to be treated fairly is not borne out in practice).
3 Misconceptions and misinformation go unchallenged; mistrust and fear of those perceived as 'different' abound and limit pupil and adult choices around relationships, work and life style.

These effects will occur whether we teach and learn in single-sex, mixed, 'all white', multi-ethnic or middle-class schools. Work to counter these effects is relevant to all of us.

STARTING THE PROCESS OF CHANGE

If it is our real intention to move towards a school environment where the chance of any pupil experiencing negative attitudes towards himself or herself or others is minimised or eradicated, where every pupil is expected to achieve highly, where diversity is perceived by everyone as an asset to enjoy and build on, how can we best set about it? How can we tackle the task in bite size chunks and avoid being overwhelmed by its apparent enormity?

Most of the work that I have done to support schools in this task since the late 1980s has involved working primarily with the whole school staff, where possible including non-teaching staff and governors. This is not the only starting point but it is arguably a very important one if a whole-school policy is to mean more than the paper it is written on. I shall describe some of the approaches and activities that have been useful in enabling everyone to engage in discussion and the development of policy and practice.

Other suggestions can be found in Appendices 3 and 4 to this chapter.

Sometimes those responsible for arranging in-service training sessions, or meetings labelled as 'equal opportunities' or other versions of the same title, are confronted with strong negative emotions from colleagues. These stem from feelings of fear or anger and are expressed in the following sorts of ways:

We're being criticised again.

I've got more important things to do.

We're doing it anyway.

Yet another thing.

This is just the latest trend.

I'll be made to feel uncomfortable, guilty, confused.

I'll be labelled or stereotyped if I open my mouth.

Will my experience be recognised?

It can be effective to invite these sorts of comments at an early stage in the process and then to agree ground rules that will help facilitate the process of learning together.

An important starting point to the debate is to clarify for ourselves, and for the collection of people we work with and for, what we mean by terms such as 'oppression' and 'equality'. Many key words and phrases which are used in this discourse are contested, subject to change in use as our understandings deepen and have different nuances for different people. Debate around the meanings of these words allows space to dispel myths and misconceptions and supports a process of coming to common understandings or at least to a point where our differences are expressed openly.

If we choose to use the word 'oppression', it is important to emphasise that what it describes is the systematic, one way, institutionalised mistreatment of one group by another group or by society as a whole. This treatment is frequently unconscious and unintentional, and should not be presented as if it were part of any deliberate, malicious individual or organisational attitude. It is often helpful at this point to provide someone from outside the school staff to facilitate a discussion to raise awareness. It will be important to allow time to explore the different understandings that staff have about the meaning of equality in the school context. Issues for debate and clarification can be structured around key phrases that attempt to define what equal opportunities mean. The facilitator will need to have a clear understanding of equality issues and be well informed about equal opportunities legislation and any supporting guidelines.

As I explained at the beginning of the chapter, the right to equal chances, access and opportunities does not necessarily mean the 'same' treatment for all. Clearly, profoundly deaf children will not be receiving equality of access if they are taught without the necessary adaptation to standard methods of communication in the mainstream classroom. This may involve the use of a loop system or of sign language. For teachers, advisers and parents this example illustrates a dilemma at the heart of the differentiation and equality debate. Many would argue that children with severe impairments are the most difficult to accommodate in mainstream schools and equality of access to the curriculum can be achieved only through specialist help and equipment provided in special schools. While this may be the best short-term solution, I believe that the development of separate schools for children with disabilities is a clear example of how oppression works. Separate education conveys a powerful message to disabled people and to able-bodied people which leads to alienation and a fear of difference in able-bodied people and to marginalisation, a sense of inferiority and low self-esteem in people who fall short of a physical or mental 'norm'. The answer is not simple. Parents of children who are different from what is perceived to be normal in the community (this difference could be in terms of physical difference, ability, ethnicity, class, etc.) experience profound and often agonising decisions about what is best for their child. Where there is no choice they may suffer the pain of knowing their child is likely to be bullied and ostracised or will receive an education separate from their able-bodied peers.

Our discussions need to probe more searchingly into what it means to respect differences. They need to be clear that positive discrimination is illegal, and focus instead on what kinds of positive actions promote good equality practice. They need to take on board a proactive element as part of our definition of equality in school: namely that equal opportunities is about building time and space into the curriculum and life of the school to teach pupils about their rights and responsibilities.

Defining what we mean by equality helps us to establish what the overall aims for our school will be. So, for example if we agree that part of what we mean by equal opportunities is that it is about positive action to address disadvantage then this will be one of our aims.

Having worked as a whole-staff group to raise awareness and share understandings of what we mean by equality, schools will wish to look at their own priorities for areas of development. One way of doing this is to develop statements of principle related to areas of school life and then to focus in on priorities and the key actions required to implement the ideals or principles. Working from a checklist of questions can help to provide a framework for developing both these principles and key actions. An example of a checklist is in Appendix 2 to this chapter.

Many schools see an urgent need to address harassment, as part of their policy and practice on pupils' behaviour, and will make this their priority. Some local authority education departments have produced helpful guidelines for schools and supporting training. The two most commonly recognised forms are racial harassment and sexual harassment. However, as has been demonstrated earlier, pupils will be harassed for belonging to or being perceived as belonging to other oppressed groups. Staff and pupils need a clear understanding of the specific features, manifestations and effects of the various forms of harassment. They should know that it is always unacceptable behaviour and what the processes are for dealing with any incidents. Staff development can take people through a process of

- identifying what we mean by harassment or incidents that we would describe as 'racist', 'sexist', etc.
- examining what hinders and what helps us to deal with these effectively in schools
- developing guidelines and procedures for dealing with incidents
- practising skills for responding in appropriate ways to incidents

CONCLUSION

The many suggestions and ideas for supporting the differing needs of pupils that the previous chapters take us through have at their core the aim of providing equality of access to learning. In our ongoing search to provide a motivating, high quality school environment it is important to recognise that first, our approach to differentiating the curriculum may have implications in terms of equality, and secondly, our classroom organisation, teaching styles, pastoral systems, curriculum content, school meetings, links with the community and staffing structures need to reflect a positive view of diversity.

The overall achievement of pupils will be influenced not only by the teaching methodology. All the messages that the institution gives out about how groups are perceived in society will have a profound effect on the way each pupil perceives herself or himself and others and on the way each pupil performs in school.

APPENDIX 1: EQUAL OPPORTUNITIES LEGISLATION

The Race Relations Act 1976 prohibits discrimination on grounds of colour, race, nationality, and ethnic or national origin. It applies to discrimination in education, employment, housing and the provision of goods, services and facilities. With regard to education it makes it unlawful to discriminate on racial grounds in undertaking any local authority or school functions under the various Education Acts.

The Sex Discrimination Act 1975 and the 1986 Amendment prohibits discrimination on grounds of sex with regard to employment practices. In relation to schools it states in Section 22 that it is unlawful for the 'responsible body' to discriminate against a girl or boy on the ground of sex. This relates to admissions (exception – single-sex schools), access to benefits, facilities or services, and exclusions.

Both these Acts define and make unlawful direct and indirect discrimination and victimisation.

Direct discrimination

Direct discrimination arises when a person is treated less favourably than others in the same circumstances on the grounds of race or sex. Discrimination can take place in the way people are recruited and selected, assessed and promoted, or in the ways that services are delivered. For example

- excluding men/women from certain work functions
- limiting options to certain gender or ethnic groups.

Indirect discrimination

Indirect discrimination occurs when a requirement or condition is placed on an activity which has the effect of disadvantaging groups or individual members of a group, such as women. Indirect discrimination is concerned with inherent or acquired disadvantage of some groups in relation to others as well as with less favourable treatment. For example

- academic qualifications to be acquired in the UK
- girls required to wear skirts.

Victimisation

The Acts define as unlawful discrimination any action against a person because they have asserted their rights under the law or supported another person in doing so.

The Disability Discrimination Act received Royal Assent in November 1995. It strengthens the rights of disabled people. For example schools are required to publish

- their arrangements for the admission of disabled pupils
- the steps taken to prevent disabled pupils from being treated less favourably than other pupils
- the facilities provided to assist access to the school by disabled pupils.

These amendments to earlier legislation do not mean that schools have to make their premises immediately accessible but do require them to address the matter.

APPENDIX 2: CHECKLIST ON EQUAL OPPORTUNITIES

When using a checklist such as this:

1 Stress the importance of the participation and contribution of groups that have less power in our society, that is women, people from minority ethnic groups, younger members of staff, and so on. This is particularly important when it comes to goal setting and methods.
2 Be realistic about what can be tackled first and what support is available. Step-by-step organisation of a goal decided upon is at least as important as the good intentions that lie behind it.
3 It is important to recognise and acknowledge good practice that already exists and to build upon it. Answers are likely to be on a continuum from 'Yes, always' to 'No, never'.

Task

For each overall area write one, two or three policy statements which summarise the intention to address the questions. Some questions will lead to specific actions as well as to more general statements.

Community

- Are all parents made to feel welcome and comfortable when they visit the school?
- Are parents from all racial, cultural, gender and socio-economic backgrounds encouraged to participate in the life of the school, e.g. on PTAs (parent–teacher associations), the governing body, etc.?
- Is the language used at meetings and functions and in the written communications (e.g. reports) accessible to all parents and interpreted or translated as necessary for some?
- Are meetings held at suitable times for working parents to attend?
- Does the school check any special arrangements that need to be made for certain pupils, e.g. diet, dress?
- Are all major religious festivals taken into account when organising an activity?
- Are venues accessible to people with disabilities?

Governors

- Does the governing body reflect the gender, racial and economic make-up of the community?
- Does the balance of power within the governing body ensure that the views and needs of the whole school community are addressed?
- How might the election process redress the balance if the above is not true?
- Does any governor have an equal opportunities brief? What other position does that person have on the governing body?

Staffing

- Do the teaching staff reflect the diverse make-up of the community?
- What are the gender, racial and age patterns for roles of responsibility within the school?
- Does the school's personnel policy make specific reference to equal opportunities practices in the recruitment, appointment and promotion procedures for staff?
- What patterns in terms of gender and race are reflected in the overall staffing of the school including administrative staff, classroom assistants, etc.?
- How do appraisal practices in the school take on board equal opportunities issues, both in terms of teachers' practices, and in terms of race, gender, age and disability issues within the appraisal process?
- Do staff development plans recognise issues of equality, e.g. taking positive action on management training for women?

Pastoral system

- Are female and male staff and staff from minority ethnic groups taking lead roles within the school's pastoral system?
- Are all staff encouraged to re-examine their views on race, gender and ability to increase their awareness of discrimination in our society, in particular to examine the effects of racism, sexism and ablism on expectations and how this affects behaviour and achievement? How is this done?
- Are all staff aware of how incidents of racism and sexism are dealt with?
- Are there assumptions that we make in our communications with parents? Whom do we contact when pupils are ill? Do we assume that every pupil has two parents?
- Has the school developed and implemented a code of practice that deals effectively with incidents of racism, sexism, etc.?
- Are sanctions and rewards applied fairly? Are there any patterns in terms of gender, race or ability?

Curriculum

- Are equal opportunities themes, dimensions and skills addressed through the whole curriculum?
- Does the school have a structure for ensuring continuity and progression of the above?
- Does the curriculum find appropriate and integrated opportunity to include the contributions and history of all racial groups and of women and disabled people?
- Are issues of stereotyping and prejudice in subject matter identified and challenged?
- Are the processes for delivering the curriculum differentiated to take on board diverse learning styles and the learning needs of different groups?
- Do materials reflect our diverse society in non-judgemental and non-stereotypical ways?
- Are teachers trained to detect – and to guide the pupils to detect – both overt and subtle manifestations of racism and sexism in materials?
- Do the displays throughout the school give positive, non-stereotypical messages with respect to all groups of people and reflect the work and interests of all pupils?
- Does the school have strategies for extending the most able as well as the least able pupils?
- Are opportunities given for bilingual pupils to communicate in their own language?
- How do school assemblies address the experiences of all pupils? Who talks about what? What themes and role models are presented?

APPENDIX 3: WHAT HELPS TO MAKE EQUAL OPPORTUNITY POLICY WORK?

1 Staff training and awareness raising.
2 Doing an audit and building on good practice.
3 Involvement and consultation with whole school community.
  - children
  - staff
  - governors
  - parents.
4 Identifying areas that need to be considered.
5 Building in key actions to implement ideals.
6 Identifying resources.
7 Prioritising and setting a time scale.
8 Monitoring outcomes and acting on results as appropriate.
9 Reviewing policy and practice.

10 Using specific materials with children.
11 Conducting small investigations.

APPENDIX 4: TAKING EQUAL OPPORTUNITIES INTO THE SECONDARY CURRICULUM

Which of the following strategies would be most applicable in order of priority for your school?

1 Including all departments in equal opportunities work by co-opting one member of each for Equal Opportunities Working Party.
2 Including all departments in equal opportunities work by personal contact to all heads of department by members of Equal Opportunities Working Party.
3 Including all departments in equal opportunities work by setting up staff meeting or conference for departmental discussions.
4 Including all departments in equal opportunities work by insisting that each department responds to equal opportunities initiative during a stated period of time.
5 Assessment of all printed materials by all departments.
6 Assessment of school-produced materials by all departments and plans for updating.
7 Planned permeation of equal opportunities issues into all curriculum areas.
8 Examination of option take-up and alternative arrangement.
9 Investigation of Year 9 curriculum, options and career advice.
10 Investigation into pupil perceptions of subjects in terms of gender and ethnicity.
11 Whole-school conference to examine the curriculum and the whole child.
12 Close examination of the school curriculum for gender, race and ability bias.
13 Looking at pastoral curriculum and codes of practice with regard to dealing with incidents of racism and sexism.
14 School-based INSET on this aspect of curriculum.
15 Monitoring by teachers of classroom interaction.
16 Monitoring of examination and SATs (standard assessment tasks) results, exclusions, extra-curricular activities, etc.
17 Encouragement of staff to attend and report back from equal opportunities courses.
18 Seeking specialist advice, such as speakers to schools.
19 School policy on non-sexist and non-racist language.
20 Conducting an equal opportunities audit based on OFSTED requirements and expectations.

Appendix
Developing practice in schools

During the course on Differentiation which led to this book, teachers reviewed INSET packs, LEA guidelines for teachers and other published material that had so far become available, and shared their comments with the group. This appendix has been compiled, based on their appraisals.

Access to history: History for children with special educational needs (Humberside County Council undated)

These guidelines discuss ways in which the history curriculum can be made accessible, appropriate and challenging to all children, and considers the implications for the full inclusion of children seen to have special educational needs. It offers suggestions for a variety of approaches, including ideas for using pictures, artefacts, documentary sources, music, dance, role play, history books and IT (information technology). Our reviewer was very impressed with the array of material presented, and the detail with which it was explained and developed. However, this is a document to read in detail rather than dip into, because you need to follow through the structure of programmes of work. One really valuable feature is that many of the ideas are illustrated with reference to actual lesson plans and classroom materials.

Further sets of guidelines are available from the same source on *Access to geography*, *Access to maths* and *Access to science*. Within the broad discussion of curriculum approaches, consideration is also given to specific needs of children with hearing, vision and physical disabilities and to children with severe learning difficulties.

Differentiating the secondary curriculum (Wiltshire LEA 1992)

This is a pack of twenty booklets, plus an introduction and guide, and a video. The booklets are written in a reader-friendly style and provide background information and suggestions for further reading, as well as practical ideas for immediate classroom use, and case studies of ideas in action in the classroom. The range of booklets serves as a useful reminder of all the different dimensions of school and classroom experience that are susceptible to positive intervention by teachers to enhance learning and achievement. The booklet titles are:

- Concept mapping
- Task analysis
- DARTS (Directed Activities Related to Text)
- Developing writers
- Computers
- Talk
- Mastery learning
- Readability
- Producing your own educational material

- Pupil motivation
- Baselining
- Metacognition
- Support for learning
- Supported self-study
- Beginnings, endings, questions
- Assessment
- Marking written work
- Classroom organisation
- Senior management team
- Behaviour management

Differentiation: A practical handbook of classroom strategies (Dickinson and Wright 1993)

This book draws on the experience of teachers and advisers who have been involved in flexible learning projects. It provides some discussion of what 'differentiation' means and why it is important, although it is mainly concerned with offering practical ideas which are immediately usable by teachers in their own classrooms. Differentiation is defined as 'a planned process of intervention in the classroom to maximise potential based on individual needs' (p. 1). The authors emphasise that the purpose is to introduce into teaching carefully planned steps that will make a difference to children's learning, by catering more effectively for individual needs.

Four areas for intervention are identified: resources, tasks, support and response. Each of these areas, and its implications for planning and teaching, is examined in detail and illustrated through the use of examples of classroom materials. Our reviewer felt that the ideas, examples and discussion were very useful as a useful springboard for teachers' own thinking, but more needed to be done to encourage questioning of the judgements and strategies involved and the impact of differential provision upon the dynamics of a learning group.

Differentiation: Making it work, ideas for staff development
(Visser 1993)

This provides a clearly set out guide to approaching staff INSET, with useful examples of activities to stimulate discussion and sharing of practice. It takes staff through a process of first exploring meanings, then examining existing practices, and finally deciding on ways forward.

Our reviewer found it both easy to read and helpful in enabling her to sort out her own approach to differentiation in her classroom. The book stresses the importance of time for reflection and observation if teachers are to improve current practice within a school. This is needed not simply to review teaching approaches but also to reflect upon how we know when successful learning is taking place.

Differentiation: Your responsibility, an inservice training pack for staff development **(Barthorpe and Visser 1991)**

This booklet is devised to help teachers lead staff development sessions on the topic of differentiation. Our reviewer found it clear, well-structured and easy to adapt to individual schools' needs. It provides an introductory framework which can be used to help schools formulate policies and develop practices for themselves. The pack contains masters for OHP transparencies, and practical hints for using the material. It is organised in three sections:

- understanding the term
- what pupils bring to their learning
- differentiation in the classroom.

Differentiation in action: A whole school approach for raising attainment **(Stradling and Saunders 1991)**

This book is presented as a handbook for school planners and managers, offering practical guidance on planning and providing for the whole range of different learning needs of all secondary school pupils. It draws on an evaluation carried out by the National Foundation for Educational Research of the Low Attaining Pupils Programme (LAPP). This was set up to encourage the development of innovative work designed to raise the attainment of pupils who had experienced limited success within the educational system.

This work was carried out in the 1980s, so it does not take into account the new expectations, opportunities and constraints of the National Curriculum. Nevertheless, the case studies could provide an interesting stimulus for discussion in schools, mapping out a range of possible responses and encouraging debate about the advantages and limitations of each. There are also suggestions for specific activities which could be used as a basis for INSET.

Guidelines for secondary schools for effective differentiation in the classroom (Essex County Council 1993)

This booklet provides a comprehensive examination of questions relating to differentiation and their implications for classroom practice. It engages in a useful way with differences of perception of what differentiation means, and presents a clear and consistent view of differentiation as a means of *'expanding the possibility for individual achievement* rather than diminishing the task to a pre-conceived level of individual ability' (p. 6, our emphasis). It sets out different models for achieving differentiation in the planning and presentation of classroom activities and examines advantages and disadvantages associated with each. Very useful in helping to clarify thinking and take a broad overview of what differentiation entails, but does not include any examples of practice in which the ideas have been applied and or show what lessons have been learnt from their application.

Partnership teaching: Co-operative teaching strategies for English language support in multilingual classrooms, an in-service pack for schools (Bourne and McPake 1991)

This pack provides material for whole-school in-service work on language and learning, and is intended for teachers working across the 9–14 age range. Based on the principle that language is central to all learning, it is about 'ways in which pairs or groups of teachers can work together inside or outside the classroom to develop classroom organisation strategies and a curriculum which meets the needs and extends the learning of all pupils'. It offers suggestions for staff development activities, background reading, and three videos with extended sequences showing ideas being developed in practice.

Additional reading

Enfield Language and Curriculum Access Service (1995) *Making progress ... Teaching and assessment in the multilingual classroom*, London Borough of Enfield.
Fielding, M. (1994b) 'Valuing difference in teachers and learners: building on Kolb's learning styles to develop a language of teaching and learning', *The Curriculum Journal* 5(3): 393–417.
Hart, S. (1992b) 'Differentiation: part of the problem or part of the solution?', *The Curriculum Journal* 3(2): 131–42.

Peter, M. (ed.) (1992) *Differentiation: Ways forward*, Stafford: National Association for Special Educational Needs.

Quicke, J. (1995) 'Differentiation: a contested concept', *Cambridge Journal of Education* 25(2): 213–24.

Bibliography

Abraham, J. (1995) *Divide and school: Gender and class dynamics in comprehensive education*, London: Falmer.

Ainscow, M. (1989) *Special education in change*, London: David Fulton.

Ainscow, M. and Tweddle, D. (1988) *Encouraging classroom success*, London: David Fulton.

Baker, D. and Bovair, K (1990) *Making the special school ordinary?*, London: Falmer.

Ball, S. (1981) *Beachside comprehensive: A case study of secondary schooling*, Cambridge: Cambridge University Press.

—— (1986) 'The sociology of the school: streaming and mixed-ability and social class', in R. Rogers (ed.) *Education and social class*, Lewes: Falmer.

Barbe, W.B. and Swassing, R.H. (1979) *Teaching through modality strengths: Concepts and practices*, Columbus, Ohio: Zaner-Blosser.

Barnes, D. (1976) *From communication to curriculum*, Harmondsworth: Penguin.

Barrs, M., Ellis, S., Hester, H. and Thomas, A. (1990) *Patterns of learning: The primary language record and the National Curriculum*, London: Centre for Language in Primary Education.

Barthorpe, T. and Visser, J. (1991) *Differentiation: Your responsibility, an inservice training pack for staff development*, Stafford: National Association for Special Educational Needs.

Bell, G. (1991) *Educating for capability*, London: Royal Society of Arts.

Bennett, N. (1991) 'The quality of classroom learning experiences for children with special educational needs', in M. Ainscow (ed.) *Effective schools for all*, London: David Fulton.

Bennett, N., Desforges, C., Cockburn, A. and Wilkinson, B. (1984) *The quality of pupil learning experiences*, London: Lawrence Erlbaum Associates.

Bodi, S. (1990) 'Teaching effectiveness and bibliographic instruction: The relevance of learning styles', *College and Research Libraries* 51 (2): 113–19.

Bourne, J. and McPake, B. (1991) *Partnership teaching: Co-operative teaching strategies for English language support in multilingual classrooms, an in-service pack for school*, London: HMSO.

Butler, K. (1987) *Learning and teaching style: In theory and practice* (2nd edn), Columbia, Conn.: The Learner's Dimension.

—— (1988) *It's all in your mind: A student's guide to learning style*, Columbia, Conn.: The Learner's Dimension.

—— (1989) *A teacher's guide to 'It's all in your mind: A student's guide to learning style'*, Columbia, Conn.: The Learner's Dimension.

Buzan, T. (1992) *Use your memory*, London: BBC Publications.

Carlsson, B., Koano, P. and Martin, J.B. (1904) 'R & D organizations as learning systems', in D.A. Kolb, I.M. Rubin and J.M. McIntyre (eds) *Organizational psychology* (4th edn) Englewood Cliffs, NJ: Prentice-Hall.

Carroll, P. (1991) 'Researching instruction while student teaching', *Research in Teacher Education Monograph Series* no. 2, Dublin University Department of Teacher Education.

Coard, B. (1971) *How the West Indian child is made educationally subnormal in the British school system: The scandal of the black child in schools in Britain*, London: New Caribbean Workers Association.

Cowie, H. and Rudduck, J. (1988) *Learning together – Working together*, BP Educational Service, PO Box 30, Blacknest, Alton, Hants GU34 4PX.

Department for Education (1994) *Education Act 1993: Sex Education in Schools*, Circular 594, London: HMSO.

Department of Education and Science (1967) *Children and their primary schools* (Plowden Report), London: HMSO.

—— (1975) *A language for life* (Bullock Report), London: HMSO.

—— (1977) *Gifted children in middle and comprehensive secondary schools*, HMI Matters for Discussion 4, London: HMSO.

—— (1978a) *Mixed ability work in comprehensive schools*, HMI Matters for Discussion 6, London: HMSO.

—— (1978b) *Special educational needs* (Warnock Report), London: HMSO.

—— (1979) *Aspects of secondary education in England. A survey by HM Inspectors of Schools*, London: HMSO.

—— (1980) *A view of the curriculum*, HMI Matters for Discussion 11, London: HMSO.

—— (1984) *Slow learning and less successful pupils in secondary schools: Evidence from some HMI visits*, London: HMSO.

—— (1985a) *The curriculum from 5–16*, Curriculum Matters 2, London: HMSO.

—— (1985b) *Education for all* (Swann Report), London: HMSO.

—— (1989) *From policy into practice*, London: HMSO.

Department of Education and Science and Welsh Office (1985a) *Better schools*, London: HMSO.

De Vesey, C. (1990) *Shared learning*, Birmingham: Development Education Centre.

Dickinson, C. and Wright, J. (1993) *Differentiation: A practical handbook of classroom strategies*, Coventry: National Council for Educational Technology.

Dunn, R., and Dunn, K. (1975) *Educators' self-teaching guide to individualizing instructional programmes*, New York: Parker Publishing.

Edwards, D. and Mercer, N. (1987) *Common knowledge: The development of understanding in the classroom*, London: Methuen.

Enfield Language and Curriculum Access Service (1995) *Making progress . . . Teaching and assessment in the multilingual classroom*, London Borough of Enfield.

Entwistle, N.J. (1981) *Styles of learning and teaching*, London: Wiley.

—— (1991) 'Cognitive style and learning', in K. Marjoribanks (ed.) *The foundations of students' learning*, Oxford: Pergamon.

Entwistle, N.J. and Ramsden, P. (1983) *Understanding student learning*, London: Croom Helm.

Essex County Council (1993) *Guidelines for secondary schools for effective differentiation in the classroom*, PO Box 47, Threadneedle House, Market Road, Chelmsford, MC1 1LD.

Fielding, M. (1994a) 'Delivery packages and the denial of learning', in H. Bradley, G. Southworth and C. Conner (eds) *Developing teachers, developing schools*, London: Fulton.

—— (1994b) 'Valuing difference in teachers and learners: building on Kolb's learning styles to develop a language of teaching and learning', *The Curriculum Journal* 5(3): 393–417.

Fitzgibbon, A. (1987) 'Kolb's experiential learning model as a model for supervision of classroom teaching for student teachers', *European Journal of Teacher Education* 10 (2): 163–77.

Francis, H. (1992) *Individuality in learning: A staff development resource book*, London: Further Education Unit.

Francis, H., Clare, M. and Simpson, E. (1990) *Individuality in learning*, London: Further Education Unit.

Further Education Development Agency (1995) *Understanding student learning*, London: FEDA.

Galton, M., Simon, B., and Croll, P. (1980) *Inside the primary classroom*, London: Routledge & Kegan Paul.

Gardner, H. (1993) *The unschooled mind*, London: Falmer.

Gibbs, G. (1988) *Learning by doing*, London: Further Education Unit.

—— (1992) *Improving the quality of student learning*, Bristol: Technical and Educational Services.

Gould, S.J. (1981) *The mismeasure of man*, Harmondsworth: Penguin.

Gregorc, A. (1982) *An adult's guide to style*, Columbia, Conn.: Gregorc Associates.

Gregorc, A. and Butler, K. (1984) 'Learning is a matter of style', *Voc Ed* April: 27–9.

Guild, P.B. and Garger, S. (1985) *Marching to different drummers*, Alexandria, Va: Association for Supervision and Curriculum Development (ASCD).

Hall, D. (1995) *Assessing the needs of bilingual pupils: Living in two languages*, London: David Fulton.

Hargreaves, D.H. (1967) *Social relations in a secondary school*, London: Routledge and Kegan Paul.

—— (1972) *Interpersonal relations and education*, London: Routledge and Kegan Paul.

Harris, D. and Bell, C. (1990) *Evaluating and assessing for learning*, London: Kogan Page.

Hart, S. (1989) 'Everest in plimsolls', in D. Mongon and S. Hart, *Improving classroom behaviour: New directions for teachers and pupils*, London: Cassell.

—— (1992a) 'Differentiation: way forward or retreat?', *British Journal of Special Education* 19 (1): 10–12.

—— (1992b) 'Differentiation: part of the problem or part of the solution?', *The Curriculum Journal* 3 (2): 131–42.

Heath, S.B. (1983) *Ways with words: Language, life and work in communities and classrooms*, Cambridge: Cambridge University Press.

Hertfordshire County Council (1992) *Equal opportunities: What's in it for boys?, A project involving two secondary and three primary schools in Hertfordshire*, Hertford: Minority Ethnic Curriculum Support Service.

Heywood, J. (1989) *Assessment in higher education* (2nd edn), Chichester: Wiley.

Heywood, J., Fitzgibbon, A. and Cameron, L.A. (1991) 'Experience versus theory in teacher education', *Research in Teacher Education Monograph Series* no.2: Dublin University Department of Teacher Education.

Hilgersom-Volk, K. (1987) 'Celebrating students' diversity through learning styles', *Oregon School Study Council* 30 (9).

Honey, P. and Mumford, A. (1986a) *The manual of learning styles*, Maidenhead: Peter Honey.

—— (1986b) *Using your learning styles*, Maidenhead: Peter Honey.

Hopson, B. and Scally, M. (1982) *Lifeskills teaching programmes no. 2*, Leeds: Lifeskills Associates.

Hudson, L. (1966) *Contrary imaginations*, London: Methuen.

Hull, R. (1985) *The language gap: How classroom dialogue fails*, London: Methuen.

Humberside County Council (1992) *Access to science: Science for children with special educational needs*, Practical Guidelines series, Humberside County Council, Coronation Road North, Hull, HU5 5RL.

—— (undated) *Access to history: History for children with special educational needs*, Practical Guidelines series, Humberside County Council.

Ignatieff, M. (1984) *The needs of strangers*, London: Chatto & Windus.

Inner London Education Authority (1984) *Improving secondary schools*, London: ILEA.

Jackson, B. (1964) *Streaming: An education system in miniature*, London: Routledge & Kegan Paul.

Jackson, R., James, S. and Myers, E. (l986) *The Romans*, London: British Museum Publications.

Johnson, D.W. and Johnson, R.T. (1987) *Learning together and alone*, Englewood Cliffs, NJ: Prentice-Hall.

Kemeny, H. (ed.) (1993) *Learning together through talk: Key stages 3 and 4*, London: Hodder & Stoughton.

Kolb, D. (1976) *Learning style inventory*, Boston, Mass.: McBer.

—— (1984) *Experiential learning*, Englewood Cliffs, NJ: Prentice-Hall.

—— (1985) *Learning style inventory* (revised edn), Boston, Mass.: McBer.

Kolb, D. and Fry, R. (1975) 'Towards an applied theory of experiential learning', in C.L. Cooper (ed.) *Theories of group processes*, Chichester: Wiley.

Kolb, D. and Lewis. L.H. (1986) 'Facilitating experiential learning: observations and reflections', *New Directions for Continuing Education* 30 (June): 99–107.

Krahe, V.A. (1993) 'The shape of the container', *Adult Learning* 4 (4): 17–18.

Lacey, C. (1970) *Hightown Grammar: The school as a social system*, Manchester: Manchester University Press.

Lawrence, G. (1982) *People types and tiger stripes: A practical guide to learning styles*, Gainesville, Fla: Center for Applications of Psychological Type.

Levine, J. (1989) *Bilingual learners and the mainstream curriculum*, Lewes: Falmer.

Lewis, A. (1992) 'From planning to practice', *British Journal of Special Education* 19 (1).

Lunzer, E. and Gardner, K. (eds) (1979) *The effective use of reading*, London: Heinemann.

McCarthy, B. (1982) 'Improving staff development through CBAM and 4MAT', *Educational Leadership* 40 (1): 20–5.

—— (1987) *The 4MAT System*, Barrington: Excel.

—— (1990) 'Using the 4MAT system to bring learning styles to schools', *Educational Leadership* 48 (2): 31–7.

Macmurray, J. (1958) 'Learning to be human', unpublishd paper.

McNamara, S. and Moreton, G. (1995) *Changing behaviour: Teaching children with emotional and behavioural difficulties in primary and secondary classrooms*, London: David Fulton.

Major, J. (1992) *Times Educational Supplement*, 28 February.

Mead, G. H. (1934) *Mind, self and society*, Chicago: Chicago University Press.

Milner, D. (1983) *Children and race ten years on*, London: Ward Lock Educational.

Moy, B. and Raleigh, M. (1985) 'Comprehension: bringing it back alive', in English and Media Centre, *The English curriculum: Reading 1, comprehension*, London: English and Media Centre.

Myers, I. B. (1962) *Introduction to type*, Palo Alto, Calif.: Consulting Psychologists Press.

—— (1980) *Gifts differing*, Palo Alto, Calif.: Consulting Psychologists Press.

National Curriculum Council (1990a) *The whole curriculum*, Guidance 2, York: NCC.
—— (1990b) *Education for citizenship*, Guidance 6, York: NCC.
—— (1990c) *The National Curriculum information pack no. 2*, York: NCC.
—— (1991) *Science and children with special educational needs*, York: NCC.
National Oracy Project (1991) *Teaching, talking and learning in key stage three*, National Association for the Teaching of English, 50 Broadfield Road, Sheffield S8 OXJ.
Norman, K. (ed.) (1992) *Thinking voices: The work of the National Oracy Project*, London: Hodder & Stoughton.
OFSTED (Office for Standards in Education)(1995) *Guidance on the inspection of secondary schools*, London: HMSO.
Peter, M. (ed.) (1992) *Differentiation: Ways forward*, Stafford: National Association for Special Educational Needs.
Pollard, A. (1985) *The social world of the primary school*, London: Holt, Rinehart & Winston.
—— (l987) 'Social differentiation in the primary classroom', *Cambridge Journal of Education* 17 (3): 158–61.
Pye, J. (1988) *Invisible children: Who are the real losers in school?*, Oxford: Oxford University Press.
Quicke, J. (1995) 'Differentiation: a contested concept', *Cambridge Journal of Education* 25 (2): 213–24.
Reid, J., Forrestal, P. and Cook J. (1989) *Small group learning in the classroom*, London: English and Media Centre.
Rist, R.G. (1971) 'Student social class and teacher expectations: the self-fulfilling prophecy in ghetto education', *Harvard Educational Review* 40: 411–51.
Runnymede Trust (1993) *Equality assurance in schools: Quality, identity, society, A handbook for action planning and school effectiveness*, London: Trentham Books with the Runnymede Trust.
Sewall, T.J. (1986) *The measurement of learning style: A critique of four assessment tools*, University of Wisconsin-Green Bay.
Simon, B. (1979) 'HMIs and mixed ability', *Forum* 21 (2): 53–5.
Simpson, M. (1995) 'Differentiation in secondary subjects: models for evaluation and development', Paper presented to European Conference on Educational Research, University of Bath, September.
Spillman, J. (l991) 'Decoding differentiation', *Special Children* 44: 7–10.
Stanford, G. and Stoate, P. (1990) *Developing effective classroom groups: A practical guide for teachers*, Acorn Books, Oak House, Bishop Sutton, Bristol BS18 4UT.
Stradling, R. and Saunders, L. with Weston, P. (1991) *Differentiation in action: A whole school approach for raising attainment*, London: HMSO.
Stradling, R. and Saunders, L. (1993) 'Differentiation in practice: responding to the needs of all pupils', *Educational Research* 35: 127–37.
Swann, W. (1992) *Classroom diversity*, Milton Keynes: Open University Press.
Thompson, J. and Hollins, M. (eds) (1991) *Investigating life key stage 3*, Bath Macmillan Science 5–16 Project, London: Macmillan.
Thorpe, M. and Thompson, J. (1993) *Learning file*, Milton Keynes: Open University Enterprises.
Thorpe, M., Edwards, R. and Hanson, A. (eds) (1993) *Culture and processes of adult learning*, London: Routledge & Open University Press.
Tizard, B. and Hughes, M. (1985) *Young children learning: Talking and thinking at home and at school*, London: Fontana.
Tobias, C.U. and Guild, P. (1986) *No sweat! How to use your learning style to be a better student*, Seattle, Wash.: Teaching Advisory.

Trenchard, L. and Warren, H. (1984) *Something to tell you: The experience and needs of young lesbians and gay men in London*, London: London Gay Teenage Group.

Visser, J. (1993) *Differentiation: Making it work, ideas for staff development*, Stafford: National Association for Special Educational Needs.

Vondrell, J.H. and Sweeney, J.M. (1989) 'Independent study: Using learning style assessment to predict student success', *Journal of Continuing Higher Education* 37 (1): 5–7.

Walker, A. (1989) *The temple of my familiar*, London: The Women's Press.

Weil, S.M. and McGill, I. (1989) *Making sense of experiential learning*, Milton Keynes: Open University Press.

Wells, G. (1987) *The meaning makers: Children learning language and using language to learn*, London: Hodder & Stoughton.

Wiltshire LEA (1992) *Differentiating the secondary curriculum*, Trowbridge: Wiltshire County Council.

INDEX